THE FORMS
AND
FUNCTIONS
OF TORT LAW

AN ANALYTICAL PRIMER ON
CASES AND CONCEPTS

By

KENNETH S. ABRAHAM

Class of 1962 Professor of Law
University of Virginia

Westbury, New York
THE FOUNDATION PRESS, INC.
1997

ISBN 1–56662–460–6

 PRINTED ON 10% POST CONSUMER RECYCLED PAPER

For Harriet

PREFACE

This book is designed to provide a concise analysis of the conceptual foundations of tort liability. Although I expect that the book will be used mainly by first-year law students, it may also be of use to upper-class students and practitioners seeking an overview of a particular area of tort law. Having taught courses in Tort Law for over twenty years, I have come to recognize students' need for something beyond the typical casebook to help them understand what is going on in the cases and in class. Yet the kind of books that are traditionally available do not always satisfy this need. Books of rules don't explain what lies behind the rules; and treatises are both too long and, often, not sufficiently analytical. What first-year students need is a book that helps them to think about "what the Professor was getting at" without spoon-feeding it to them. I hope that this book does exactly that.

The organization and strategy of the book are as follows. I have found that students often are much better able to understand the cases they study during their first few weeks in law school if they appreciate something about the procedure that has brought the case to the point where it can be decided on appeal. In addition, often some part of the earliest classes is devoted to discussion of the purposes served by the imposition of tort liability. Therefore, Chapter One provides a primer on procedure and discusses the functions of tort liability. Thereafter the book follows the pattern of most of the major casebooks, beginning with material on intentional physical injury and then moving on to negligence, causation, defenses, products liability, limited duties, and damages. This material pretty well coincides with what is taught in the typical one semester course in Torts. There follow Chapters on subjects that are usually taken up in a second-semester or Torts II course, on tort reform and alternative compensation systems, defamation, invasion of privacy, misrepresentation, and interference with contract and prospective contractual advantage.

My strategy throughout the book is to provide a brief summary of the rules that govern a particular area, but then to devote the majority of the analysis to an examination of the purposes the rules serve and the arguments that can be made for and against the rules as they stand. Where some knowledge of the way the law has developed over time can help the reader to appreciate the current state of the law, I have tried to provide a capsule history that puts things in context. In short, the reader will find a conceptual analysis of virtually all the major issues in tort law. Ideally, the student who has read the material on a particular subject before he or she goes to class will be prepared to discuss not only what the cases hold, but their implications as well. Although I have discussed most of what would be covered in two semesters of tort law, inevitably there have been a few omissions. I have barely talked about the torts of trespass to land and conversion of property, for example, and have entirely omitted malicious prosecution.

The greatest help I have had in writing this book has come from the students to whom I have taught Torts for over twenty years. They have been a continuing source of excitement, insight, provocative confusion, and stimulation. Without their participation with me in the great venture of the course in Torts, I could never have written this book. I am also grateful to my colleagues, and to the many torts scholars whose work has influenced me over time, though I have occasionally distilled that work in ways that can never reflect all of its richness. Susan Baker, of the University of Virginia Law School Class of 1998, provided very capable research assistance. And as always, my family gave me the inspiration to press on when the spirit lagged.

KENNETH S. ABRAHAM

Charlottesville, Virginia
August, 1996

TABLE OF CONTENTS

TABLE OF CONTENTS

THE FORMS
AND
FUNCTIONS
OF TORT LAW

AN ANALYTICAL PRIMER ON
CASES AND CONCEPTS

*

1

The Nature and Functions of Tort Law

T he law of torts (a name derived from the Latin word for "twisted")
governs the rights of private parties to obtain compensation from
those who have caused them injury or damage. Most of tort law is
"common law," that is, law made by courts rather than legislatures. And
most of that law is made by state rather than federal courts. So although
reference often is made to "the" law of torts, in fact there are fifty separate
state regimes of tort law that are nonetheless sufficiently similar in
important respects to constitute one "body" of law with variations within
it.

It is useful to begin at a general level before addressing particular
areas of tort law and specific legal doctrines. This Chapter starts with a
brief discussion of the nature of tort law in order to introduce the
subject. As in many areas of the law, however, it is impossible to
obtain the fullest appreciation of substance if one does not understand
the procedural setting in which a substantive rule has been made. The
Chapter therefore turns next to the procedural context in which tort law
is made, surveying the points of procedure that arise most frequently in
tort cases. Finally, the Chapter takes up the functions of tort law,
surveying briefly the different purposes that tort law serves and that
figure prominently in the Chapters that follow this one.

I. What Is A Tort?

Courses in Torts often begin with the question, "What is a tort?"
Students give puzzled responses until the correct answer, "A civil
wrong not arising out of contract," eventually emerges. This answer is
a good enough starting point, but it is both overinclusive and underin-
clusive. Not all civil wrongs that do not arise out of contract are torts.
For example, many statutory schemes that create civil liability, such as
Civil Rights statutes, involve neither contract nor tort liability, although they resemble tort in attenuated way. And some torts actually

do "arise" of out contract, at least in a loose sense. Certain legal actions for personal injury or property damage caused by defective products, as well as claims for bad-faith breach of contract, are examples. But these are, so to speak, exceptions that prove the rule. For the most part tort law is in fact a residuary category of civil liability. Legally cognizable wrongs that do not fit elsewhere often fall under the rubric of tort law.

Tort law itself can be subdivided into two general categories, based on the "standard of care" whose breach may result in liability. *Accident law* is comprised of cases imposing strict liability or negligence liability, usually for physical injury—bodily injury or property damage. Strict liability is imposed without regard to the degree of care that the defendant, or "tortfeasor," exercised. Negligence liability is imposed only upon proof of some kind of carelessness—technically, the failure to exercise reasonable care under the circumstances. In contrast, in what are sometimes called the *intentional torts* liability is not imposed for negligence, but upon proof of the defendant's intention to invade the legally protected interest of another. The intentional torts involve a wide variety of non-accidental behavior. Some of this behavior obviously merits the name "intentional" in the sense of an intention to cause harm. A good deal of what falls in the category of the intentional torts, however, does not necessarily require or involve an intent to cause harm. Certain forms of defamation and some invasions of privacy, to give just two examples, are actionable even in the absence of intent to cause harm, as long as the defendant intended to take the action that caused the plaintiff harm. Nonetheless, this crude distinction between the torts that fall in the general area of accident law and those informally classified as intentional is worth recognizing.

The distinction between tort liability for accidental and intentional harm, however, goes only to the standard of care at issue. Proof that the defendant violated the applicable standard of care is not enough to warrant the imposition tort liability. Breach of the standard of care is merely the first element of any "cause of action"—basis for imposing liability—in tort. In addition, there must be proof that the plaintiff suffered harm, and that the defendant's action in breaching the applicable standard of care caused that harm. Combining these requirements yields the four elements of any cause of action in tort: 1) Duty (i.e., the legal duty to comply with a particular standard of care); 2) Breach of Duty (i.e., failure to comply with the applicable standard of care); 3) Causation; and 4) Damages.

II. Procedure in a Tort Suit: Where Tort Law Comes From

There are five major phases of a tort suit: pleadings; pre-trial motions; discovery; trial; and appeal. The pleadings initiate the suit. Discovery is the process by which the parties obtain information about each side's position and about the facts as they will be presented at trial. Pre-trial motions raise legal issues that may clarify or narrow the range of the dispute. At trial evidence is introduced, there are findings of fact, and legal rules are applied to those facts, yielding a verdict either for the plaintiff or for the defendant. And on appeal the party who was unsuccessful at trial is entitled to identify what it contends were legal errors committed by the trial judge.

A. *Initial Pleadings*

Tort suits proceed much like other civil actions. A suit, or action, is commenced when the injured party, or *Plaintiff*, files in court a *Complaint* or *Declaration*, alleging facts giving rise to a *cause of action*. The Complaint is said to contain "allegations" because the assertions in it do not count as facts unless and until the defendant admits them, or a jury finds them to be true at trial. A "cause of action" is the plaintiff's legally actionable claim, or basis upon which he asserts a right to damages or other relief. Typically a cause of action is the name of a particular tort, such as negligence, or battery, or defamation.

The *Defendant* is then served with the Complaint and a summons requiring the filing of an *Answer*, which may admit or deny the allegations of the Complaint and also may state what are known as *Affirmative Defenses*—defenses that the defendant is required to raise specifically and prove at trial. Commonly the defendant admits some of the plaintiff's allegations and denies others. By comparing the Complaint and the Answer the parties can determine what is disputed and what is not. All the documents mentioned thus far, as well as pre-trial motions filed later, are typically referred to as the *Pleadings*.

B. *Discovery*

In the *Discovery* stage of the suit the parties are permitted to seek information from each other about the nature of their positions and the evidence supporting them. Through written *Interrogatories* the parties may propound questions to be answered in writing, and through oral

Depositions witnesses (including the plaintiff and the defendant) may be examined to determine the scope and details of their possible testimony at trial. The information sought in discovery need not be admissible in evidence to be discoverable, as long as it has the potential to lead to admissible evidence. For example, through discovery the defendant may learn the precise nature of the injuries the plaintiff claims to have suffered, and the basis for the plaintiff's claim that the defendant was negligent. Similarly, the plaintiff may learn what features of her claim the defendant contests and the basis for the defendant's contentions. Discovery reduces the element of surprise at trial, thereby permitting the parties to prepare and focus only on the issues actually in dispute, and promotes settlement before trial by helping to inform the parties of the strengths and weaknesses of each side's position.

In the simplest of cases there is little discovery, but these days discovery is an important part of virtually all cases. A single deposition may take a day, two days, or even occasionally a week, and may be preceded or followed by written interrogatories. Even in a simple auto accident case discovery can take some time if there are eye witnesses and medical experts who are in the possession of potentially relevant information. On the other hand, in a complicated tort suit discovery may take months or even years, if there are large numbers of documents to be obtained and many witnesses to be deposed. For example, think of how many people may have information that is potentially relevant when the manufacturer of a prescription drug is sued for negligently failing to warn of a side effect that injured the plaintiff. Research scientists, marketing personnel, financial analysts, and management officials all may know something relevant to the decisions that led to the failure to warn. The plaintiff is likely to depose many, and perhaps all, of these individuals.

C. Pre-Trial Motions

Pre-trial motions may be made before or after discovery. This is the first stage at which important "procedural" decisions are made. But anyone who turns off his mind when he comes to a procedural issue in the course of examining a body of substantive law is making a big mistake, for it is in the resolution of procedural issues that substantive law emerges. For our purposes the important pre-trial motions are the *Motion to Dismiss* and the motion for *Summary Judgment*. The former tends to be made before discovery and the latter after discovery.

The function of a motion to dismiss the plaintiff's complaint is to test the legal sufficiency of the plaintiff's allegations. For purposes of the motion the plaintiff's allegations are accepted as true. By making the motion the defendant asserts that even if the allegations are true the plaintiff does not have a valid, legally cognizable claim. For example, suppose that the plaintiff alleged that he was walking down the street when the defendant frowned at him, and that as a result he experienced emotional pain and suffering. The defendant's motion to dismiss for failure to state a cause of action (or as it is described in the federal system, for failure to "state a claim upon which relief can be granted") would in effect admit that the defendant frowned at the plaintiff, and admit that the plaintiff experienced emotional pain and suffering as a result, but would deny that this behavior is actionable—i.e., deny that this behavior constitutes a tort.[1]

These motions are made prior to discovery. In contrast, after discovery a motion for *Summary Judgment* by either side asserts that 1) that there is no genuine issue of material fact, and 2) that based on the undisputed facts, the party making the motion is entitled to judgment "as a matter of law." For example, if discovery reveals no dispute between the parties that while driving blindfolded down Main Street the defendant struck and injured the plaintiff, the plaintiff would move for summary judgment. The only question would be whether the defendant was negligent "as a matter of law" or, on the contrary, a jury could legitimately conclude on the basis of the undisputed facts that the defendant was not negligent. In all probability the plaintiff would be granted summary judgment under these circumstances. Thus, whereas typically a motion to dismiss or a demurrer tests the legal sufficiency of mere *allegations*, a motion for summary judgment tests the legal sufficiency of a party's position based on undisputed and therefore established *facts*. But in other respects the two kinds of motions function in a very similar way: they take certain facts to be established, and then assert that on the basis of these facts (and sometimes notwithstanding these facts) the party making the motion is entitled to prevail as a matter of law, without the need for decision by a jury.

From these examples it should be obvious that these motions are not "mere" procedure. Rather, their proper resolution depends on the

---

[1] A similar motion in some states is known as a *Demurrer*. But demurrers can be filed by either side, and simply test the legal sufficiency of the pleading to which they respond. For instance, a defendant's demurrer to the plaintiff's complaint is in effect a motion to dismiss; a plaintiff's demurrer to a defendant's answer is in effect a motion to strike the answer as a legally insufficient defense.

applicable substantive rule of tort law. The motion to dismiss a suit claiming damages for injury caused by being frowned at cannot be granted or denied without knowing whether frowning under those circumstances constitutes a tort (which of course it does not). And the motion for summary judgment cannot be granted or denied without identifying the applicable rule governing the role of the jury in determining whether driving blindfolded down Main Street is negligent. If the question whether the defendant was negligent must always be decided by a jury, then the plaintiff's motion for summary judgment must be denied. But if there are cases in which it can be said "as a matter of law" that the defendant is negligent (and as we shall see in Chapter Three there are such cases), and this is one of those cases, then summary judgment should be granted. Much of tort law, in fact, is made and applied through rulings on motions such as these.

D. Trial

If a ruling on a motion has not disposed of the case and the parties have not settled, then the case proceeds to trial. At trial the allocation of responsibility between the court (i.e., the trial judge) and the jury is of crucial significance: courts *only* decide issues of law; juries *only* decide issues of fact. When there is a trial without a jury—a "bench trial"—then the trial judge wears two hats. Then the trial judge both rules on the law and serves as the "trier of fact."

1. Fact-finding

There are two different kinds of fact-finding that juries perform. One is making "pure" findings of fact. This requires answering *empirical* questions about the world: did the defendant strike the plaintiff, how long had the banana peel been lying on the supermarket aisle before the plaintiff slipped on it, would the plaintiff have chosen to use the defendant's product if he had been warned of the risks it posed, how much suffering has the plaintiff experienced as a result of her injury? I do not mean to minimize how difficult it sometimes is to answer merely empirical questions. Predicting how much an injured person will suffer from her injury twenty years from now is a pure empirical question, but that does not make it any easier to answer.

Another kind of finding that juries are required to make involves what are sometimes called *mixed* questions of fact and law. In answering these questions the jury does not make empirical findings. Rather, it evaluates or characterizes empirical facts that it has already found, or applies the law to these facts. To do this the jury answers such questions as, was the defendant negligent, did the plaintiff assume the risk of harm, was the defendant's product in a defective condition unreasonably dangerous to the user?

These two kinds of findings of fact are made in a trial in which the plaintiff presents evidence directed at proving and the defendant seeks to refute the four necessary elements of the plaintiff's case: 1) duty; 2) breach of duty; 3) causation; and 4) damages. Typically the plaintiff bears the *burden of proof* on all elements of the claim. That burden in turn consists of two parts. The "burden of production" requires the plaintiff to introduce evidence from which the jury "could" find that each element of the case has been proved. Introducing evidence that satisfies this standard constitutes making out a *prima facie* case. For instance, in an intersection collision case the plaintiff might testify that he was proceeding through the intersection with the traffic signal green when the defendant's vehicle collided with his own vehicle, breaking his arm. Ordinarily this testimony would make out a *prima facie* case. That is, if the jury believed the testimony, it *could* find, but would not be required to find, that the defendant had a duty to stop at the light that was red for him, that the defendant was negligent in failing to do so, and that this negligence caused damage to the plaintiff's vehicle and a broken arm.

In contrast, the "burden of persuasion" requires the plaintiff actually to persuade the jury by a *preponderance of the evidence*, of each element of his or her claim. To satisfy this preponderance standard, the jury must be persuaded that it is "more probable than not" that each element of the claim (duty, breach of duty, causation and damages) is true. Whether the plaintiff satisfied this standard would depend on whether the jury believed his testimony, what the defendant and other witnesses testified, and whether the jury believed them.[2] If the evidence on any element on which a party bears the burden of persuasion is in "equipoise," or evenly balanced, then the party bearing that burden has not satisfied it.

2. Legal Rulings

The legal function of the judge and the fact-finding function of the jury operate (and interact) at trial in connection with the admissibility

---

[2] On certain affirmative defenses (e.g., that the plaintiff is barred from recovery because she assumed the risk of the defendant's negligence) and in a few unusual situations, the defendant rather than the plaintiff bears the burden of proof.

of evidence, on motions for a directed verdict, and in the court's instructions to the jury. First, when oral or documentary testimony is offered into evidence, the court rules on its admissibility. The principal rule governing admissibility is that evidence which is irrelevant to the issues to be decided is not admissible. This rule does not rule evidence in, since not all relevant evidence is admissible, but it rules evidence out. This is a simple enough, but very important rule: nothing irrelevant is admissible. By applying the substantive rules of tort law, the court can determine whether evidence is or is not irrelevant and therefore whether or not it is automatically inadmissible. For example, if intent to cause physical harm to the plaintiff is not a necessary element of the tort of battery, then testimony by the defendant that he did not intend to cause the plaintiff harm when he slapped him on the back after telling a joke would be inadmissible, because it would be irrelevant. On the other hand, if failure to comply with a safety statute enacted by the legislature is negligence, then evidence that the defendant violated the statute is obviously relevant and (absent special circumstances) will be admissible. A number of the rules of tort law are reflected in, and can be deduced from, rulings on the admissibility of evidence of this sort.

Second, the court decides legal questions in applying the rule that a factual contention may only be submitted to the jury for decision if there is evidence to support it. If there is no evidence to support a contention whose proof is essential for a party to prevail, then that party has not met the burden of production, and the opposing party prevails. But if there is evidence to "make out a jury question" on all the elements of the case, then the case is submitted to the jury. The significance of the decision to submit an issue to the jury cannot be emphasized enough: submitting an issue to the jury means that the jury may decide the issue for or against the plaintiff, for or against the defendant. The same issue, submitted to different juries, might be decided differently. That is why the standard for making out a jury question is often said to be whether "reasonable people could disagree" about the question. If reasonable people could disagree, the case goes to the jury; if reasonable people could not disagree, then either the plaintiff wins as "a matter of law" (having prevailed on all the elements as a matter of law) or the defendant wins because, as matter of law, the plaintiff failed to provide evidence sufficient to make out a jury question on one or more of the necessary elements of his case.

The question whether an issue poses a question for the jury is raised at the close of each party's evidence when the opposing party typically moves for a *directed verdict* (or in the federal system, a motion for judgment as a matter of law). This phrasing is a holdover from the time when, if the motion was granted, the court literally "directed" the jury to bring in a verdict for the party whose motion prevailed. But the granting of a motion for a directed verdict today means that the court determines as a matter of law, rather than the jury finding as a matter of fact, which party wins. There is necessarily some judgment involved when a trial court decides whether reasonable people could disagree about a particular question. Nonetheless, that decision is considered a question of law even though it requires the court to make a judgment about a whole set of facts, and is subject to legal review on appeal as described later.

Like decisions on the admissibility of evidence, rules of tort law are also embedded in rulings on motions for directed verdicts. For example, there is liability in tort for injuries caused by defective products, as the discussion of products liability in Chapter Nine indicates. Suppose that the plaintiff is injured when he dives into an above-ground swimming pool with aluminum sides. He submits evidence of the dangers that this product design poses (as well as proof of causation and damages). The defendant then moves for a directed verdict on the ground that the plaintiff submitted no evidence that an alternative safer design of the product was feasible. The court would grant the motion in a state where the rule is that a product design is not defective unless an alternative safer design was feasible. On the other hand, the court would deny the motion in a state where the rule is that such proof is not required to show that a product's design is defective. In effect, a motion for a directed verdict is the trial equivalent of the pre-trial motion to dismiss for failure to state a viable claim or cause of action. Whereas the motion to dismiss tests the legal sufficiency of the plaintiff's *allegations* by assuming them to be true and contending that the plaintiff nevertheless is not entitled to recover, the defendant's motion for a directed verdict tests the legal sufficiency of the plaintiff's *evidence* by assuming it to be true and contending that the plaintiff nevertheless is not entitled to recover. By the same token, the plaintiff's motion for a directed verdict tests the legal sufficiency of the defendant's position by assuming the defendant's evidence to be true and contending that the plaintiff is nevertheless entitled to recover as a matter of law.

Sometimes courts decline to grant directed verdicts even when they believe that doing so would be proper, so as to obtain a record of what the jury verdict is in the event that, contrary to what the court expects, the case does pose a question for the jury. For example, suppose the court concludes that the plaintiff is entitled to a directed verdict. The court nonetheless submits the case to the jury for decision. If the jury finds for the plaintiff, the court enters a judgment in the plaintiff's favor. But if the jury finds for the defendant, the court then grants the plaintiff's motion for *judgment notwithstanding the verdict*—also know as or "j.n.o.v.", which stands for judgment *non obstante veredicto* (or in the federal system a judgment as a matter of law). The court thereby has on record the decision of the jury if it turns out on appeal that it was correct to submit the case to the jury—i.e., that it would have been incorrect to grant a directed verdict for the plaintiff and was incorrect to grant the plaintiff's motion for a j.n.o.v. In this manner the same issue that is raised by a motion for a directed verdict can be decided, but without the burden of a new trial if granting the motion was error. The appellate court either affirms the trial court, or reverses and enters a judgment for the party in whose favor the jury brought back its verdict, without the need for a new trial simply to see what the jury would have done decided had it only been given the chance to decide. It was given that chance.

The third way in which the allocation of responsibility between court and jury operates is through the court's *instructions* to the jury at the close of the evidence. In its instructions the court describes the rules of tort law to be applied by the jury. The judge identifies the factual disputes the jury should resolve and the rules of law the jury should apply to its factual findings in order to determine whether to bring back a verdict for the plaintiff or the defendant. The substantive rules of tort law are thus expressed in these instructions. In the instructions the court states and then explains the four elements of any tort claim: duty, breach of duty, causation, and damages. For example, in a negligence case the judge will explain the concept of negligence; the meaning of the requirement that the defendant's negligence, if any, have caused the plaintiff injury; the rules governing the assessment of damages; and the way in which the jury is to determine whether any defenses interposed by the defendant should prevail. The jury then retires to deliberate and bring back its verdict.

3. Verdicts

In most cases the jury is asked to return a *general verdict*, simply indicating whether it finds for the plaintiff or defendant, and if the former, the amount of damages awarded. In most states, however, the court has discretion to ask the jury to return a *special verdict*, answering each of the specific questions posed by the instructions as to whether there was proof of each element of the plaintiff's case and any defenses available. There are number of differences between these two approaches. Since instructions typically are given orally and except in very lengthy cases jurors do not take notes, jurors must try to remember the instructions given them when they are asked to return a general verdict. In contrast, when a jury is asked to return a special verdict, the jury normally is given a written list of the questions to be answered. The jury can therefore use this list of questions, or "special verdict form," to guide its deliberations.

In addition—and perhaps more importantly—when the jury is required to bring in a special verdict, the court can examine the verdict to determine whether the jury's answers are internally consistent. For example, after being properly instructed, if the jury indicates on its special verdict form that it finds that the defendant was negligent but that the defendant's negligence did not cause the plaintiff any injury, yet the jury still makes an award of damages to the plaintiff, the court will detect this inconsistency: the jury found that the plaintiff did not meet her burden of proving causation, but the jury nonetheless imposed liability on the defendant. The court will therefore grant the defendant's motion for judgment notwithstanding the verdict. If the jury had made a similar mistake in its deliberations prior to returning a general verdict in favor of the plaintiff, the mistake would not be detected. Indeed, asking the jury to return a general verdict not only forfeits the opportunity to detect honest mistakes, but in a sense gives the jury the power deliberately to ignore the instructions.

The natural question to ask at this point is why special verdicts are not used more often, or universally required, in order to preclude the jury's inadvertent or even deliberate circumvention of the court's instructions. One possible answer is that using special verdicts more frequently would in fact be a good idea, and that the prevalence of the general verdict procedure simply reflects the stubborn conservatism of the law. But there is something more going on here than the mere stubborn refusal of the law to change. Tort law has undergone a great deal of change over the years, after all, much of it in the hands of the very judges who continue to employ general verdict rather than special verdict procedure. It makes more sense to infer that there is something desirable about the insulation of jury deliberations from judicial review that results from asking juries only for general verdicts.

What might that be? The answer, I think, is that tort law is ambivalent about the relationship between its rules and the function of the jury. On the one hand, the trial judge must strictly apply the rules of tort law in making decisions about the admissibility of evidence, in ruling on motions, and in formulating instructions to the jury. On the other hand, rules are rigid things. We have juries in tort cases not because we need fact-finding robots, but because they can bring the common sense of the community into the courtroom. Asking juries for general verdicts reflects the recognition that not everything that is relevant to the outcome of a lawsuit can be fully captured by a judge's oral summary of a set of legal rules. The request for a general verdict implicitly permits jurors to take other factors into account, not because they are told that they are permitted to do so, but because under a general verdict approach there is no way to police such behavior. At its extreme, of course, this approach permits *jury nullification* of the law. But in its more moderate manifestations, this approach permits juries to soften the hard edges of rules, without paying painstaking attention to the precise verbal formulations in which the rules are embodied. Under a special verdict approach, that is much more difficult, because the jury's task is defined and contained by a set of specific questions whose answers are supposed to be the jury's only concern. To oversimplify only a bit, the request for a special verdict seeks specific answers; but the request for a general verdict seeks justice.

E. Appeal

After a judgment is entered, the losing party may appeal. The party appealing is referred to as the "appellant" (sometimes the "petitioner") and the opposing party is referred to as the "appellee" (sometimes the "respondent"). An appellate court has three alternatives available to it: affirm, reverse, or reverse and remand for further proceedings, such as a new trial. The key point to understand about appeal, whether in tort or other cases, concerns what appellate courts can and cannot do. Like trial judges, appellate courts make decisions of law only. Appellate courts have no authority to make factual findings. There is no new evidence introduced on appeal, there is no jury, and there is no fact-finding. Rather, appellate courts accept the factual findings made by juries at trial, or accept as facts the findings that logically must be inferred from general verdicts returned by juries.

This latter point is worth a bit of explanation. Suppose that in a negligence case the plaintiff testifies as follows. He was a passenger in the defendant's car when he said to the defendant, "Slow down." The defendant then nodded his head up and down. However, the defendant testifies that the plaintiff never said those words to him. The contention that the defendant failed to heed the plaintiff's warning is the only evidence of negligence in the case. The jury finds for the plaintiff. At this point it is therefore established as a fact that the defendant heard and failed to heed the plaintiff's warning and that this failure was negligent, because that failure was the only evidence of negligence. On appeal, the appellate court is not permitted to hold that, although the jury found that the plaintiff did warn the defendant by saying "Slow down," the appellate court (unlike the jury) believes the defendant's testimony and doubts that such a warning was given. On the contrary, the appellate court must accept it as established that, for purposes of the legal issues that the court has authority to decide, there was such a warning.

It follows from the fact that appellate courts make only legal decisions that they review only the decisions of the trial judge. In tort cases, this means that appellate courts review the "procedural" moves of the trial court, which of course reflect the substantive rules of tort law: rulings on the admissibility of evidence, disposition of the parties' motions, and the formulation of instructions to the jury. Thus, the following are examples of typical issues raised on appeal: "Did the trial court err in admitting evidence that the defendant did not intend to cause the plaintiff harm?"; "Did the trial court err in denying the defendant's motion for a directed verdict?"; and "Did the trial court err in instructing the jury that the defendant could not be held liable for battery if he did not intend to harm the plaintiff?"

Just as at trial each of the court's "procedural" moves reflects a particular substantive rule of tort law, so on appeal the appellate court's decision reviewing the correctness of the trial court's actions reflects a substantive rule. Suppose that in a battery case the evidence was that the defendant intended to touch the plaintiff without permission, but that the defendant did not intend to cause harm in doing so. The trial court then instructed the jury that if the defendant did not intend to cause the plaintiff harm, liability cannot be imposed. The jury then found for the defendant. The plaintiff appealed, arguing that this instruction was incorrect, because a defendant can be held liable for battery if he touches the plaintiff without permission, even without intending to cause harm. The appellate court will then apply the correct rule governing liability for battery to determine whether the trial court's instruction was or was not correct.[3] This ruling will be embodied in a written opinion explain-

---

[3] For an appellate opinion addressing this issue, see *Vosburg v. Putney*, 80 Wis. 523, 50 N.W. 403 (1891).

ing the basis for the appellate court's decision and indicating whether the court's instruction was or was not correct in light of the substantive rules of battery.

* * *

In summary, tort suits—and indeed all civil lawsuits—are ordered by the rules of civil procedure, and tort rules emerge mainly through rulings in which the substantive rules of tort law determine the proper procedure to be followed. In the pleading, trial, and appeals, procedure mediates substance, and substance is reflected in "procedural" decisions. To understand substance, one must understand procedure; and to understand procedure, one must understand substance.

III. The Functions of Tort Law

Fields of law normally do not come labelled with self-designated functions. As a field that is predominately common law—law made by courts adjudicating individual disputes over a period of centuries—the law of torts has grown and evolved, state-by-state, without any central, self-conscious authority to make it responsive to a clear set of express goals. Although much of modern tort law scholarship has been concerned with analysis of and debate about the proper functions of tort law, they remain contested. The functions of tort law are "mixed": they co-exist, sometimes in tension with each other, with one or more dominating in some contexts and others coming to the forefront at other times.

A. Corrective Justice

When one party wrongs another, correction of the wrong may help to restore the moral balance between them. In tort law, when bodily injury has occurred, the injurer cannot literally rectify the injury. Liability is therefore imposed for monetary compensation, though it is admittedly often a poor substitute for prior good health. In cases involving only economic loss the correction can be more nearly adequate and complete. The case of the intentional wrongdoer is most obviously an occasion for corrective justice. But in many cases of negligence and even sometimes when there has been neither intention to cause harm nor negligence, corrective justice may have appeal as a justification for the imposition of liability.

The way in which correction actually occurs, however, may affect the strength of the appeal of corrective justice as a justification for imposing tort liability. The core of the notion of corrective justice envisions an individual injurer who directly compensates an individual victim, with the injurer's own money. Here the correction of the wrong by the injurer is direct and close. In contrast, as the connection between injurer and victim becomes less direct, corrective justice seems less relevant. For example, if the injurer is protected by liability insurance, she does not pay her victim directly. Instead, she has paid premiums for this insurance that may or may not bear a close relation to the degree of risk that her activities pose. Similarly, if the injurer is a corporation, then ultimately the shareholders or customers of the corporation may bear the cost of compensating the victim. In these situations an injustice still is corrected, and the injurer is the one who has undertaken to assure correction. But these situations are at some remove from the core concept of corrective justice as the face-to-face correction of a moral imbalance between individuals. For this reason, there is a difference of opinion among the commentators as to the value of preserving corrective justice as a function of modern tort law in settings where defendants typically are large corporations and individuals who are covered by liability insurance.

B. Optimal Deterrence

The imposition of tort liability not only corrects wrongs that have already occurred; it also helps to prevent future tortious actions, by threatening potential wrongdoers with liability if they cause actionable harm. Not all risky activity is worth deterring, however, or we would be required to take endless safety precautions at unlimited cost. Rather, the function of tort liability in this respect is to promote *optimal* deterrence—that is, to deter *excessively* risky activity so that only those losses worth avoiding are avoided.

Two points about this notion are worth emphasizing, for they are sometimes difficult to appreciate. First, it follows from the principle of optimal deterrence that deterring certain losses is not worth what it would take to deter them. That is, imposing liability for activity that poses some risk but that is not excessively risky would require foregoing some of the benefit of that activity. Virtually every activity poses some risk, and therefore sometimes results in loss—safely driven automobiles sometimes collide, knives sometimes cut fingers, and so forth. Up to a point tort law threatens liability for risky activity, but beyond that point it does not, and the law tolerates the losses that result. Put harshly, some losses—and this includes some personal injuries—are not worth avoiding. Otherwise we would not require proof of negligence in a whole series of cases, but would instead always impose liability regardless of negligence. The negligence requirement implies that some losses are worth avoiding (those caused by negligence) but that some (those caused without negligence) are not.

Second, nothing in the principle of optimal deterrence dictates what values should be taken into account in determining which losses are and which losses are not worth deterring. Some supporters of the principle of optimal deterrence promote it as an economic concept that compares the monetary costs of risking losses with the monetary costs of preventing losses. And some opponents of the principle object to it for precisely that reason, since it seems to them to ignore important human values. But the economic approach to optimal deterrence is merely one among a number of possible conceptions. One might reasonably take the position that the economic conception of deterrence is unacceptable and that the pain and suffering that results from personal injury should not be reduced to a monetary value in comparing it to what must be done to reduce the risk that injury will occur. But that is not the same as saying that no effort should be made to compare the social benefits gained by reducing the risk of personal injury with the social costs, economic and otherwise, that must be incurred in order to reduce this risk. Making such a qualitative rather than an economic or quantitative comparison may be difficult, but being willing to make it is consistent with accepting the principle of optimal deterrence, even while rejecting an economic conception of that principle.

C. Loss Distribution

Defendants who are held liable in tort actions often do not shoulder the burden of compensation themselves. Sometimes defendants are covered by liability insurance and the insurer literally pays the plaintiff on behalf of the policyholder/defendant. On other occasions even an uninsured defendant may be able to include its prospective liabilities in the price of the products it sells; or the defendant may have shareholders whose investments decline in value as a result of the payment of a liability by the company whose shares they own. In each of these situations the cost of the loss suffered by the plaintiff is not simply transferred to the defendant, but is distributed through the defendant to a larger number of individuals. Promoting the broad distribution of losses is therefore often considered one of the functions of tort liability.

Whether loss distribution in itself is a good thing, and even if it is, whether imposing tort liability is a good way to achieve loss distribution, are both disputed questions. Suppose you suffer a $500 loss, and the law pays you for that loss by charging $1 to each of 500 people. Unless the sum of the value that each of these individuals attaches to the $1 they pay is less than the value you attach to the $500 you have lost, nothing has been gained by the transfer. There is still a total loss of $500. On the other hand, when people purchase insurance they are confirming the notion that losing a small sum for certain (the premium they pay) is a lesser loss than the low probability of suffering a larger loss later. This is much like saying that 500 losses of $1 do in fact entail less loss than a single loss of $500. Tort law has long reflected the similar intuition that, other things being equal, having a large number of people bear a small loss is better than having a single person bear a large one. Thus there has been an inclination to develop rules of law that permit the imposition of tort liability on businesses and institutions that can distribute their liabilities through the purchase of insurance or by raising the price of their products or services.

This rationale has some power, but it also has a weakness. This common rationale for the imposition of tort liability contains no stopping point. Like the compensation justification for imposing liability, it cannot explain why tort liability often is *not* imposed on parties who might, in fact, be good loss distributors. Moreover, imposing tort liability through a lawsuit is a cumbersome and expensive mechanism for achieving loss distribution. Simpler and more broadly applicable insurance systems (e.g., health insurance, disability insurance, social security) can broadly distribute losses at lesser cost if that is desired. Nonetheless, despite the objections that can be levelled at loss distribution as a rationale for the imposition of tort liability, there can be no denying that loss distribution has been and is likely to continue to be one of the functions performed by the imposition of tort liability.

D. Compensation

It is sometimes said that a principal function of tort law is to promote the compensation of those who have suffered injury. For most analysts of tort law, this is only true in a very limited sense. There is no doubt that anytime tort liability is imposed, a plaintiff is awarded compensation. There is also no doubt that, other things being equal, most of us feel enough natural sympathy for the victims of injury (especially physical, as opposed to solely economic, injury) to view the event giving rise to the injury as an appropriate occasion for considering

17

whether (and how) society might assist the victim of the injury. And it is probably true that up to a point we are all better off—because we feel more secure and are therefore willing to take socially productive risks that we would not otherwise take—knowing that if we suffer certain kinds of injury, then compensation for that injury may be forthcoming. If by a "function" of tort law we mean a beneficial effect of the imposition of tort liability, then it is accurate enough to say that providing compensation to victims is a function of tort law.

But if by the term "function" we mean a "goal" of tort law, the notion that providing compensation is a function of tort law is debatable at best. The desirability of providing compensation to a particular class of injury victims rarely explains the lines that are drawn to distinguish those who are and those who are not entitled to prevail in a tort claim. Rather, time after time, some other factor or factors explain the occasion for the imposition of tort liability, or tort law's refusal to impose liability. As Holmes put it with characteristically ruthless clarity over a century ago,

> The general principle of our law is that loss from accident must lie where it falls, and this principle is not affected by the fact that a human being is the instrument of misfortune. * * * The undertaking to redistribute losses simply on the ground that they resulted from the defendant's act would not only be open to [other] objections, but * * * to the still graver one of offending the sense of justice.[4]

Since the time Holmes wrote, the scope of liability in tort has expanded substantially, but the principle he expressed still stands. Liability is not imposed in order to provide compensation to victims. Rather, victims are provided compensation in order to serve the other goals of tort law. If it were otherwise then the basis of liability would be the suffering of misfortune, not the commission of a tort by another. Since in order to justify the imposition of liability, we require something in addition to the bare fact that the plaintiff suffered an injury caused by another party, describing "compensation" as one of the functions of tort liability cannot tell us why or when tort liability will or will not be imposed. At best, the desirability of providing compensation will be a factor that, when linked with others yet to be described, increases the probability that liability will be imposed. And even on that view, providing compensation *under certain circumstances* rather than in general is what is really going on when tort liability is imposed.

---

[4] Oliver Wendell Holmes, Jr., THE COMMON LAW 76–78 (M.Howe ed. 1963).

For that reason, these "other circumstances"—whatever they turn out to be—are likely more clearly to reflect the actual functions, or goals of tort liability, than the goal of compensating victims. Compensation is a good thing when the prerequisites to the imposition of liability are satisfied, but victims go uncompensated when these prerequisites are not satisfied.

E. Redress of Social Grievances

Even in situations in which the foregoing rationales for the imposition of tort liability will not be served or are shown to be inapt, people sometimes have the sense that tort liability should be imposed anyway. Of course, one view is that such people are wrong and that tort law should never be imposed if it would not effectively serve one of the functions described above. But another view is that, even apart from these functions, the right to sue in tort promotes the redress of social grievances, especially against large, impersonal institutions. In this sense tort law is a populist mechanism that permits ordinary people to put authority on trial. Surely the lawsuits involving the Dalkon Shield, asbestos-related lung disease, and breast-implants exhibit some of this quality. Standing alone, this justification for the imposition of tort liability may not be strong; but when allied with one or more of the other functions of tort liability, the possibility that imposing liability on an impersonal institution will help to redress social grievances may well help to explain why some close cases are decided the way they are.

F. Summary: A Mixed System

It should be obvious from the preceding discussion that tort law does not serve any single goal, but a set of different goals whose strength is likely to vary with the situation. Tort law thus performs a "mixed" set of functions. In some cases concern for corrective justice will dominate, but in others deterrence or concern for loss distribution will be the key. And in many cases, because the imposition of liability would not serve any of the goals of tort law effectively, liability is not imposed. For those who seek perfect clarity, this may be an unsatisfying state of affairs. But it makes life interesting for anyone who wants to understand the forms and functions of tort law. That is a task to which the remainder of this book is addressed.

2

Intentional Harms

I t is common to begin thinking about tort law by considering the intentional torts of battery and assault. Although only a small percentage of tort litigation involves these torts, the concepts at their core as well as the interests they protect are easy to identify and therefore good conceptual building blocks. Everyone understands the difference between an injury inflicted on purpose and a mere accident. Cases involving a deliberate punch in the nose typically are therefore fairly simple. As might be expected, however, more difficult issues often arise in some intentional tort cases. In addition, two other torts that are close relatives of the torts of battery and assault—false imprisonment and intentional infliction of emotional distress—pose interesting and challenging issues. After considering these four personal injury torts, we turn to a brief discussion of torts involving intentional harm to property and their defenses, including a more extended discussion of the conditional privilege of necessity.

I. The Personal Injury Torts

A. Battery

Battery involves actual physical contact, whereas assault is the threat of contact. Technically, a battery is a harmful or offensive contact with another, resulting from an intention to cause that contact, or from an intention to put another in apprehension that a harmful or offensive contact is imminent. Unpacking this definition reveals each of its features.

1. The Physical Contact Requirement

There must be some physical contact with the plaintiff, or at least something that is in contact with the plaintiff. Ordinarily this is direct physical contact between the plaintiff and the defendant. But the contact may be by some object set in motion by the defendant, such as a weapon, or by some force such as electricity. In fact, the force need not literally be set in motion by the defendant, as long as the contact results from the defendant's intention. For example, in *Garratt v. Dailey*,[1] the defendant a pulled chair out from under the plaintiff as she was about to sit down. The plaintiff was injured when she fell to the ground. Literally speaking it was the plaintiff who, by attempting to sit down, set in motion the force that caused her injury. But the harmful contact with the ground was intended by the defendant, and that was sufficient to satisfy this element of the tort. That was as it should be, since what is at stake in battery is the plaintiff's interest in protection of his or her bodily well-being and dignity from intentional invasion, not merely in avoiding specific methods of invading that interest.

2. Harmful or Offensive Contact

The contact at issue in battery need not cause actual physical injury to the plaintiff; an offensive but not harmful contact is sufficient. What is "offensive" is likely to be context-dependent. Certainly it would be a jury question, at the least, whether an unwanted kiss was offensive even if planted politely on the cheek. And many courts probably would grant a motion for a directed verdict for the plaintiff on this issue if the circumstances spoke of sexual harassment rather than romantic excess. Similarly, in most circumstances a pat on the back is both harmless and inoffensive. But a pat on the back of a female employee by a male supervisor whose romantic advances the employee has rejected in the past is likely to be offensive in context. The point is that the tort of battery protects more than just physical well-being; it protects bodily autonomy as well. A certain amount of touching and jostling might be expected in a crowded world, but an "invasion" of bodily autonomy—a touching without consent—may be offensive even if it is not physically harmful.[2]

---

[1] 46 Wash.2d 197, 279 P.2d 1091 (1955).

[2] Probably the outer reaches of this concept are reflected in *Fisher v. Carrousel Motor Hotel, Inc.*, 424 S.W.2d 627 (S.Ct. of Texas, 1967), in which the defendant grabbed a plate from an individual in a buffet line, stating, "a Negro could not be served in the club." The plaintiff sued for battery. Although the defendant's action in that case was offensive, one might wonder whether it was the contact that took place when the defendant grabbed the plate that was offensive, or the defendant's motive in taking the plate. To put it another way, perhaps it was not the plaintiff's *bodily* autonomy that was invaded in that case as much as his integrity as a human being. That might be another tort, such as intentional infliction of emotional distress, even if it were not a battery.

Sometimes everything depends on whether the touching in question is or is not to be expected under the circumstances. For example, in *Vosburg v. Putney*,[3] the defendant (age eleven) reached his foot across the aisle of their classroom and either touched or kicked the plaintiff's leg. The defendant did not intend to harm the plaintiff, but the contact aggravated an earlier injury. The court held that the plaintiff could maintain an action for battery under these circumstances, emphasizing that the defendant's behavior was a violation of the order and decorum of the classroom. The court even called the behavior "unlawful," by which it apparently meant "inappropriate" under the circumstances and therefore not impliedly consented to by the plaintiff. In reaching this conclusion, the court distinguished what might be expected in a classroom—order and decorum without physical contact—from what might be expected on a school playground, and therefore what is impliedly consented to in other such settings—a certain amount of non-malicious physical contact.

3. Intent

There can be no battery without the requisite intent on the part of the defendant. But that intent is not necessarily an intent to harm. The defendant must intend the consequences against which the law protects the plaintiff, but need not have a malicious intent or even any understanding that what he is doing is wrongful. Thus, in *Vosburg*, the circumstances in which the parties found themselves (a classroom) gave the plaintiff the right not to be touched by the defendant. That the defendant intended the touching was sufficient, even though the defendant did not necessarily intend the touching to be harmful or offensive. The defendant must either desire to bring about such contact, or act with substantial certainty that the contact will result from his actions. In *Vosburg*, for instance, it was substantially certain that the touching would occur. It is not sufficient, however, for the defendant to know that his action merely *risks* harmful or offensive contact if there is no intent to cause such contact.

The result of this two-fold approach to intent is that, if the defendant acts with an intent to cause a harmful or offensive contact, it does not matter that the probability of harm or offense is low; liability is imposed if what was intended occurs. On the other hand, if the defendant does not intend contact there must be a near certainty that it will occur. This makes pretty good, straightforward sense. Acting with the

---

[3] 80 Wis. 523, 50 N.W. 403 (1891).

intent to cause harm or offense is sufficiently objectionable that even when the probability of harm or offense is low the intent standard is satisfied. But when one does not desire harm or offense to occur, his conduct is merely risky until he knows that harm or offense is substantially certain to result from it. Such low-risk action might constitute some other tort, such as negligence, but it is not battery.

The intent standard is subjective. The question is whether this defendant had the requisite state of mind, not what people similarly situated would have intended under the same circumstances. But it is important to distinguish the nature of the intent standard in battery from the evidence that might be employed to prove that the standard was or was not breached. Truly "direct" evidence of the defendant's state of mind usually is not available, unless the defendant actually has voiced his intention to cause harm. So the plaintiff's proof often is "external" to the mind of the defendant and therefore is only "circumstantial" evidence of intent. That is, the jury is permitted to infer that the defendant did or did not intend the harm at issue from the surrounding circumstances. The jury must determine the likely internal, subjective state of mind of the defendant based on the objective, or at least external, facts. What facts were staring the defendant in the face? What is his explanation for the action he took? What was the history of relations between plaintiff and defendant? Answers to these and similar questions are the typical basis for the jury's decision about the defendant's subjective state of mind.

Why is there liability not only when the defendant desired to cause harm, but also when he knew that harm was substantially certain to occur? Surely part of the answer is obvious: ordinarily, acting in the face of knowledge that one's act is substantially certain to cause harm is only slightly less morally objectionable than acting with the desire to cause harm. In addition, however, the difficulty of proving the defendant's state of mind directly also helps to explain the substantial-certainty basis for battery liability. A defendant who acted with substantial certainty that harm would result from his act will very often have desired this harm to occur. It is the rare, though not unheard of case in which a defendant knows that he is very likely to cause harm but does not desire that harm to occur. Why else act if one knows that what he is doing will very likely harm someone? Only when the defendant had some other end in view and the harm that would certainly occur as a result was a mere side effect of achieving that end will the defendant have acted with substantial certainty yet not intended the harm (e.g., shooting at a target with a crowd of people standing near it). For this reason, often it will be valid to infer intent to cause harm from evidence that the defendant knew that harm was substantially certain to occur. However, what the defendant *knew* often can be more reliably proved than what the defendant *intended*. So the substantial-certainty basis for battery liability is in this sense not merely an independent basis for liability, but also a surrogate for proof of the intent to bring about harm.

The intent standard is double-barrelled in another way as well. The standard is satisfied when the defendant intends to cause an offensive contact but a harmful contact results, and also when he intends to cause a harmful contact but an offensive contact results. A number of justifications can be offered for this approach. One justification is that the underlying wrong is the intention to invade another person's bodily integrity, and that both harmful and offensive contacts are simply different consequences of this same underlying wrong. A second justification is that each form of contact is sufficiently likely to result from an intent to cause the other that an act intended to cause one form of contact should be regarded as intended also to cause the other. Still another justification (though only for one-half of the approach) is that all intentionally harmful contact is also offensive; intention to cause harm therefore is necessarily intention to cause offense. And a final justification is that it sometimes it is difficult for the plaintiff to prove which form of contact the defendant intended, even though the plaintiff can prove that the defendant definitely intended one or the other. If the defendant brings a dog to the home of a person whom he knows has a phobia about being bitten and the dog jumps on the that person, it should not matter whether the defendant intended a harmful contact or an offensive one. The consequence of requiring proof of the kind of contact the defendant intended would be that sometimes the defendant would avoid liability for tortious contact, because of the difficulty of determining which form of tortious contact he intended. It would be odd, for example, if the defendant who intended harmful contact could avoid liability for an offensive contact on the ground that he had intended something worse (harmful contact) than what actually occurred.

4. Transferred Intent

A fourth feature of the definition of a battery also relates to the intent standard. Although the defendant must intend a harmful or offensive contact with another person, the individual who actually suffers the contact need not be the person whom the defendant intended to harm or offend. This rule is known as the doctrine of *transferred intent*. The core explanation for this doctrine is that the defendant's conduct is so blameworthy that it would be inappropriate to allow him to escape liability on the ground that he did not harm or offend the particular person he intended to harm or offend. But practical problems of proof also play a role in supporting the doctrine. The doctrine does not simply apply to the clear case in which the defendant's intentions were directed at A, but B was injured. Rather, sometimes a plaintiff will easily be able to prove that the defendant intended harm to someone, or acted with knowledge that harm to someone was substantially certain to occur, but the plaintiff will be unable to prove precisely to whom. Suppose, for example, that a defendant surreptitiously disposes of hazardous waste in a community's water supply. If the defendant must intend harm to a particular individual or group of individuals, then there will be no liability for battery under these circumstances. The doctrine of transferred intent solves this problem, by making the identity of the particular target of the defendant's intentions irrelevant.

B. Assault

An assault occurs when the defendant, intending either to cause a battery or to put another person in apprehension of imminent harmful or offensive contact, does put the plaintiff in apprehension of imminent harmful or offensive contact. In contrast to battery, the interest protected in assault is the plaintiff's mental peace, rather than his physical well-being and bodily autonomy. The operative word in the definition of assault is "apprehension" of harmful or offensive conduct. Although typically the plaintiff "fears" imminent conduct, fear is not required. Rather, only "anticipation" of such contact is required, for even anticipation of a battery without fear of it substantially disturbs one's mental peace.

The elements of an assault are virtually identical to those of battery, with the absence of a requirement of actual contact with the plaintiff's person. In fact, virtually every battery is also an assault, since normally the plaintiff is first put in apprehension of imminent physical contact, and then suffers the contact. The converse, of course, is not true. Sometimes an assault is only an assault, either because it was intended only as an assault, or because it was an attempted battery that missed.

Aside from the issues that also arise in battery (such as intent and offensiveness), there are two key issues in assault. The first issue is how close to consummation a threat must be to become an assault. The answer, not entirely helpful standing alone, is that the harm threatened must be "imminent." The cases make clear, however, that imminent means a number of things. The threat must be *immediate* in terms of time: a statement by the defendant that he is going home to get his rifle and will return to kill the plaintiff is not an assault. The threat also must be *close* in terms of space: a threat made over the telephone is not an assault. And the threat must be *actual* rather than potential. The defendant's statement that "If I were a violent man I would tear your eyes out" is not an assault.

These requirements make sense on several grounds. The idea behind assault is to protect the mental peace that is breached when one is about to suffer a battery. Talk is cheap; until the plaintiff faces immediate action by the defendant his concern is about a future battery, not a present one. In addition, until a battery is in fact imminent, the defendant's intention and therefore the amount of blame that should be ascribed to him is uncertain. Imminence strengthens the inference of the defendant's intent. Finally, the courts could have their hands full with all manner of claims if there were liability not only for the mental suffering caused by the imminent threat of battery, but for concern over potential future battery as well.

A second issue that arises distinctively in assault involves the extra-sensitive plaintiff. Some people are of course more sensitive than others. Ordinarily there is no liability for the making of threats that would not satisfy the demands of the tort of assault if made to a typical person, even if the extra-sensitive plaintiff did actually regard a battery as imminent. Imposing liability for conduct that the defendant could not reasonably have understood to be tortious would deter conduct that would not ordinarily be tortious. That rationale for this limitation on liability for assault, however, also suggests its own exception. Once the defendant knows of the plaintiff's extra-sensitivity, the reason for declining to impose liability for threats of battery that fall just short of imminent disappears. Because in this situation the defendant knows of the effect his threat will have on the plaintiff, he has the requisite intent to put the plaintiff in apprehension of imminent harm, even if the ordinary person would not feel such apprehension.

C. False Imprisonment and Intentional Infliction of Emotional Distress

These two torts, the first long-established and the second of more recent vintage, are worth some discussion not only in their own right, but also because of what they illustrate about the nature of legal rules more generally. These torts reveal that at times the desirability of expanding the degree of protection afforded by the law of torts is in tension with the need for easily administrable rules governing the scope of liability. A choice must often be made about the mix of predictability of outcome and flexibility of application that should be combined in a particular rule.

1. False Imprisonment

Battery and assault do not protect against all intentional interferences with personal well-being and autonomy, because they require physical contact or apprehension of it. Early on it was recognized that one particular form of interference that does not involve contact or apprehension is nonetheless sufficiently objectionable to be made actionable in tort. The essence of this tort of false imprisonment is the unjustified (i.e., "false") restriction of the plaintiff's freedom of movement, not harmful or offensive contact. To be actionable, a confinement must be total—forcing the plaintiff to take the long way around is not sufficient to constitute imprisonment. But giving him no way out of where he is, even no way out of a large space, constitutes the necessary confinement.

Note the interests that the tort of false imprisonment does and does not protect. The tort is narrowly tailored to meet a particular need—the failure of the torts of assault and battery to remedy a different, discrete form of interference with bodily autonomy. The cause of action is specifically and exclusively for false imprisonment, not a general claim for intentional interference with bodily autonomy. In fashioning the cause of action to deal with this one problem alone, the courts were able over time to develop rather specific rules about what does and does not satisfy the elements of the tort. Thus, *total confinement* rather than partial confinement is required; generally the plaintiff must have *conscious awareness* of the confinement; and the restraint on the plaintiff's freedom must be *intentional*, but physical force is not necessary if there is a threat of force. Although these requirements are not self-applying and leave some room for judgment, often they enable the courts to determine as a matter of law whether a valid claim exists. The result is a substantial amount of predictability that can help potential litigants sort out by themselves the cases that should and should not be brought or defended. Instead of operating under a rather general cause of action which is likely to send most questions to the jury, potential litigants can understand in advance the limits of what is actionable, and make decisions about whether to institute a claim and whether to defend against or settle it.

This predictability is achieved, however, by limiting the discretion of the trial courts and juries to determine, on a case-by-case basis, which intentional interferences with bodily autonomy should be actionable. That decision has already been made at a "high level of generality": assaults, batteries, and false imprisonments. Any intentional interference that does not fall within one of these categories is not actionable, no matter how unsavory the defendant's conduct or how deserving the plaintiff. Denying liability to the occasional sympathetic plaintiff who has clearly been wronged, but by conduct that is not quite assault, battery, or false imprisonment, is just the cost of having rules, whose very purpose is to draw lines between situations that are and are not actionable. Sometimes a case simply falls a hair short of being within one of the actionable categories.

This bright-line approach becomes less and less tolerable, however, as the number of instances in which the need for more flexibility increases. Then the predictability tail seems to be wagging the justice dog. This is a generic problem in the formulation of legal rules. And what happened next is also common.

2. Intentional Infliction of Emotional Distress

A typical avenue of development was taken by what became the tort of intentional infliction of emotional distress. The courts began to be presented with a cluster of cases that fell outside the existing three categories of actionable intentional interference with bodily autonomy, but that had certain common features. Although in these cases there was no physical contact, no threat of contact, and no confinement, in each case the defendant had acted in a manner that was intended to interfere severely with the plaintiff's peace of mind. At first the defendants were innkeepers or common carriers, who it was said were under a "contractual" obligation not to engage in such conduct. But eventually the contractual prerequisite disappeared, and defendants of all sorts were subjected to liability for what came to be recognized as the tort of intentional infliction of emotional distress.

It is no surprise that even before the tort had a name, the cases in which the courts first felt compelled to permit the imposition of liability involved extremely outrageous conduct by the defendant. For example, malicious practical jokes, such as a false story that the plaintiff's husband had been grievously injured, were typical of the cases in which the courts felt justified in imposing liability. In such cases the defendant had not merely intended to distress the plaintiff, but also had gone beyond the reasonable bounds of decency in doing so. The courts were understandably concerned, however, about what they might be letting out of Pandora's box in authorizing a general cause of action for intentional infliction of emotional distress. Such a cause of action could have created a potentially unlimited expansion of liability for the kind of unmannerly conduct that, while distressing, is only too common and therefore to be expected by almost anyone who has contact with other people. An unbounded tort of intentional infliction of emotional distress would also have risked fraudulent claims by those who had merely been insulted or aggravated rather than truly and deeply distressed.

The result was that the "extreme outrageousness" that characterized the defendants' conduct in the early cases became an element of the tort itself. The requirement of extreme outrageousness helps to meet the two concerns that would otherwise be troubling about the tort. Because only extraordinary instances of misbehavior satisfy this requirement, there is no chance that liability will be radically expanded; and because this kind of misbehavior is more likely than ordinary rudeness to cause emotional distress, the requirement reduces the risk of fraudulent claims.

3. Some Observations about the Nature of these Legal Rules

The development of the tort of intentional infliction of emotional distress can tell us something more generally about the nature of legal rules. The very concept of a rule implies a division—a line—between the situations in which liability is imposed and those in which it is not. Some fact situations fall squarely within the confines of a tort, such as battery, assault, or false imprisonment, and some situations fall outside those confines. When a situation falls far outside those confines, typically there is no reason for concern. But when an appealing fact situation falls just outside the confines of an established cause of action, the courts sometimes are inclined to create an exception to the rule that will make that fact situation actionable.

There is nothing necessarily right or wrong about this tendency. The prior rule may have been too limited, and the combination of that rule plus the exception—in effect a new, broader rule—may be just right. But a rule is not a rule if it does not have limits. If any situation that falls just outside the confines of the rule may nonetheless be made the subject of a new exception, then the rule is infinitely malleable and infinitely expandable, and in effect is no rule at all. That is not what happened in the development of the tort of intentional infliction of emotional distress. Rather, a few cases that were not quite battery, not quite assault, and not quite false imprisonment were held to be actionable, and then a new rule governing a new tort emerged, based on the common characteristics of those few cases and subject to its own limits.

Things might have developed otherwise. Instead of fashioning a new rule to fit the new, actionable fact situations, the courts might have decided that in actuality a whole series of hard-to-specify wrongs ought to be actionable, including but not limited to battery, assault, false imprisonment, and intentional infliction of emotional distress. The courts might then have dispensed with the use of rules to determine which such wrongs were actionable, and instead could have employed what might be called a *standard*—a less specific principle that could loosely guide decisions about what was actionable but that would have been too indefinite to decide particular cases. For example, the standard might have reflected the putative tort of "wrongful and intentional interference with personal autonomy or dignity," but left the courts and juries in particular cases to decide which such intentional interferences would be actionable. Eventually more specific guidelines, very much resembling rules, might have emerged; or perhaps it simply would have been left to juries to decide what was actionable, on a case-by-case basis. Things never developed that way, however, and the intentional injury torts remained governed largely by rules and not standards.

In practice, the distinction between rules and standards is a bit less firm than I have described it. No rule is perfectly specific and no standard is entirely indefinite. The distinction between the two kinds of legal "norms" is a matter of degree. The closer a legal norm comes to the rule side of the spectrum, the more predictable the application of the norm to any particular fact situation is likely to be. The cost of such predictability, however, is the relative incapacity of the norm to accommodate situations that do not qualify according to the norm's strict limits. Conversely, the closer a norm comes to the standard side of the spectrum, the less predictable its application will be, but the more discretion decisionmakers will have to distinguish between situations that are and are not actionable. At one extreme lie rules with highly predictable applications and very little flexibility. At the other extreme lie standards that afford enormous discretion and whose application is very difficult to predict. In between lie most of the actual rules of tort law.

II. Defenses

Even after the plaintiff in a tort case proves a *prima facie* case—i.e., submits evidence supporting each element of his or her case—the defendant may avoid liability by making out a defense to liability. In connection with the four personal injury intentional torts, most of these defenses fall into the category of "privileges"—that is, actions taken under circumstances that justify or excuse what would otherwise be tortious. Although there are a number of defenses, the main ones are consent (which is not a privilege) and the privileges of self-defense and defense of others.

A. *Consent*

If the plaintiff has consented to conduct by the defendant that would otherwise be tortious, an essential element of the plaintiff's case is missing, because the defendant's conduct is not wrongful. For example, an intentional touching by the defendant to which the plaintiff consented is not a wrong at all. Procedurally, consent is a defense in the sense that the defendant is the party who typically raises the issue and bears the burden of proving it; ordinarily the plaintiff can make out a *prima facie* case without making reference to consent. Naturally there are often questions of fact regarding the existence of consent. Some questions are purely factual—what did the defendant say, what did the plaintiff reply? Other questions are interpretive, since consent may be not only express but implied—what physical contacts does a person playing touch-football or someone taken unconscious to an emergency room impliedly consent to? And in other situations nominal consent has been given, but is not legally effective because there was fraud, duress, certain forms of mistake, or the legal incapacity of the plaintiff to give consent.

Even when consent has been given, the defense does not apply when the scope of the consent is exceeded. For example, in *Mohr v. Williams,*[4] the plaintiff consented to have the defendant surgeon perform an operation on her right ear. While the plaintiff was under anesthesia, the defendant examined both ears, and decided that the condition of the plaintiff's right ear was less serious than expected and

---

[4] 95 Minn. 261, 104 N.W. 12 (1905).

that the left ear required surgery. He therefore operated on the left ear. The plaintiff sued for battery. On appeal, the court held that plaintiff's consent to an operation, and indeed an operation on one of her ears, did not constitute consent to an operation on her other ear. The defendant had therefore exceeded the scope of the plaintiff's consent and was liable for a battery.

One of the most vexing problems regarding consent involves inter-subjectivity. Consent must be communicated, but communication sometimes misfires. An uncommunicated consent, if there could be such a thing, probably is a defense. But what about the situation in which the plaintiff has not consented but the defendant incorrectly, yet honestly, believes that the plaintiff did consent? Often cases involving sexual conduct such as alleged "date rape" raise such issues. These issues are highly charged, but they cannot be avoided in a discussion of consent simply because they are controversial.

The traditional rule holds that the defendant cannot escape liability merely by honestly believing that there was consent, but must have "reasonably relied" on a manifestation of consent by the plaintiff. For example, suppose that the defendant John suggests, after a certain amount of physical intimacy with the plaintiff Jean, that they engage in sexual intercourse. The plaintiff then says, "Oh John, I love you but I'm just not sure I want to," after which she simply freezes up and says nothing more. They then have sexual intercourse. The plaintiff sues for battery, and the defendant alleges consent.

Under the traditional approach it probably would be a question of fact whether the defendant reasonably relied in that situation. But even determining whether the defendant has submitted enough evidence to make the defense of consent a jury question is highly situation-dependent. Whether the defendant could reasonably have understood the words "I love you but I'm just not sure I want to" as consent depends very much on how the plaintiff and defendant had communicated in the past, and on how they had interpreted seemingly ambiguous statements about their intentions, such as "I just don't know." If the plaintiff and defendant had little or no history of communication that could help to resolve the issue, then whether the defendant could reasonably have understood the plaintiff to be consenting might depend on prevailing cultural norms regarding consent to sexual contact. And if the plaintiff and the defendant came from settings in which these norms differed, then the traditional approach might well permit the defense of consent even where the plaintiff was, in effect, communicating one message ("I do not consent") and the defendant was hearing another

("I do not object"). The very formulation of the consent defense in these reasonable-reliance terms means that sometimes there is no liability even when the plaintiff did not in fact intend to consent, as long as some people would reasonably have understood her to have consented. The traditional approach might therefore be regarded as being somewhat pro-defendant, which in most sexual offense cases will translate into "pro-male."

On the other hand, it would be possible for the law to take the position that unless there has been an express, affirmative consent by the plaintiff, the defendant can never have reasonably relied. Then the message "I do not object"—even assuming that "I just don't know" could reasonably be understood to mean "I do not object"—normally would not count as affirmative consent: not objecting is not the same as consenting. This approach would emphasize the plaintiff's state of mind rather than the defendant's. The question would not be whether the defendant reasonably relied, but whether the plaintiff actually consented. However, although the ultimate issue under this formulation of the defense would be the plaintiff's state of mind, often the only evidence of this state of mind aside from the plaintiff's own subsequent assertions are her words and actions at the time. As a consequence, for practical purposes the issue in such cases often still would be whether, objectively speaking, those words and actions actually constituted consent.

There is room for some variation under this approach. On the one hand, the approach could be formulated so as to be nearly identical to the traditional approach—directing the jury to determine whether the plaintiff consented by asking how a reasonable person would have understood the plaintiff's words and actions. On the other hand, the defense could be formulated so as to be noticeably less pro-defendant than the traditional approach, by instructing the jury that the consent defense must be rejected unless there was an actual, affirmative indication of consent by the plaintiff. Under this formulation the consent defense is less likely to prevail even when some people would have believed that there was consent.

It is worth remembering, however, that except in the unusual case in which the court could rule that there was no consent as a matter of law, the differences between these formulations will be reflected mainly in the language in which instructions are given to the jury. Under any of these formulations, whether there was consent is very likely to raise a jury question, since even under the alternative to the traditional approach the defendant will contend that the plaintiff's words or gestures should be interpreted as an express affirmative consent. The outcome of claims involving unwanted sexual behavior will therefore still depend more on the values and experiences of the members of the jury than on the subtleties of the particular instructions read to them by the trial judge.

B. Self-Defense and Defense of Others

The defenses of self-defense and the defense of others are known as "privileges;" that is, they afford the defendant the privilege of causing what would otherwise be tortious harm to the plaintiff, in order to prevent himself or others from suffering such harm. To be entitled to engage in self-defense or the defense of another, the defendant must reasonably believe that the use of physical force is necessary to prevent or repel an attack or imprisonment. Thus, when there would actually have been no attack, the defendant can avoid liability for a mistaken belief that an attack was about to occur, or was occurring, only if that mistake was reasonable. What constitutes a reasonable belief that an attack is likely to occur can be highly situation-sensitive. A person who feigns a threat against someone whom he knows to be unusually nervous because of a recent mugging risks a privileged effort at self-defense by the person threatened, even though self-defense might not be privileged under other circumstances.

The general rule is that the use of reasonable force in defense of oneself or others is privileged, but that the defendant is liable for injury caused by the use of unreasonable means or excessive force. Commonly the defendant has been required to make a split-second decision about the need for defense and the amount of force to use, however, and as a consequence the jury is likely to afford considerable leeway when the defendant or the person he was protecting was actually at risk of serious harm by the plaintiff. The only important limitation on the jury's discretion in this regard is the "equivalence" rule: if there is a threat of death or serious bodily harm, then the defendant is privileged to defend himself or another with an equivalent amount of force; but if the threat is of lesser harm, then lesser force must be used in defense or the privilege is lost. Sometimes it is also said that if there is a means of escape the use of force in defense is not privileged, except in one's home. Probably it is more accurate, however, to say that on some occasions discretion is the better part of valor, and that the jury's decision whether the defendant used a reasonable amount of force in defense may take into account both whether there was an avenue of escape, and whether it would have been reasonable under all the circumstances to have chosen escape rather than defense.

A number of the issues relating to defense of self and others are similar to those that arise in connection with the consent defense. In each situation the plaintiff communicates something to the defendant (an alleged threat or an alleged consent, respectively) that the defendant later claims authorizes or justifies the taking of an action that would otherwise be tortious. In each case it is possible that the defendant has misunderstood that communication, mistakenly believing that there has been consent, or the threat of an immediate attack. In each case the law is that a subjectively honest but unreasonable mistake is no defense, but that an objectively reasonable honest mistake does excuse what would otherwise be tortious. Finally, even when inflicting harm that would otherwise be tortious is authorized, the law places limits on the amount of force that may be used, depending on the scope of the consent or the severity of the threatened attack.

III. The Property Torts

A. *The Nature of the Torts*

There are three torts concerned with intentional injury to property: trespass to land, trespass to personal property, and conversion. The two forms of trespass are just what they appear to be: wrongs in which the defendant breaches the boundary of or touches the plaintiff's real or personal property, or otherwise physically interferes with the plaintiff's right of possession, which includes the right to exclude others from occupying or using that property. The defendant need not have intended to trespass, but only to have intended to be present on or interfere with the possession of property that turns out to be owned by the plaintiff. Trespass is actionable without proof of actual damage, although in modern times it would be highly unusual to bring a trespass action only as a matter of principle. In contrast to trespass, in which the defendant himself interferes with the plaintiff's right of possession, the defendant in conversion typically has undertaken the unauthorized transfer of the plaintiff's personal property to another person.

The essence of all three of these torts is interference with the plaintiff's right to possess and control his or her property. Although the concern with bodily autonomy that characterizes the personal injury torts is not present here, it would be a mistake to suppose that the property torts are concerned only with monetary loss resulting from damage to property. On the contrary, while few such tort actions would be brought unless there were monetary damage, often more is at stake than money alone. Property ownership is not merely an economic but also a personal right. The way people live their lives may be influenced, sometimes even protected by, their property. Think of people who live on rural tracts of land to obtain privacy and solitude, or derive great pleasure from unique paintings or sculpture. Interference with the rights of possession and ownership of such property, especially intentional interference, is likely to engender indignation or outrage. The person whose property is trespassed upon typically feels personally invaded. Sometimes there is no way entirely to separate these intangible losses from the more easily measured monetary losses that may be the result of trespass or conversion.

B. Defenses: Especially The Privilege of "Necessity"

A series of related privileges may serve as defenses to actions for trespass and, occasionally, conversion. These include public or private necessity, defense of property, recapture of chattels, recapture of land, and action in pursuance of legal process. Necessity is by far the most important privilege for our purposes, however, since this defense raises issues that can help us make a conceptual transition from the intentional torts to those involving negligence and strict liability.

In a sense, all the privileges that serve as defenses to liability for intentional harm to persons or property are based on necessity. But the term necessity is reserved for those cases in which the defendant has damaged or destroyed the plaintiff's property in order to avoid harm to himself or his property, but the risk of harm to the plaintiff has not been created by the plaintiff. In contrast, when such privileges as self-defense, defense of others, or defense of property are invoked, the risk of harm has been created by the plaintiff.

Two forms of necessity must be distinguished. In cases of *public necessity* a risk to the property of a sufficiently large number of people to make the risk "public" can be reduced or eliminated by damaging or destroying the property of the plaintiff. For example, the plaintiff's house may be torn down in order to prevent the spread of a fire to the remainder of a town. In cases of public necessity the privilege is "absolute;" that is, the privilege of necessity is a complete defense to liability. Since the privilege exists, the defendant has the right to make use of the plaintiff's property. And because the defendant possesses a

37

privilege, the plaintiff does not have the right to prevent him from using the plaintiff's property.

In contrast, in cases of *private necessity* there is a risk to one party or his property only, and this party can reduce or eliminate that risk by damaging or destroying someone else's property. In such cases the privilege of necessity is said to be "qualified" or "conditional." Because the privilege is only qualified rather than absolute, the defendant is liable to the plaintiff for the damage done to the latter's property. That is, the privilege is conditioned on the privileged party's later compensating the other party for using the latter's property.

1. *Ploof* and *Vincent*: The Basics

These principles are illustrated by two celebrated cases. In *Ploof v. Putnam,*[5] the plaintiffs were sailing on Lake Champlain when a sudden storm forced them to tie up at the defendant's dock. The defendant then had his servant untie the ship, as a result of which the boat and its contents were destroyed and the plaintiffs were injured. The court held that the privilege of necessity had entitled the plaintiffs to tie up at the defendant's dock. Because doing so therefore did not constitute a trespass, the defendant did not have the right to exclude them from the dock, and having the plaintiffs untied in effect trespassed on the plaintiffs. That is, private necessity afforded the plaintiffs what amounted to a limited property interest in the defendant's dock (the right to tie up for the duration of the storm), with which the defendant had interfered. The defendant therefore was liable to the plaintiffs for the harm that ensued when they were untied.

Two years later, however, in *Vincent v. Lake Erie Transportation Co.,*[6] the defendant's ship had been unloading at the plaintiff's dock when a storm arose. By the time the unloading was completed it would have been dangerous to venture out into the storm, so the ship remained moored to the dock. As the mooring lines parted or chafed they were replaced. The plaintiff sued for the damage that resulted from the buffeting of the ship against the dock during the storm. The defendant argued that because it would have been negligent, perhaps even foolhardy, to untie the ship from the dock because of the risk to life and the ship, it should not be liable for the damage to the dock. But the court disagreed, holding that the defendant had a conditional privilege only.

---

[5] 81 Vt. 471, 71 A. 188 (1908).

[6] 109 Minn. 456, 124 N.W. 221 (1910).

Although the defendant had done nothing wrong, it had saved the ship at the expense of the dock and was liable for the damage that resulted.

2. The Property Rights Explanation

The notion that because the defendant in *Vincent* did nothing wrong it should not bear liability may seem appealing on the surface, but is not persuasive. To say that the defendant did nothing wrong is simply another way of saying that it had the privilege of staying moored to the dock and that the plaintiff had no right to exclude the defendant in an emergency. As the court put it, "the ordinary rules regulating property rights were suspended by forces beyond human control * * *". The whole point of the conditional privilege, however, is that when such property rights are suspended and the defendant is privileged to use the plaintiff's property, the defendant is obligated to pay for any damage that results.

But why? It may seem self-evident that if I use someone else's property, I should pay for doing so. If that were the principle underlying *Vincent*, however, then the defendant should be liable only for the rental value of the dock for the period in question, since this was what he was entitled to use without needing permission. This was not a case, that is, in which a starving man has a privilege to enter a cabin in the woods and open canned goods for food, as long as he pays for the food. The defendant did not choose to consume or to damage the dock, but only to risk damaging it.

The explanation for the law's refusal to credit this distinction between intending harm and merely risking it has to be that the risk in *Vincent* was sufficiently high to bring it within the confines of the rule governing conditional privilege. After all, we choose to risk damaging other people's property all the time, yet are usually held liable for damage that actually occurs only if it was negligent to take the risk. For example, I create a risk of non-negligently damaging nearby property when I drive to work, since I may have a tire blowout that causes my car to run off the road and damage a neighbor's house. But the risk is very low. I am therefore liable for such damage only if I have been negligent. In *Vincent* the risk must have been high, or the case would in fact more closely resemble my driving to work. Moreover, the fact that as the mooring ropes parted or chafed the defendant replaced them highlights the element of choice by the defendant, although I would argue that the replacement of the ropes ultimately should not affect the outcome of the case, since this merely risked harming the dock.

39

But the question why liability is imposed remains. Why not apply the public necessity rule to all cases in which the defendant was privileged to use the plaintiff's property, by making the privilege absolute? A perfectly respectable answer is simply that, as between two innocent parties, the one whom nature put at risk should bear the cost of saving himself or his property, rather than the owner of the property that does the saving. For many people that is a sufficiently persuasive answer to end the inquiry.

The trouble with this answer is that if both parties are innocent— i.e., neither was negligent—then the conditional privilege rule looks more like a way to break the moral tie between the parties than a method of achieving corrective justice. It will not do to argue that the shipowner made a choice to risk the dock, but that the dockowner made no such choice, since the dockowner chose to have a dock where ships might tie up when storms arose. Until we know what legal rule governs the rights of ship and dock owners, we cannot make assertions about what they did and did not "choose" to risk. This is an important point, for it reflects the fact that legal rules not only honor expectations of safety; sometimes expectations of safety are derived from legal rules. In such situations the decision about what legal rule to have is in essence a decision about what expectations of safety to create.

For example, if the governing rule were that the dockowner cannot recover from the shipowner unless the shipowner was negligent in staying moored to the dock, then the dockowner could be said to have "chosen" to risk being non-negligently damaged by ships moored to the dock during storms. We cannot deduce the scope of the dockowner's property rights from the governing tort liability rule, because what we are arguing about is the scope of the "property" rights the governing liability rule should or should not give the dockowner. One of these rights, though only one, involves the dockowner's possible right of recovery for damage resulting from ships moored during storms. The dockowner's right in this regard might be the broad one afforded by *Vincent*, or it might be a narrower one that would make the shipowner liable for damage only when it was caused by the shipowner's negligence.

Thus, the scope of the dockowner's rights does not determine the appropriate liability rule; rather, the appropriate liability rule determines the scope of the dockowner's rights. To put it another way, the dockowner's rights do not come to us already established and independent of the issue. On the contrary, what is at issue is the scope of those rights. One way to understand this is to imagine how things would change if the shipowner were not liable in the *Vincent* situation. Then the risk to dockowners would rise, and the risk to shipowners would fall. Presumably docks would be worth slightly less than they would otherwise be (since owning a dock would entail one less "right") and ships would be worth slightly more than they would otherwise be (since owning a ship would entail one more "right").

When the issue is understood in this light, the question is whether there is some moral or other basis for favoring dockowners over shipowners, or vice versa. We might say that when we talk in ordinary language about property "ownership," we include in that notion the right not to have the safety of our property consciously and deliberately risked by others. If pressed we might acknowledge the limitation on property rights that was recognized in *Ploof v. Putnam*, but only on the condition that if our property were damaged when another person used it in an emergency, that person be required to compensate us for the damage. It might follow that unless there were some good reason for departing from this instinctive conception of property rights, the law should reflect that conception, in order not to upset people's expectations and undermine confidence in the firmness of property rights.

In my view, however, this explanation—though many people find it congenial—is just short of being circular, since the explanation rests on a pretty vague and probably not universally shared notion of what it means to "own" property. Nonetheless, for those who still think that the proper explanation of *Vincent* is that the shipowner really did "take" something from the dockowner, the property rights explanation does work.

3. The Deterrence Explanation

The question then becomes whether there could be a good reason for departing from the ordinary conception of what it means to "own" property and denying the dockowner a right to recover. Up to this point we have been talking only about compensation for damage to the dock, without reference to the possibility of avoiding such damage. We have been talking about corrective justice, but not about deterrence. Perhaps a concern for reducing losses can supply a justification for departing from the ordinary conception of what it means to own property.

a. Who Should be Liable?

Suppose that dockowners were much better situated than shipowners to determine the best way to prevent damage to their docks when ships stayed tied to them during storms. This is a plausible supposition, since dockowners are likely to know more about docks than shipowners. If dockowners can nonetheless recover from shipowners for damage to docks during storms, then dockowners will have less incentive to take measures to reduce the risk of damage to their docks, since they will have to pay for those measures themselves, whereas shipowners will have to pay if the measures are not taken and damage occurs. Denying dockowners the right to recover from shipowners for damage done to docks during storms might therefore tend to increase dockowners' incentive to take additional precautions that would protect their docks.

But this is only half the story. Sometimes it would make sense to stay moored at the dock, but at other times the total risk to both the dock and the ship might be reduced by untying and venturing out into the storm. Denying dockowners the right to recover from shipowners in such situations will increase the tendency of shipowners to risk damaging docks, because shipowners will not have to pay for damage to docks. Shipowners will tend not to venture out into a storm, risking damage to the ship, if they can stay moored at the dock without having to pay for damage to the dock. In contrast, under the rule in *Vincent* the shipowner always has an incentive to compare the risk to the dock if the ship stays moored, against the risk to the ship if the ship does not stay moored, because under *Vincent* the shipowner must pay for whatever damage occurs: he is liable to the dockowner for damage, and as the owner of the ship he must bear the cost of any damage that occurs if the ship ventures out into the storm.

Thus, threatening a party with liability gives that party an incentive to compare the cost of liability with the cost of alternatives that may avoid liability. Sometimes the threat of liability induces more careful behavior; but if, all things considered, it is cheaper to bear liability than to avoid it, then the threat of liability gives the party that is threatened an incentive to make the right choice. One way to view the issue in *Vincent*, therefore, is not to ask which party should be liable for the damage to the dock, but rather, which party is in the better position to compare the risk to the dock with the risk to the ship. I suspect that this is a close question, since while dockowners are likely to know a lot about their docks and at least something about ships and storms, shipowners are likely to know a lot about their ships and about storms, and at least something about docks. In other situations, however, it may be that one party knows a whole lot more about both sides of the comparison than the other party. Then, on this theory, the party with both the most relevant knowledge and the capacity to act on it should be liable.

b. When Does It Matter Who Is Liable?

Since it is probably a close question which party is in a better position to make the decision in cases like *Ploof* and *Vincent*, we are likely to get pretty good decisions whether or not the shipowner is liable for damage to the dock, as long as the party who is liable has the right to choose between the two alternatives of staying moored or venturing out. The privilege of necessity gives the shipowner the right to make this choice, but charges him with the cost of doing so. The converse of this approach would deny the shipowner the privilege of tying up at the dock, but would make the dockowner liable for damage to the ship if he denied it the right to use the dock during a storm. The *Vincent* approach makes sense if shipowners know more about ships and docks than dockowners know about docks and ships.

If we are not sure who knows more, or if the answer varies depending on the kind of ship and kind of dock, then giving shipowners and dockowners freedom to bargain in advance about what will happen during storms may help to solve the problem. For example, if there were no legal privilege of necessity, shipowners might be willing to pay dockowners for the contractual privilege of staying moored to docks during storms, but dockowners might grant them this privilege only in return for higher mooring fees that would compensate the dockowner in advance for damage that might be done. Shipowners might look at these higher costs and decide that they could more cheaply bear liability for damage to docks by installing cushioning devices such as tires on the dock-sides of their ships, and offer to bear liability in return for lower mooring fees. The point is that, when the parties themselves can identify the most cost-effective approach and can inexpensively set aside the prevailing tort liability rule, then the cost of the courts' adopting the "wrong" rule, so to speak, is simply the cost of setting the rule aside in advance by contract. The parties themselves will contractually arrive at the best rule for them if they can. This was one of the insights flowing from the famous theorem developed by Nobel Laureate Ronald Coase, that in the absence of "transactions costs" the rule of liability does not matter.[7]

When the parties are strangers and transactions costs are in effect prohibitive, however, the Coase theorem does not apply and whether liability is imposed can make a big difference. The plaintiffs in *Ploof* could not contract in advance with every dockowner on Lake Champlain. And because I cannot go around bargaining with everyone whose drives on the same roads as I do about how to order our liability relationship if our vehicles collide, it is important that tort law adopt a rule governing automobile collisions that creates the correct incentives for reasonably safe driving. That rule, whatever it is, must be the "right" rule, because it could not be set aside contractually even if we were willing to let do so.

Interestingly, all this leads us back to public necessity. If at least one of the fundamental purposes of imposing liability is to give those who risk doing injury or damage the incentive to make the correct comparison between taking such risks and avoiding them, then why is there an absolute privilege in cases of public necessity? Why isn't the party who destroys the plaintiff's property entitled to do so, but also liable to the plaintiff for the damages that result? For example, it would seem that when a house in the path of a fire is torn down to save the remainder of a town, the owner should be able to recover for his loss. Otherwise those who tear down the house will be like the shipowner who never has to pay for damage to the dock, tearing down houses whenever there is even a slight risk to the remainder of the town, even if there were other, more prudent courses of action.

A partial explanation for the seemingly anomalous rule that there is no liability in such a situation—i.e., that there is an absolute rather than only a conditional privilege—is that in the vast majority of public necessity cases, the plaintiff's property would have been destroyed anyway by the oncoming fire or other force that threatened the public's property. When this is true, the plaintiff really has not lost anything, and the decision to destroy the plaintiff's property was in fact correct. But a more satisfying explanation, I think, is that when the public necessity rule emerged, there would have been no feasible way to hold the appropriate parties liable. Because towns and municipalities did not exist as legal entities until relatively recently, there was no way for the plaintiff to hold a "town" liable. And because the individual or indi-

---

[7] Ronald H. Coase, *The Problem of Social Cost*, 3 J.L. & Econ. 1 (1960).

viduals who actually tore down the plaintiff's house were acting not only for themselves but also for others and the public good, it would have been inappropriate to hold them and only them liable. Yet it would have been difficult if not impossible to identify and recover from the large number of people whose property had benefitted enough from destruction of the plaintiff's property to warrant imposing liability on them. By the time municipalities gained a legal existence and consequently a means of raising funds, the public necessity rule had already crystallized.

* * *

My discussion of necessity may seem to have wandered far from the defenses that may be raised in suits for intentional injury to property. But the discussion illustrates the way in which any effort to reject superficial answers and to dig more deeply into the reasons that tort liability is or is not imposed inevitably leads to considerations of principle and policy at a general level. The issues raised in considering the defense of necessity run throughout the law of torts: in fashioning the rules governing tort liability and the defenses to it, how much stress should be placed on the goal of corrective justice; what is the best way to promote optimal deterrence; and when should liability be imposed even in the absence of a wrong by the defendant? These issues return, again and again, whether intentional torts, negligence, strict liability, or other torts are involved.

3

The Negligence Standard

E ven if the defendant did not intend to injure the plaintiff or to invade
another interest of the plaintiff that the law of torts protects, liability
may be imposed for injury or damage caused by the defendant's
negligence. In fact, most tort claims are for negligence. Negligence is
easily defined: it is the failure to exercise reasonable care to avoid injury
or damage to another person or property. What is "reasonable care,"
however, depends on the circumstances. Negligence cases are therefore
heavily fact-driven and usually are decided by the jury. Nonetheless, a
number of important rules of law regarding negligence have developed
over time. These rules affect the admissibility of evidence, rulings on
motions for summary judgment, rulings on motions for directed verdicts
and judgments notwithstanding the verdict, and the wording of jury
instructions, among other things. At the core of all of these rules is the
meaning of the concept of negligence.

This Chapter examines the meaning of negligence, first looking
briefly at the history of negligence law, and then scrutinizing the modern negligence standard by exploring a number of subjects within it:
the reasonable person standard; Judge Learned Hand's negligence
"calculus;" the role played by evidence of compliance or non-compliance with custom; professional negligence, or malpractice; violation of
statutes; and finally, *per se* rules and the role of judge and jury in
negligence cases.

I. A Page of History

When Oliver Wendell Holmes, Jr. said that "a page of history is
worth a volume of logic," he meant that understanding how a rule of
law developed over time may provide a more satisfactory explanation
for its current character than exclusively logical analysis of the rule.

For us as well as for Holmes, a bit about the history of negligence law can help to place the modern law of negligence in a more comprehensible context.

A. *The Scope of Liability in Trespass*

Tort law emerged out of criminal law, and was therefore originally concerned principally with violent breaches of the peace. The early tort actions were for what amounted to battery or trespass to land. To bring a tort action one needed a *writ*. The writs for battery and trespass to land were called "trespass *vi et armis*" (trespass by force of arms) and "trespass *quare clausum fregit*" (trespass by breaching the plaintiff's boundary). The allegations of the plaintiff's complaint had to conform to the requirements of each writ or the action could not be brought. For example, trespass required that the injury to the plaintiff be direct and forceful.

If the plaintiff's claim fell perfectly within the contours of trespass he had a very strong chance of recovery. This was because, early on, the defendant was liable virtually without regard to whether he was to blame for the plaintiff's injury, as long as he caused it. Thus, in *The Thorns Case*,[1] the defendant was sued for trespassing on the plaintiff's land in order to retrieve the branches of a hedge of thorns that had fallen while the defendant was cutting the hedge. The court held that the defendant was liable simply by virtue of having trespassed. There was some language in the case, however, leaving open the possibility that if the defendant had proved that he had done all in his power to keep the thorns off the plaintiff's land, the result might have been otherwise. But in the absence of such a showing, trespass was what we would today call a strict liability tort.

Over time the courts made increasing reference to the possibility that a defendant could avoid liability in trespass by proving that he was, as they sometimes put it, "utterly without fault," or that the injury to the plaintiff was an "inevitable accident." But for both substantive and procedural reasons, the defense apparently was very narrow. For example, in perhaps the most noteworthy case on the issue, *Weaver v. Ward*,[2] the parties were both English soldiers. The plaintiff's complaint alleged that in the course of a military training exercise the defendant shot the plaintiff. This bare allegation made out a *prima*

---

[1] Y.B. Mich. 6 Ed. 4 f.7, pl. 18 (1466).

[2] 80 Eng. Rep. 284 (K.B. 1616).

facie case of trespass *vi et armis*. The defendant could then avoid liability only by pleading and proving that he was utterly without fault. What the defendant actually pleaded in *Weaver* was that the shooting was accidental. From the modern point of view this plea seems to come pretty close to alleging that the defendant was "utterly without fault."

The court in *Weaver* held, however, that the facts pleaded by the defendant did not show him to be utterly without fault. To avoid liability, the court said, it would have been necessary for the defendant to plead and prove that the plaintiff had run across the line of fire while the defendant was shooting, or otherwise to have shown that the accident had been "inevitable, and that the defendant had committed no negligence to give occasion to the hurt." Given this language, the best interpretation of *Weaver* is that there was liability in trespass for direct and forceful injury except when the defendant could not be said in any way to have been responsible for what happened. Merely having exercised what today we would regard as reasonable care was not enough to show that the defendant was "utterly without fault" and therefore not enough to avoid liability. In addition, *Weaver* makes it clear that as a matter of procedure the defendant in trespass had the burden of proving that he was utterly without fault. The plaintiff could recover for direct and forceful injury unless the defendant succeeded in proving that the circumstances fell within the substantively narrow defense of "utterly without fault."

Indeed, the meaning of "utterly without fault" was so narrow that there are few recorded cases over a period of centuries in which the defense prevailed. There may be unreported cases—trials that did not result in appeals, for example—in which the defense prevailed. And there was often a procedural explanation for the defendant's loss that makes it difficult to pinpoint the substantive scope of the defense "utterly without fault." Over time two distinct defenses emerged. One was a "general" defense that was raised by a general plea or denial. This plea denied the facts alleged, or at least the critical allegation that the defendant's act caused the plaintiff's harm. The other was a "special" defense or plea that admitted that the cause of the plaintiff's harm was the defendant's act, but further alleged that the defendant was utterly without fault. In some cases the defendant seemed to lose because he had entered a general plea when he should have pleaded specially, and vice versa.

Consequently, it may be that some defendants even in the recorded cases would in fact have prevailed on the defense that they were "utterly without fault" had they employed the proper plea in raising their defenses. That is, there may well have been more scope for escaping liability because of the absence of fault than the recorded cases suggest. But even if this were true, it is fair to say that there was precious little room for avoiding liability on this basis, although there seemed to be more and more room as the beginning of the nineteenth century approached.

B. The Rise of Trespass on the Case and the Transition to a Negligence Standard

Plaintiffs had their problems too. For a while (centuries, perhaps) there was no liability for personal injury that did not fall within the contours of trespass—i.e., that was not direct and forceful. Eventually, however, liability sometimes was imposed when the harm was indirect, or consequential, as long as the defendant was negligent in risking the harm. But the plaintiff shouldered the burden of proof on the negligence issue. Since the writ system was still operating when this form of liability emerged, it first became actionable as "trespass in a similar case," then as "trespass on the case," and finally (more or less for short) as "case." The question that was often raised after this alternative approach to liability became established was whether the plaintiff should have sued in trespass or in case, since the requirements of these two alternatives varied. Trespass would lie (that is, was the appropriate form of action) when the harm alleged was direct; the defendant could escape liability for trespass only in narrow circumstances, by proving that he was utterly without fault. On the other hand, case would lie when the harm was indirect or consequential, and in case the defendant was only liable for negligence. Trespass was obviously a more favorable form of action for the plaintiff, because liability was imposed virtually without regard to whether the defendant was at fault, and even the utter absence of fault was an affirmative defense to be proved by the defendant, whereas in case there was only liability only if the defendant was negligent, and the plaintiff had the burden of proving it. But if the plaintiff sued in trespass (for direct harm) when he should have sued in case (for indirect harm), he lost.

This was precisely the issue in the memorable case of *Scott v. Shepherd*.[3] There the defendant threw a lighted squib (a firecracker or torch of some sort) into a marketplace, and it was tossed like a hot potato from person to person until it injured the plaintiff, who sued in trespass. The defendant argued that because the harm was not direct, the plaintiff should have sued in case. The court found that the harm was direct and that trespass therefore would lie, but in so holding revealed how arbitrary the distinction between trespass and case actually was. A plaintiff "lucky" enough to be able to sue in trespass usually recovered very easily; but a plaintiff forced to sue in case had a harder time, since he had to prove negligence. Similarly, a defendant unfortunate enough to have caused direct injury and to be sued in trespass was almost certainly going to be liable, whereas a defendant who was sued in case could avoid liability if he had exercised what came to be understood as reasonable care. And these differences depended on something that increasingly seemed morally and practically irrelevant: whether the harm had occurred in a direct or indirect manner.[4]

Although it took more time than one might expect to sweep away this distinction between trespass and case, eventually it did happen. On this side of the Atlantic the leading decision was *Brown v. Kendall*,[5] the dogfight case. The plaintiff and defendant owned dogs that were fighting, and in attempting to break up the fight with a stick, the defendant accidentally struck the plaintiff in the eye. The plaintiff sued in trespass, alleging that the defendant was liable for a direct and forceful injury. The opinion for the highest court of Massachusetts was written by Chief Judge Lemuel Shaw, who happened to be the father-in-law of Herman Melville and in all probability served as the model for Captain Vere in Melville's novel, BILLY BUDD.

Shaw's opinion in *Brown v. Kendall* inaugurated a new era in American tort law. The plaintiff claimed that because his action properly was brought in trespass, he needed only to prove direct, forceful injury, and that the defendant could only escape liability by showing that he had exercised extraordinary care (presumably, something like being "utterly without fault"). Shaw rejected this contention outright. He said that the statements in the cases to the effect that trespass will lie in cases of direct injury all had been made in reference to the

---

[3] 96 Eng. Rep. 5525 (K.B. 1773).

[4] See Charles O. Gregory, *Trespass to Negligence to Absolute Liability*, 37 Va. L.Rev. 359 (1951).

[5] 60 Mass. (6 Cush.) 292 (1850).

question whether trespass and not case will lie, *assuming that some action would lie*. But neither trespass nor case will lie, he said, unless the defendant had intended to injure the plaintiff or had negligently injured him. And Shaw went on to say that the plaintiff has the burden of proving either intent to injure or negligence, whether the action is brought in trespass or in case. Finally, Shaw indicated that while there may be instances in which the reasonable thing to do would be to exercise extraordinary care, the standard by which the defendant is to be judged is always one of "ordinary" or reasonable care. If the defendant has exercised ordinary care then he is not liable, whether the action is brought in trespass or in case.

As legal history, this was inaccurate to say the least. *Brown v. Kendall* did not merely redescribe existing law, but changed it substantially. No longer could there be any question whether a plaintiff could recover for a direct injury even if the defendant had acted carefully: there was no such recovery. And no longer did the defendant bear the burden of proving that he had met the requisite standard of care: the plaintiff now had the burden of proving breach of that standard. In short, there was no longer any substantive difference between trespass and case; that difference was merely procedural, affecting the kind of writ the plaintiff had to obtain, but not what the plaintiff had to prove in order to succeed. There could be no recovery in the absence of negligence or conduct even more blameworthy.

Very quickly this approach became nearly universal. *Brown v. Kendall* is only the most famous of the mid-nineteenth century decisions out of which this new negligence regime emerged. But although there is no doubt about the fact of this development, there is controversy among legal scholars about the way in which the new regime meshed with nineteenth century social and economic attitudes. Certainly the idea that there would be no liability unless the defendant had done something wrong was consistent with the rugged individualism and industrial expansionism of the age. Some scholars have gone further, however, asserting that the new negligence regime was designed to provide a subsidy to infant industry, by removing the threat of strict liability that might have hindered industrial development. In the view of these scholars, the development of contributory negligence (i.e., negligence by the plaintiff) as a complete defense to a negligence action further subsidized potential defendants by further narrowing the scope of liability. Other scholars have examined the facts of large samples of negligence cases during that era, however, and concluded that the "subsidy thesis" is too simplistic, since the move to negligence aided all kinds of defendants. *Brown v. Kendall*, after all, did not involve an industrial or commercial defendant, but two individuals. Moreover, although trespass may until that time have been a strict liability action, both trespass and case had limited applicability in earlier centuries. But over time the number of situations in which liability might be imposed at all had slowly expanded. Although *Brown* and cases like it did narrow the basis of liability, certainly the cumulative effect of all these developments was the expansion of liability between the seventeenth and the nineteenth centuries.

Regardless of the way one views the issues posed by the subsidy thesis, it is indisputable that by the late nineteenth century, negligence was the dominant standard. Even today, while the areas in which strict liability is imposed have slowly expanded, negligence remains the dominant basis for imposing liability in cases of non-intentional personal injury or property damage. The question, then, is what it means to be negligent.

II. The Reasonable Person Standard

Negligence is the failure to exercise the care that would have been exercised by the reasonably prudent person under the circumstances. Standing alone this definition is useful only as loose guidance for the jury. It is not a concrete rule, but a general standard that asks for a normative judgment. In many negligence cases, therefore, enormous reliance is placed on the jury to resolve the "mixed" question of law and fact, "should the defendant have behaved more carefully?" Karl Llewellyn once drew an analogy between legal rules and the game of golf. Rules, he said, are like chipping from off the green. They can get the ball onto the green, but you still have to putt to get the ball in the hole—i.e., to apply the rule to the facts. What Llewellyn said of concrete rules is even more true of general standards. In negligence cases the jury does the putting.

A general negligence standard can work well in many negligence cases. When jurors are familiar with the activity that gave rise to the plaintiff's injury, then they can easily apply the conscience of the community in evaluating the defendant's conduct. The kind of activities juries are likely to know about will vary with the time and place. For example, in *Vaughan v. Menlove*,[6] the defendant was sued for damage to the plaintiff's cottages resulting from a fire that started in

---

[6] 132 Eng. Rep. 490 (C.P. 1837).

one of the defendant's hay stacks. The question was whether the defendant had behaved negligently in placing a hay stack so near to the plaintiff's cottages, in light of the dry condition of the hay. I doubt that many of today's readers would feel competent to make that judgment without some assistance from expert witnesses. But in rural England in 1837, jurors probably would know how the community would expect the defendant to behave. The issue was one on which the jurors were likely to have had experience and an opinion.

The equivalent today would be an ordinary intersection accident between automobiles. Virtually everyone drives, and virtually everyone would feel capable of judging whether the defendant drove reasonably under the circumstances. In contrast, in cases involving complex or technical activities with which most of us are not automatically familiar—the provision of medical care or the design of products, for example—the task is more difficult and the jury must be educated by the parties before it can be expected to render an informed verdict. As we shall see, the law has ways of helping this process of education along, but even with this help the result must sometimes fall short of the ideal of the well-informed decisionmaker invoking settled community norms.

The idealized picture of the jury as the informed conscience of the community in negligence cases sometimes is unrealistic in another way as well. In some cases there may be well-developed and fairly uniform standards regarding the proper way to engage in a particular activity. Farmers may know and agree on the proper way to build hay stacks, and citizens may know and agree on the proper way to change lanes on a four-lane divided highway. But often, perhaps even usually, there are no pre-existing, uniform norms that jurors can invoke in order to decide whether the defendant was negligent. The facts of actual cases are so varied that general norms do not definitively resolve them. For example, in a highway accident case the jury's sense of the proper way to change lanes might depend on how much traffic there was on the highway; how fast the vehicles were travelling; and how much space between vehicles the drivers on that highway ordinarily maintain. To the extent that this is true, there is no precise rule that the jury can use to resolve the negligence issue. Rather, in effect the jury must create a rule for the particular case at hand based on the general "reasonableness" standard and then apply that rule to evaluate the defendant's behavior.

In situations such as this when no firm, pre-existing rule applies across the board, different juries are likely to resolve the negligence issue differently in cases involving the same or highly similar facts. Nothing in negligence law requires that like cases be decided alike by different juries. Rather, when there is no applicable rule that makes the reasonableness standard more concrete, instead of having negligence rules that resolve disputes on their own, we have a "process" for resolving negligence cases by submitting them to the jury. Fortunately, however, over time the law has put a bit of meat on the bones of the reasonableness standard by creating some rules that give the jury guidance as to the proper way to make its negligence/no negligence decision. The most important guidelines are the objective standard, the special rules governing children and the infirm, and the foreseeability requirement.

A. *The Objective Standard*

Perhaps the most important clarification of the negligence standard is that it is objective, not subjective. That the defendant did his best or acted in good faith is no defense. Rather, the question is how the reasonably prudent person would have acted under the circumstances, not whether the defendant meant well. Indeed, evidence of the defendant's benevolent state of mind ordinarily is not even admissible, because under the objective standard it is irrelevant. It is admittedly somewhat anomalous to hold that a defendant was negligent even if she could not have done any better. How can the defendant be at "fault" if she did her best? If the defendant is still at "fault" when she did her best, then legal fault obviously differs from moral fault. There are nonetheless a number of arguments that she should be held liable.

First, a subjective standard would be infinitely variable, depending on the particular strengths, weaknesses, and experiences of the individual in question. Applying such a standard would require much more complicated and difficult fact-finding than applying an objective standard. To apply a subjective standard the jury would have to determine how careful the defendant was capable of being, and whether she employed all her abilities. But to apply an objective reasonableness standard the jury need only compare the actual conduct of the defendant with that standard. Second, a subjective standard would encourage fraud and deception. If the negligence determination depended on the characteristics of the defendant, then the defendant would have an incentive to mislead the jury about those characteristics, understating her strengths and overstating her weaknesses. An objective standard does not create this problem because those strengths and weaknesses do not count.

Third, because the defendant's strengths and weaknesses do not count, the objective standard has greater potential for encouraging the defendant to exercise all the care and skill that she can. Admittedly, the defendant can only do as well as she is capable of doing; but under a subjective standard she may not even do that, relying on the vagaries of the fact-finding process for protection. In contrast, the objective standard is unforgiving; the threat of liability under an objective standard may therefore push potential defendants to do their best, especially if the reasonable person standard is set (as juries typically set it) at a level that is well within the reach of most people. Fourth, an objective standard gives the public assurance that those to whose actions they are exposed will either act with a predictable level of care or be liable for the consequences of failing to do so. Members of the public can therefore more accurately gauge the level of self-protective care that they need to employ than would be possible if the amount of care that could be expected varied with the characteristics of each individual. Finally, the great advantage of an objective standard is that it asks the members of the jury to judge the defendant based on their own knowledge and experience in the world. They need not engage in psychology or attempt to look into the defendant's mind. They need only decide how the reasonable person would have behaved, and measure the defendant's behavior against that standard.

As arguments for the objective standard, these points have considerable weight. But for a series of reasons, they are not indisputable. It would be far from unthinkable for jurors to inquire into the state of mind of the defendant in deciding whether she was negligent. Juries must do exactly that in cases involving battery and assault; they could do so in negligence cases as well, assessing the credibility of the defendant in order to minimize perjury. It is also true that a benefit of the objective standard is that it may create an incentive for defendants to exercise all the care they can; but this incentive cannot be created unless the fact that the standard is objective is communicated to and understood by the below-average individuals who are most likely to be affected by the standard but least likely to appreciate its significance for them. And although the objective standard may make some people's behavior more predictably safe, in light of the variable application of even the objective standard from jury to jury the size of this effect is debatable. Finally, it may be an advantage of the objective standard that it does not require the jury to engage in psychology; but if in many instances the jury must in effect construct a rule to govern a particular complex or technical situation with which it has no first-hand experience, its task is at least as challenging as deciding whether the defendant did his best.

Despite the strength of some of these counterarguments, the law has long adhered in the conventional case to the objective standard. There are situations, however, in which the standard is relaxed and at least some subjectivity is permitted to find its way into the negligence decision. The main cases involve children and the infirm.

B. Children and the Infirm

Notwithstanding the objective standard, the law has always made certain accommodations for children and the infirm. The scope of these accommodations sheds some additional light on the overall purpose of the objective standard.

1. Children

Children below about the age of five cannot be negligent at all, presumably because they cannot be expected to exercise care. Until about the mid-twentieth century the rule governing children above that age was that they are expected to exercise the degree of care that would be reasonable in a child of similar age, intelligence, and experience. This is what might be called a semi-objective standard, in that the reasonableness of the child's behavior is measured against the capacities of similar children in that age group. But a child of unusual intelligence or experience might be expected to exercise more care than would usually be expected of children of his age.

This rule was a concession to the reality that there is a limit to the degree of care that can be expected of children. The incentive-creating effects of an objective standard on adults whose capacities are below average are highly unlikely to influence children. Those who come into contact with children understand this and can exercise additional self-protective care when necessary. Moreover, until several decades ago there was little point to suing children in tort, since parents are not liable for the torts of their children (though they may be liable in their own right for negligent supervision) and children ordinarily have no substantial assets of their own.

The semi-objective children's reasonableness standard has now been qualified in many jurisdictions, however, by the proviso that when children engage in *adult activities*, they are held to an adult standard of care. The point made in the cases that have established this proviso is that potential victims of children who drive motor vehicles, fly airplanes, or operate motor boats, for example, have no way to anticipate which driver or pilot is a child. There is therefore no realistic way to exercise the additional self-protective care that is required when one encounters children engaged in children's activities. Furthermore, there is no particular social benefit to be gained by immunizing children against liability for harm caused by engaging in adult activities; unless a child is capable of complying with an adult standard of care he or she should not be driving, flying, or operating a motor boat. In addition, with the post-World War II rise of auto and homeowner's liability insurance, children are much more likely than in the past to be covered by their parents' liability insurance policies and thereby able to satisfy judgments rendered against them in negligence cases. Where insurance has gone, tort law has followed.

2. Adults

Pinpointing the standard that applies to physically and mentally infirm adults is more complicated. Typically, physical infirmities are taken into account in judging the reasonableness of behavior, but mental infirmities are not. The common law rule is that even insane people are liable for their torts. What might account for this difference? Indeed, why would there be a departure from the objective standard at all where physical infirmities are concerned? The answers tell us something about both the objective standard and the exceptions to it.

The main difference between physical and mental infirmities is that the former are typically visible, measurable, and verifiable. By contrast—especially in the nineteenth century when these rules developed—mental infirmities are invisible, hard to measure, and incompletely verifiable. The whole focus of the objective standard, in fact, is the classic case of this problem: the defendant in *Vaughan v. Menlove* (the haystack case) and others like him, who may assert that he just doesn't have the judgment or intelligence to be as careful about avoiding risk to others as the average or reasonable person does. The objective standard rejects this assertion, not because it is necessarily false, but because it is not necessarily true and it is difficult to know when it is true and when it is not. One might respond that those who have serious mental illness can now be easily and reliably identified and diagnosed. Perhaps, but even now psychiatric diagnosis is a dicey enterprise. Moreover, people who suffer delusions often have periods of lucidity. During such periods it may be negligent not to take action to prevent oneself from causing harm while delusional. This was the basis of the court's decision, for example, in *Breunig v. American Family Ins. Co.,*[7] in which the defendant thought that she and her car could fly "because Batman does it." Finally, often people who are psychotic or delusional are also capable of being careful. Just because I think that I am Napoleon doesn't mean that I don't know I should stop at a red light. In any event, such people commonly have guardians who have an interest in preserving their assets and therefore an incentive to monitor and control their behavior. This incentive would be diminished if the mentally ill were not liable for negligence. In contrast, physical infirmities pose measurement and verifiability problems to a much lesser degree and are therefore subject to a semi-objective standard. A blind person cannot read a sign that says "Warning: Highly Flammable Vapors. Do Not Smoke." If his smoking starts a fire, the jury will be instructed in a suit by the owner of the property damaged by fire that it may (probably must) take into account the defendant's blindness in determining whether he behaved reasonably or negligently under the circumstances. However, although usually a semi-objective standard is more lenient than an objective standard, there are times when the existence of the defendant's infirmity can cut the other way. The jury is permitted to take the defendant's physical infirmity into account in deciding whether his physical limitation should have led him to take precautions different from or additional to those expected of a reasonable person without the physical infirmity in question. Most obviously, a blind person should not drive a motor vehicle; a person in a wheelchair should be more hesitant about "jaywalking" than others.

It is worth noting, however, that over time our social attitudes toward physical and mental infirmities have evolved in favor of greater and greater involvement of people with those infirmities in everyday activities. At the very least evidence of what people with the same handicaps as the defendant's are capable of doing would be admissible

---

[7] 45 Wis.2d 536, 173 N.W.2d 619 (1970).

in his defense. And given evolving attitudes, in making the negligence decision at least some juries would be likely to reflect the evolution of our attitudes in this regard. What once would have been considered the taking of an imprudent risk by a handicapped person might not be today.

C. The Foreseeability Requirement

The logic of reasonable care involves a connection between knowledge and behavior. The defendant is not negligent unless he knew or reasonably should have known of the risk of harm to the plaintiff. Even then, the defendant is not negligent unless a reasonable person in under the circumstances would have taken precautions that the defendant did not take in order to avoid that risk. It would be nonsensical to say that someone was negligent for failing to reduce or eliminate a risk about which he did not and could not know. Consequently, a person cannot be negligent for failing to take precautions regarding an unforeseeable risk of harm.

For example, in one of the early cases on this issue, *Blyth v. Birmingham Water Works*,[8] a record freeze apparently caused leakage from one of the defendant's underground water mains, damaging the plaintiff's house. The trial court left it to the jury to decide whether the defendant was negligent (presumably either in the design of the system, or in failing to inspect it, or both), and the jury found for the plaintiff. However, on appeal the court held, in effect, that a directed verdict should have been granted for the defendant, reasoning that it was not unreasonable to fail to take precautions against a frost that "penetrated to a greater depth than any which ordinarily occurs south of the polar regions." For practical purposes the court seems to have concluded that the risk that materialized in harm to the plaintiff simply was not foreseeable.

Today, *Blyth* would almost certainly pose a question of fact for the jury. Few risks are so unforeseeable as to warrant granting a directed verdict to the defendant on that ground alone. That is especially true of weather. Nothing is so foreseeable as more severe weather than is normally foreseen. That is what is meant by 100 year floods and even 1000 year floods. It is foreseeable that such things will happen, though on a very infrequent basis. But even if the mere improbability of the risk that caused harm is not, in itself, a basis for exonerating the defen-

---

[8] 156 Eng. Rep. 1047 (Ex. 1856).

dant, this factor may figure in the overall negligence calculation. To put it another way, rarely does a defendant escape liability purely because a risk was utterly unforeseeable. Yet how likely or unlikely it was that a particular risk would materialize in harm is very relevant. We turn next, therefore, to what has been called the negligence "calculus," in which the probability of harm plays an important part.

III. The Negligence "Calculus"

Despite the different clarifications of the reasonable person standard that tort law has developed, the notion is still very general. A different angle of analysis that has emerged to help clarify what it means to be negligent has come to be called the negligence "calculus." The negligence calculus affords a way of thinking about when a reasonable person would risk harm and when a reasonable person would instead take steps to reduce that risk. The calculus unpacks the general notion of reasonable behavior into three components: the probability that a particular act or omission will cause harm; the magnitude of that harm if it occurs; and the value of the interest that must be foregone or sacrificed in order to reduce the risk of harm.

A. The Learned Hand Formulation

The negligence calculus received its most famous expression in an opinion by Judge Learned Hand in *United States v. Carroll Towing Co.*[9] In that case the question was whether it was negligent not to have personnel at all times on a barge under tow. Hand put the issue this way:

> the [barge] owner's duty, as in other similar situations, to provide against resulting injuries is a function of three variables: (1) The probability that she will break away; (2) the gravity of the resulting injury, if she does; (3) the burden of adequate precautions. Possibly it serves to bring this notion into relief to state it in algebraic terms: if the probability be called P; the injury, L; and the burden, B; liability depends upon whether B is less than L multiplied by P: i.e., whether B is less than PL.

Although Hand's use of even simple algebra might be overly technical for some people, the intuition behind the negligence calculus is straightforward. To determine whether taking a particular risky action

---

[9] 159 F.2d 169 (2d Cir. 1947).

is or is not reasonable, these three factors can be taken into account. The first two factors—the probability of harm and the magnitude of harm if it occurs—measure the "cost" of taking risky action. The last factor—the interest that must be sacrificed to reduce the risk of harm—measures the "cost" of reducing or avoiding the risk of harm. When the first two factors are more weighty than the last, then the cost of risking harm is greater than the cost of avoiding or reducing it. And when the cost of risking harm is greater than the cost of reducing or avoiding that risk, taking the risky action is unreasonable according to the negligence calculus. Conversely, if the interest that must be sacrificed to reduce or avoid a risk (normally, the cost of safety precautions) is more weighty than the risk of harm, then it is not unreasonable to take the risk.

The substance of the negligence calculus has been embodied in the Restatement (Second) of Torts §§ 291–293 (1965). As a clarification for the tort law theorist the calculation may be insightful, but can the calculus actually be used in litigation? There are a number of ways, though its litigation usefulness should not be overestimated. Conceivably a jury could be instructed that it might take the factors comprising the negligence calculus into account in deciding whether the defendant (or plaintiff) was negligent. But such instructions are rare and even when given probably should leave the jury the option of ignoring them. Certainly the calculus could also help a court to determine whether certain evidence (about the factors comprising the calculus) is relevant. And the intuition behind the negligence calculus, or reference to the specific factors articulated by the calculus, may help a court to rule on a motion for a directed verdict.

For example, in *Eckert v. Long Island R.R.*,[10] the plaintiff's decedent had saved a small child from near-certain death by sweeping the child off the tracks of a negligently-operated train. In the course of the rescue, however, the rescuer was killed. At the trial of an action by the rescuer's estate against the defendant railroad, the defendant moved for a "nonsuit"—in effect, a directed verdict—on the ground (among other things) that it was negligent as a matter of law for the rescuer to have risked his life as he did and that such "contributory" negligence by the plaintiff barred recovery. The court rejected this contention, stating that "[t]he law has so high a regard for human life that it will not impute negligence to an effort to preserve it, unless made under such circumstances as to constitute rashness in the judgment of prudent

---

[10] 43 N.Y. 502 (1871).

persons." But in a passage making it clear that something like the negligence calculus was at the heart of its reasoning, the court went on to indicate that if the rescue had been attempted merely to protect property from harm, the result would have been different.

If all this seems like ordinary common sense, it is. In these circumstances the negligence calculus is merely a way of identifying the factors that may lead to common-sense conclusions about which risks are worth taking and which are not, depending on what is at stake: the probability of harm (the chance that the child will be hit by the train); the magnitude of harm if it occurs (death or serious injury); and the interest that must be sacrificed to avoid the harm (the risk of death or serious injury to the rescuer). In other, more complex cases, reference to the factors that comprise the negligence calculus may also help to guide a judge's or a jury's thinking: How many people's safety did the defendant's action risk? How likely was it that harm would occur? What would have been involved in developing safety measures that would have reduced the risk of harm? How much could different possible safety measures have reduced the risk? When counsel for the parties direct some of the evidence in the case to these factors, they will assist the judge or jury in making sense out of the negligence question: whether one or both of the parties' conduct was reasonable under all the circumstances. This does not necessarily even have to take place under the rubric of the negligence calculus. Rather, the calculus is a clarification of why it makes sense to do what, in all probability, we would intuitively do anyway—think about the factors that might make a risk too dangerous to take.

B. Is the Calculus an Economic Theory of Negligence?

Some academics in the "law and economics" school have pressed the concept of the negligence calculus further, suggesting that Hand was articulating what amounts to an economic theory of negligence. Most notably, Judge (then Professor) Richard Posner argued in a famous article that the factors in the calculus are essentially economic.[11] Posner said that multiplying the probability of loss times the amount of loss that will be suffered if it occurs yields a measure of the economic benefit to be derived from avoiding the loss. Similarly, the cost of preventing the loss may be the cost of installing safety equipment or the benefit foregone by curtailing or eliminating the activity. If the cost of preventing the loss is greater than the benefit to be gained by avoid-

---

[11] See Richard A. Posner, *A Theory of Negligence*, 1 J. Legal Stud. 29 (1972).

ing it, said Posner, then society would be better off, in economic terms, to have the accident that results in the loss than to avoid it. In such a situation a defendant should not be considered negligent for failing to take precautions that would have been more costly than the result they would have avoided. Conversely, if the cost of a loss is greater than the cost of preventing it, society benefits from avoiding the loss and a defendant who fails to avoid it should be considered negligent.

Many who encounter the economic theory of negligence find it repulsive because it seems to reduce the entire accident problem to a question of money. *Should* negligence law be designed exclusively to promote economic efficiency by deterring only those accidents that are economically worth avoiding? When the question is posed in that manner it is easy to answer in the negative. There are, of course, other values worth promoting besides economic efficiency. But in a sense the question is a caricature when it is posed in this fashion. Remove the words "exclusively" and "economics" from the formulation and it seems so obviously true as to be trivial: *Should* negligence law be designed to deter only those accidents that are worth avoiding? Well, of course. Presumably the reasonably prudent person takes action to avoid those accidents that are "worth" avoiding, and does not take action to avoid accidents that are not "worth" avoiding. The whole question is how we should decide which accidents those are. That was Learned Hand's point in *Carroll Towing*. The implication of this point—that sometimes we will tolerate injury rather than require that it be avoided—is not entirely comfortable, but is a fact that most people are willing to live with after they understand what Hand was saying.

When this point is rephrased as a choice between injury and money, however, many people are unwilling to go along, for a number of reasons. First, it is not clear that economic efficiency—understood as maximizing resources and minimizing the waste of resources—is necessarily a goal to be preferred over others. Second, to be operational the economic theory of negligence requires that we place a dollar value on human safety in order to decide how much it is worth paying to avoid injury. It seems wrong to value human safety only in this way. Finally, the notion that the factors that would figure in the negligence calculus in many cases—human safety, convenience, the value of jobs foregone, and so forth—can all be reduced to a single currency of exchange and balanced against each other seems unrealistic.

As to the first objection, certainly economic efficiency is a value, other things being equal. While the economic theory of negligence may err in its exclusive focus on efficiency, it would be foolhardy to say that the law should simply ignore the impact that its rules have on the allocation of resources. Virtually everyone would agree that negligence law shouldn't encourage people to "waste" money on safety precautions. If that is true, then the issue is when we would consider money wasted, not whether being efficient about the way the law encourages people to spend money on safety is desirable. Of course whether safety precautions are cost-effective is something to take into account—even if it is not the only thing.

As to the second objection, whether we like it or not, in tort law we are forced to place a monetary value on human safety and physical well-being. For a jury to determine how much compensation to award an injured plaintiff it must engage in monetary valuation of precisely this kind. If a jury must do this in order to make an award after it has decided that the defendant was negligent, then it does not seem at all outrageous to imagine that such a valuation would be made as part of the process of determining whether the defendant was negligent to begin with.

This brings us to the third objection. Probably it is unrealistic to suppose that all the factors that could properly be taken into account under the negligence calculus could very often be reduced to a monetary value and then be accurately compared. Learned Hand himself recognized this point early on, when he noted that his calculus required a choice between "incommensurables"—things that cannot be compared.[12] More than that, however, the factors that make up the negligence calculus are likely in most cases to be difficult even to quantify, let alone to compare with each other. Statistics about the probability of particular kinds of injury in particular situations generally are not available, and when such statistics are available their relevance is debatable and their implications are complex. For example, the probability of harm depends on the severity of the injury with which one is concerned. Typically minor injury is a more probable consequence of any risk than major injury. The cost of safety precautions is likely to be easier to pinpoint on occasion, but not always. As a consequence, the precise comparison of quantitative values that seems to make the economic theory of negligence unpalatable—the economic cost of avoiding injury as against the economic benefit of doing so—will rarely be

---

[12] *Conway v. O'Brien*, 111 F.2d 611, 612 (2d Cir. 1940).

possible. Instead, as Hand envisioned, more or less loose efforts at quantification ordinarily can do no more than center the jury's attention on the factors that might be determinative in a given case.

Even staunch opponents of the economic theory of negligence, however, would do well to remember one additional point. Whether or not tort law adopts an economic theory of negligence, the parties that find themselves frequently involved as defendants in negligence suits—most notably sizable corporate enterprises—are likely to behave in accordance with the theory. Even if the law were to employ a thoroughly non-economic approach to negligence, such defendants still would attempt in advance to compare the cost of risking liability for particular categories of injury against the cost of taking safety precautions to reduce that risk. Such enterprises would attempt to avoid the accidents "worth" it to them to avoid, but would prefer to incur liability for the accidents not "worth" avoiding, because by taking this approach their liability costs would be lower than their avoidance costs. Whether we like it or not, therefore, the economic theory of negligence is likely to be relevant in at least this way to tort law's calculations about the best way to affect the behavior of those whose actions risk causing accidents. In this sense the theory is highly practical, for it predicts how defendants who are economically motivated will behave in response to the threat of liability for negligence, however that concept is defined.

C. *The Poor Man's Calculus: The Untaken Precaution*

It is often said that the plaintiff is under no obligation to prove the particular safety measure that the defendant should have employed; rather, the plaintiff need only prove that in acting as he did, the defendant did not behave with reasonable prudence. This may be true, but in many cases the plaintiff goes farther than he or she is required to, and actually attempts to prove that there was a particular precaution that the defendant should have taken, and that, more probably than not, if this precaution had been taken the plaintiff would not have been harmed.[13] Often the nature of the untaken precaution is obvious. If a defendant is alleged to have collided with the plaintiff at an intersection controlled by a traffic signal, the untaken precaution is the defendant's failure stop at the red light. In many cases, however, the best

---

[13] See Mark F. Grady, *Untaken Precautions*, 18 J. Legal Stud. 139 (1989).

way to show that the defendant did not exercise reasonable care is to prove some less obvious precaution or safety measure that was available, inexpensive, and potentially effective.

Disputes over the viability of an untaken precaution are often the core of negligence cases involving activities with which jurors are not ordinarily familiar. Such disputes presuppose something like the negligence calculus, even when it is not made explicit. The plaintiff points to a precaution and proves—sometimes through expert testimony, sometimes not—that it would have been easy enough for the defendant to have taken the precaution, especially in light of the risk of severe injury that the precaution would have reduced or avoided. Then the defendant attempts to show that the precaution could not easily have been employed, either because it would in fact be expensive, or would interfere with the easy or safe conduct of the activity. The dispute is formally about whether the reasonably prudent person would have taken the precaution, but that dispute is informed by evidence and argument about the factors that enter into the negligence calculus. But of course the evidence may not be quantitative in the way that the economic theory of negligence envisions.

IV. Custom

The rules governing "custom" are well-developed and reasonably clear. By far the dominant rule is that evidence of compliance or non-compliance with an industry custom is relevant and admissible, but not dispositive. That is, even in the face of uncontradicted evidence of the defendant's compliance or non-compliance with custom, the jury may find that the defendant was or was not negligent. The interesting points in this area involve the application and rationale for this rule.

A. Application

Whether a particular practice is sufficiently widespread to constitute a "custom" may itself be a jury question. A practice need not be universal to constitute a custom, although it must be more than just one of a number of different practices. At the very least it must be something done by most people or entities. If the practice in question does qualify as a custom, then the party on whose behalf the evidence of compliance or non-compliance was admitted is entitled to an instruction expressly permitting the jury to consider the fact that there was compliance or non-compliance with that custom. This kind of instruction may give the evidence weight with the jury. That is why the parties may fight over the issue. But even if a practice does not qualify as a custom, evidence of non-compliance with a practice in which some others engage may be admitted and considered by the jury anyway. The plaintiff is certainly entitled to point to an untaken precaution that he or she contends the reasonable person would take. Evidence that some others take the precaution helps to prove that it is reasonable to take it, even if it is not so widespread as to be customary. Thus, failing to prove that a practice with which the defendant did not comply is a custom ordinarily will not prevent the plaintiff from proving what he wishes—that the defendant failed to take a precaution that some others take.

It is less clear whether a defendant who wants to show that the practice it followed is also followed by others may do so when the practice is not so widespread as to constitute a custom. As the next section indicates, one of the reasons for admitting evidence of the defendant's compliance with custom is to inform the jury that, if it finds the defendant negligent, it is in effect finding an entire industry negligent. If a particular practice is not a custom, however, the evidence that the defendant followed the practice is not necessary for this purpose. For this reason, failing to prove that a practice is a custom may well disadvantage defendants more than it disadvantages plaintiffs.

B. Rationale

Evidence of non-compliance or compliance with custom is only relevant, not dispositive. As to non-compliance, the defendant may be able to explain why he departed from the custom of his industry: complying with custom may have been dangerous under the circumstances, or he may reasonably (and perhaps correctly) believe that his precautions are superior to customary precautions. As to compliance, an entire industry may, conceivably, be negligent in the way it conducts itself.

For example, in *The T.J. Hooper*,[14] the defendant was an operator of tug boats towing barges that were lost in a storm along with their cargo. The negligence alleged was the failure to supply the tugs with radios which would have warned them of the approaching storm. Although many tug boat captains carried their own radios, the court

---

[14] 60 F.2d 737 (2d Cir. 1932).

concluded that it was not the custom of tug owners to supply radios. Nonetheless, the court upheld a finding of negligence on the part of the tug owner for failing to supply radios:

> Indeed in most cases reasonable prudence is in fact common prudence; but strictly it is never its measure; a whole calling may have unduly lagged in the adoption of new and available devices * * * [T]here are precautions so imperative that even their universal disregard will not excuse their omission.[15]

Thus, evidence regarding compliance with custom can never be automatically dispositive. But why is it even relevant? The principal reason that evidence of custom is relevant is of course that it reflects the judgment of a large number of those who engage in a risky activity about the best way to conduct the activity. Compliance therefore *tends* to prove reasonableness, and non-compliance *tends* to prove negligence. In addition, potential victims sometimes are aware of the customary practices of potential injurers. On this basis potential victims can make judgments about the necessary levels of self-protective care they should take. Non-compliance with custom may thus tend to show negligence if the plaintiff can also show that the defendant knew or should have known that potential victims were relying on the defendant's taking customary precautions. Similarly, proof of compliance with custom may show that the defendant took the precautions that potential victims generally anticipate, and therefore may tend to show that the defendant's behavior was reasonable.

Evidence regarding custom may be relevant in one or both of two other ways as well. First, proof that the defendant did not comply with a custom of the industry tends to show that the precaution the plaintiff claims was feasible was in fact feasible. After all, the rest of the industry takes the precaution. Second, although under the rule in *T.J. Hooper* the jury may find the defendant negligent despite compliance with industry custom, evidence of the custom's existence serves to impress upon the jury the seriousness of what it would be doing by finding the defendant negligent. A finding of negligence under these circumstances amounts to a finding that the defendant's entire industry—not the defendant alone—has been behaving negligently. The jury has the authority to make such a finding, but it ought not do so without appreciating the implications of its decision.

---

[15] Id. at 740.

Beyond all this, the general function of this body of law governing custom should be put in context. As negligence cases move from simple to complex activities, from the familiar to the unfamiliar, juries need increasing assistance in understanding the nature of the activities under scrutiny and in forming judgments about the way in which to evaluate the degree of care that it is reasonable to employ in conducting these activities. Many jurors in the nineteenth century were capable of making such judgments about farming accidents almost without assistance, just as modern jurors are readily capable of determining whether the defendant in a run-of-the-mill automobile collision drove reasonably. But modern jurors are likely to know a lot less, for example, about the shipping industry, or about the various advantages and disadvantages of shatterproof glass. Evidence of industry custom—as well as of non-compliance with custom—can help to educate jurors about these activities and thereby to put them in a position to make informed decisions. Thus, among other things the rules governing custom perform an "educational" function for the jury.

V. Malpractice

In contrast to the rules that apply in ordinary negligence cases, different rules govern the conduct of professionals, including physicians, attorneys, and accountants. Most of the "action" in this field, however, involves medical malpractice suits. This form of litigation has grown exponentially in the last several decades. In 1960 across the nation, physicians and hospitals paid under $100 million for insurance against liability for medical malpractice—a rough measure of the direct cost of medical malpractice litigation. In contrast, in the late 1990's, physicians and hospitals are paying nearly $10 billion annually for such insurance—an increase of about 10,000 percent. A variety of factors have contributed to this enormous expansion in the cost of medical malpractice liability: legal changes permitting more suits; increases in the cost of health care, which is of course a component of the damages awarded for medical malpractice; the greater willingness of some people to bring suit against physicians, some of whom are merely "specialists" with whom the plaintiff has no longstanding relationship; the increased specialization and consequently greater ability of plaintiffs' attorneys; and, ironically, medical advances themselves, which create greater opportunities for medical "error" than in the past.[16]

A. *The Special Standard of Care for Professionals*

In ordinary negligence litigation, failure to comply with custom is not automatically negligent, and complying with custom is not automatically reasonable care. In contrast, in cases involving professionals, the rule is that compliance with custom insulates the defendant from liability, and failure to comply with custom is malpractice. And in medical malpractice, the standards of the medical profession are the relevant "custom." Thus, the plaintiff's proof that the defendant committed malpractice consists entirely of proof that the defendant violated the standards of the profession. Conversely, the defendant's case on the issue consists entirely of proof that the defendant complied with the standards of the profession. Indeed, in many jurisdictions a "respectable minority" rule obtains, under which non-compliance with a standard rejected by much of the profession is not malpractice, as long as the defendant complied with a school of thought or practice followed by a respectable minority.

What justifies so radical a departure from the treatment of custom in ordinary negligence cases? The answer must lie in necessity. Certainly as a general matter the activity that is the subject of scrutiny in professional liability cases is considerably more complex, and the jury is substantially less familiar with it, than the activities that are the subject of ordinary negligence cases. In a medical malpractice case, for example, to ask the jury to go beyond professional standards to determine whether it was reasonable for the defendant to follow a particular medical course of treatment would in effect ask for the jury's medical judgment—something that no member of the jury is likely to be capable of giving.

For the reader who thinks that this approach lets physicians and other professionals off too easily, remember that the dispositive effect of custom in medical malpractice cases cuts both ways: although compliance with custom automatically insulates the physician from liability, deviation from custom automatically triggers a finding of malpractice. One might even argue that, to the extent that the justifica-

---

[16] For more extensive discussion of these and other factors, see generally Paul C. Weiler, MEDICAL MALPRACTICE ON TRIAL (1991).

tion for this overall approach is the jury's inability to adjudicate cases involving complex, technical, and scientific issues, the problem is not that malpractice law departs from the normal treatment of custom, but that the law ought to find a way to apply the approach to custom taken in professional liability cases to complex cases involving non-professional liability as well. After all, the jury is just as likely to be at sea in making judgments about what constitutes reasonable care in other technically complex and unfamiliar cases as it is in medical malpractice cases. Yet largely for reasons of history and continuing solicitude for professionals—one group of whom are appellate judges who are former practicing lawyers—the special rule governing professional liability has not spread to other areas.

Another reason for the application of the special standard to professionals alone is that in practice the standard may not operate so differently from ordinary cases. Like most legal issues, most difficult medical issues cannot be resolved by reference to a definitive, black-letter rule; medical judgment is required. Expert testimony therefore does not usually point to a precise "standard" that governs the problem that the defendant faced. Rather, experts for each side tend to testify about what they would have done in the defendant's place, and what they believe good medical practice required. Often this kind of testimony could be interpreted to be about medical custom and to trigger the insulation from liability afforded by the "respectable minority" rule referred to earlier. But a number of courts interpret such testimony as being in conflict about what the prevailing medical standard actually is, and leave that question to the jury. In addition, of course, many malpractice cases turn heavily on disputed facts and must therefore go the jury regardless of the prevailing standard of care. Given the maze of facts and issues presented to it, the jury may well give the court's instruction on the respectable minority rule less consideration than might otherwise be expected. This may help to explain how it is possible that malpractice costs have risen 10,000 percent during a forty-year period in which compliance with custom purportedly has provided physicians with immunity from malpractice liability.

B. The Demise of the "Strict Locality" Rule

The demise of the strict locality rule is another factor that has contributed to the escalating cost of medical malpractice liability. That rule operated in the following way. Proof of the relevant medical standards almost always is provided in the form of expert testimony by physicians practicing in the defendant's specialty. Without such testimony the plaintiff could not survive the defendant's motion for a directed verdict, since the jury is rarely familiar on its own with the relevant standards. For many years this testimony had to come from a physician competent to testify as to the medical standard prevailing in the defendant's own community. Often courts held that only a physician actually practicing in that very community could provide such testimony. This "strict locality" rule made it extremely difficult for a potential plaintiff to secure an expert both competent and willing to testify. In any locale where physicians knew each other well and worked together, personal colleagues often were reluctant to testify against each other. The result came to be called the "conspiracy of silence," since it often appeared to plaintiffs and their attorneys that physicians "conspired" not to testify against their colleagues. When plaintiffs could not secure an expert witness whose testimony would be admissible pursuant to the strict locality rule and such a witness was a prerequisite to making out a *prima facie* case, there was no point in going to trial, and sometimes no point even in making a claim.

The strict locality rule may have made sense when medical standards varied significantly from community to community, especially when the limited resources available in small communities influenced or dictated the kind of treatment that could be provided. As the degree of variation declined and medical standards became increasingly uniform and national, however, the justification for the strict locality rule diminished. At that point the rule served mainly to place an artificial obstacle in the way of plaintiffs' search for experts willing to testify on their behalf. A rule that had once been grounded in the substantive differences between localities became a technical requirement without much substance to support it.

It is no surprise, therefore, that the rule broke down in a variety of ways and then eventually disintegrated. For example, some courts held that although the standard to be applied in assessing the defendant's conduct still was that of the locality in which she practiced, physicians from other localities who had familiarized themselves with the standards of the defendant's locality were competent to testify about those standards. Other courts went further, holding that the strict locality rule was too restrictive, and that the appropriate test to measure the defendant's conduct was the standard of practice prevailing in the same locality or localities "similar" to the locality where the defendant practiced. With the increasing nationalization of medical standards, this approach is tantamount to the adoption of a national standard but with a soft restriction on those who can testify to the standard, perhaps with

73

some leeway taking into account any limitation on resources available in smaller communities. Finally, many courts (including some of those that first took only one of the intermediate steps just described) have gone all the way in rejecting any form of locality rule, holding instead that national standards govern and that any expert familiar with such standards can testify about them.

The result has been a much more freewheeling litigation environment, in which some physicians have become professional witnesses, spending most or even all of their time as experts in litigation rather than practicing medicine. A number of states have enacted rules limiting potential witnesses to those who still practice medicine. In some states things have thus come full circle from the old days of the conspiracy of silence, and concern is frequently voiced about excessive numbers of frivolous malpractice suits. Although available data do not support the claim that more than a negligible proportion of malpractice suits are completely groundless, other criticisms of the system can be made. For example, only a fraction of those who are injured by medical malpractice actually sue and obtain recoveries. Conversely, many of those who do obtain recoveries appear, from retrospective examination of their records, not to have been the victims of malpractice.[17] Apparently the system is not terribly good at compensating deserving claimants, or at denying compensation to claimants whose claims do not warrant it. In short, there is a considerable mismatch between those who deserve compensation under the rules governing malpractice and those who receive compensation.

C. Informed Consent

Over time there has developed a cause of action distinct from ordinary malpractice, based on the physician's failure to obtain the patient's informed consent to treatment. The interest protected by this cause of action is the patient's right to determine whether to take the risks associated with any given form of medical treatment. A totally unconsented to treatment would of course constitute battery. In contrast, actions for informed consent sound in negligence or malpractice, for they involve the claim that although the patient consented to treatment, consent was not sufficiently informed because of the physician's failure to provide the patient with the requisite information about the risks associated with the treatment.

---

[17] See P. Weiler et. al., A MEASURE OF MALPRACTICE 69–76 (1993).

1. Informed Consent Standards

Most medical treatments involve some risk. The treatment itself may not succeed; pain, inconvenience, or disturbance of normal bodily functions may accompany treatment; and some treatments or procedures may risk serious, permanent side effects such as incontinence or paralysis. The doctrine of informed consent requires the physician to inform the patient of these risks, so that the patient may decide whether to take the risks of submitting to treatment, to seek alternative treatment, or to select no treatment at all. Because for most people the decision whether to risk the possible side effects of medical treatment depends on what is to be gained from the treatment, the physician must also inform the patient of the benefits of the treatment, including the probability that it will or will not be successful. Note that to prevail on a claim sounding in informed consent the plaintiff need not show that the treatment that was provided was malpractice. Rather, the plaintiff may prevail even when the treatment was provided in accordance with all relevant medical standards, *if* the treatment resulted in bodily injury and *if* the plaintiff would have decided not to have the treatment if he or she had been adequately informed.

There are two different standards for determining whether the requirements of the doctrine of informed consent have been satisfied. The *reasonable-patient* standard requires the physician to disclose information about the risks and benefits of treatment that a reasonable patient in what the physician knows to be the patient's situation would wish to know.[18] This standard does not ask the physician to be a mind-reader; if the patient has unusual interests or concerns of which the physician is unaware, then disclosure of information that a reasonable patient would not desire but that this patient would in fact have desired is not required. On the other hand, once the physician knows of the patient's unusual interests or concerns, then the disclosure necessary to satisfy those interests or concerns is required. The reasonable-patient standard employs what amounts to an ordinary negligence test to determine whether informed consent has been obtained. Medical custom regarding information disclosure may be relevant in actions brought under this standard, but is not dispositive: under the reasonable-patient standard, the failure to obtain informed consent is not actionable as malpractice, but as negligence. Consequently, expert testimony still is ordinarily required in order to establish what the risks

---

[18] See *Canterbury v. Spence*, 464 F.2d 772 (D.C. Cir. 1972).

and benefits of the treatment in question were; but there need be no expert testimony regarding the defendant's violation of the standard of care, since the jury is competent to determine what a reasonable patient would have wanted to know under the circumstances.

In contrast, under a *reasonable-physician* standard the failure to obtain the patient's informed consent is actionable only as malpractice. The plaintiff-patient must therefore meet the requirements of a malpractice action by proving that the defendant-physician failed to comply with the standards of the profession regarding disclosure of information to patients in the plaintiff's position. Expert testimony is required not only as to the relevant risks and benefits, but also as to the applicable medical standard regarding disclosure of these risks and benefits.

On their face these two standards seem to represent very different philosophies. The reasonable-patient standard appears to put the patient in complete control, rejecting medical determination of the information to be disclosed. The reasonable-physician standard seems to place the medical profession in control, permitting the professional to determine what information the patient needs to know. In practice, however, these days most physicians are likely simply out of concern for their patients to disclose the information that they think their patients want, regardless of the jurisdiction in which they practice. Consequently, the medical standard for disclosure and patient desires for information are likely to converge, notwithstanding the logical possibility that under the reasonable-physician standard the profession as a whole could decide to disclose only a little information, without fear of liability. In fact, the courts probably would not be comfortable with the reasonable-physician standard if that were to occur. The major differences between the two approaches, therefore, lie in the requirement that there be expert testimony as to the applicable standard of disclosure under the reasonable-physician standard, and in the possibility that liability will be imposed less often under that standard where the respectable-minority rule obtains.

2. Causation in Informed Consent Cases

Even after the plaintiff has proved the failure of the defendant to make proper information disclosure, proof of a causal connection between that failure and the plaintiff's injury is required. The matter of causation is the subject of another Chapter, but a brief exploration here helps to tell us a bit more about informed consent. To prove causation, the plaintiff must show that "but for" the defendant's failure to disclose the requisite information, the plaintiff would not have suffered the harm resulting from the treatment provided. Ordinarily this means that the plaintiff must show that he would have declined the treatment that caused his injury if he had been given the requisite information about the risks posed by the treatment. Some courts also require the plaintiff to show that the treatment he would have selected (including no treatment) would have caused less injury.

Proving causation in an informed consent case often is difficult, because many people—perhaps most—take the advice of their physician even after he or she has disclosed the information required by the doctrine of informed consent. People are likely to decide to follow a physician's advice except in two situations: when there are two plausible courses of treatment and the physician recommends one but believes the other also to be reasonable; and when the patient is sufficiently idiosyncratic that the physician's sense of what risks are worth taking and the individual's sense of this are very different. Of course, the plaintiff would not even be suing if he did not contend that, had the requisite information been disclosed, he would have chosen a different course of treatment. Consequently, the plaintiff's own conclusory testimony on this score may not be worth very much as proof for the jury.

Many courts have therefore adopted what amounts to an objective standard governing the causation issue. Under this standard the jury is instructed to resolve the issue by asking whether a reasonable person in the plaintiff's position would have declined treatment if the requisite information on risks and benefits had been disclosed. The plaintiff is permitted to testify, but his testimony is simply one piece of evidence for the jury about what he would have done had his informed consent been properly sought. In retrospect the plaintiff may believe that he would have declined treatment; but the question for the jury is what a reasonable person in the plaintiff's position would have done. In this regard the plaintiff's testimony can be either almost useless or extraordinarily helpful. If the plaintiff merely asserts that he would have disregarded his or her physician's advice without providing a persuasive explanation for this conclusion, the jury may regard the testimony as merely self-serving. But if the plaintiff identifies an idiosyncrasy or value that would have caused him to disregard his physician's advice, such testimony can be very persuasive. The plaintiff may have an unusual concern about scarring, or prefer a shorter life expectancy without the rigors of chemotherapy. As the court in *Scott v. Bradford* put it, "the causation question must be resolved by examining the

credibility of the plaintiff's testimony."[19] If these sorts of idiosyncracies or values asserted by the plaintiff can be corroborated through
evidence about plaintiff's past behavior or even serious conversations
with others in the past reflecting these values or idiosyncracies, then
the plaintiff's testimony will be all the more credible.

These considerations suggest that the doctrine of informed consent
really is serving two functions at once. First, the doctrine protects the
interest of idiosyncratic patients who do not share the values of their
physicians or of most patients, and who would therefore act very differently from the ordinary patient if adequately informed of the risks
and benefits of proposed treatment. Second, the doctrine encourages
the dissemination of information to the great mass of "ordinary" patients who will take their physicians' advice with or without the information, but whose autonomous right to make informed decisions is
promoted by encouraging physicians to make disclosure of the risks
and benefits of treatment.

In recognizing the need to protect these interests, however, we
must take care not to adopt too unrealistic a view of the process by
which informed consent is obtained. There is a difference between an
"informed" decision by the patient and an "independent" decision by
the patient. The doctrine of informed consent attempts to secure the
former, not the latter. Sometimes the opinions in cases involving the
doctrine speak as if the two were the same, and that the physician's
disclosure of information transmits to the patient everything needed for
the patient to make a treatment decision. This ultra-rationalistic model
of patient decisionmaking is unrealistic. Many patients who find that
they have serious medical problems become psychologically depend-
ent on others, including their physicians. This condition of dependency, along with genuine ambivalence about what treatment to pursue,
is not compatible with the ultra-rationalistic model of patient decision.
The doctrine of informed consent quite properly requires that patients
be informed of the risks and benefits of proposed treatments. But patients in a condition of dependency and vulnerability are unlikely simply to take the information and make entirely independent decisions
about treatment. They will want to talk at length with their family and
their physicians to obtain the opinion of these other people about the
right course of treatment to follow. It may be that the most salutary
function of the doctrine of informed consent, therefore, is not simply to

---

[19] 606 P.2d 554 (Sup. Ct. of Oklahoma 1979).

inform the patient, but to help the patient's family and friends to open an informed dialogue with the patient about the course of treatment that will best reflect and protect the patient's values and concerns.

VI. Violation of Statutes

We live in an age of statutes. For this reason, many acts alleged to be negligent also violate statutes. The standard approach holds that the unexcused violation of a statute is negligence "per se"—that is, negligence as a matter of law. That was the rule enunciated by Judge Cardozo in the famous case of *Martin v. Herzog*.[20] If the legislature actually provided in each statute it enacted that there shall be an action in tort for injuries caused by violation of the statute, then the reason for this standard approach would be easy to see. But most statutes do not contain such provisions. Occasionally statutes provide for such causes of action, but more often they provide only for criminal penalties in the event of violation. One might even speculate—though probably inaccurately—that since the legislature knows how to include a cause of action for statutory violation in the laws it enacts, the absence of such provision should be taken as an expression of legislative intent that there be no such cause of action. Consequently, legislative intent is not a satisfactory explanation of the rule that violation of a statute is negligence per se.

It is more accurate to understand the rule as a common law creation, based on the notion that the reasonable person does not violate statutes. The result is that in the ordinary case, the jury is not permitted to decide whether the violation of a statute was or was not negligent: the unexcused violation of a statute is negligence. But since sometimes the violation of a statute can be "excused," technically there is only a presumption that violation of a statute is negligence per se. Under this formulation, in the absence of a competent excuse the jury is required to find that violation of a statute is negligent.

A. *Legally Cognizable Excuses*

A great deal may then turn on when a party may be "excused" for the violation of a statute. But the categories of excuses are none too helpful because they are so general: incapacity, emergency, and necessity. For example, in *Tedla v. Ellman*,[21] the plaintiff was struck by the

---

[20] 228 N.Y. 164, 126 N.E. 814 (1920).

[21] 280 N.Y.124, 19 N.E. 2d 987 (1939)·

defendant's vehicle while she was walking with her back to the traffic on her side of a road instead of walking with her face to the traffic on the other side of the road, as a statute required. The plaintiff argued that she was not negligent, because on that day the traffic was much heavier on the side of the highway where the statute seemed to require her to walk, and that it would therefore have been much more dangerous for her to comply with the statute than to violate it. In an opinion not distinguished for its clarity, the court agreed, seeming at least in part to suggest that a statute (such as the one in question) that codified a common law rule rather than reversing it should be read to contain an implied exception for cases in which compliance with a statute would involve a greater risk of harm than violation. But it may also be sensible to think of *Tedla* as involving the excuse of necessity.

B. The Defense of Limited Statutory Purpose

A second defense permits the defendant to show that the plaintiff was not in the class of persons intended to be protected by the statute which the defendant violated. For example, in *Di Caprio v. New York Central Railway Co.*,[22] the defendant violated a statute requiring that fences be erected to keep livestock off its tracks. There was no recovery when the plaintiff's young son was killed after wandering onto the tracks, because protection against this risk was not the object of the statute.

Despite the theoretical availability of this defense in cases involving violation of statute, the defense rarely prevails in practice. Statutes usually do not carry their purposes on their face. Rather, their purpose is a matter of judgment and of judicial construction. Unless the plaintiff could not by any stretch of the imagination have been an intended beneficiary of the statute's protection, modern courts are likely to hold that at least a "secondary" purpose of the statute was to protect individuals in the plaintiff's situation. There are a number of cases in which defendants have violated statutes apparently designed mainly for the protection of persons other than the plaintiff, yet the courts hold that those in the plaintiffs' situation do fall within the class of those protected. For example, "dram shop" shop statutes in many states prohibit the sale of alcoholic beverages to those who appear to be inebriated. In a number of cases the individual who has been served in

---

[22] 231 N.Y. 94, 131 N.E. 746 (1921).

violation of the statute is shortly thereafter involved in an auto accident in which a third party is injured. The plaintiff third party then sues both the driver and the server, and the server's defense is that the statutory protection does not extend to the plaintiff. Many courts reject this defense, construing the statutory purpose broadly.[23] Similarly, statutes or municipal ordinances sometimes prohibit leaving vehicles parked with keys in the ignition. When a thief steals a vehicle parked with a key in the ignition and his negligent driving injures the plaintiff, the courts typically hold that the purpose of these enactments is not only to protect the vehicle's owner, but also to protect those who might be injured by the negligent driving of the thief. The defense of limited statutory purpose is therefore not available to the owner or custodian of the vehicle in a suit by a third party injured by the thief's negligent driving.[24]

There are two ways of predicting how the courts will rule on this scope-of-statutory-purpose of issue. The first is to see whether there is legislative history or a preamble to the statute in question, indicating its purpose or purposes. If there is any reference at all to those in the plaintiff's situation, then the courts are highly likely to find that the plaintiff is an intended beneficiary. The absence of such reference, however, is not determinative: the courts may still find the plaintiff to be an intended beneficiary. The second predictor is more complicated. If violation of the statute does not at all increase the risk of harm to those in the plaintiff's situation, then the courts are very unlikely to hold that the plaintiff is an intended beneficiary. It would not be sensible to say that a statute is intended to protect a particular class of persons if violation of the statute does not increase the risk to those in the class. For instance, suppose that I borrow your car and the car is damaged by lightning while I am exceeding the speed limit. I am negligent per se; and if I had not been speeding, the car probably would not have been damaged by the lightning, because it would have been at a different place when lightning struck. Violating the statute, however, did not increase the risk of lightning damage; therefore you are not in the class of intended beneficiaries, at least as to this risk. In contrast, if violating a statute does increase the risk of harm to those in the plaintiff's situation—such as the plaintiffs in the dram shop and key in the ignition cases—then the courts may well hold that the plain-

---

[23] See, e.g., *Vesely v. Sager*, 5 Cal.3d 153, 486 P.2d 151, 95 Cal. Rptr. 623 (1971).

[24] See, e.g., *Ross v. Hartman*, 139 F.2d 14 (D.C. Cir. 1943).

tiff falls within the class of the statute's beneficiaries. The greater the increase of risk to those in the plaintiff's situation resulting from a violation of the statute, the greater the probability that the court will hold that the statute protects the plaintiff. All this sometimes takes place under the rubric of "proximate cause" (a subject that we take up in Chapter Six) rather than negligence per se, but the analysis is essentially the same.

Perhaps the most celebrated case in which something like this notion lurks is *Brown v. Shyne*.[25] In that case the defendant, a chiropractor, violated a statute prohibiting the practice of medicine without a license. The treatment the defendant provided the plaintiff injured him, and the plaintiff sued. The court held that violation of the statute was irrelevant to the plaintiff's claim. A license to practice medicine, said the court, confers no additional skill on its holder, and therefore is irrelevant to the question whether the defendant committed malpractice in his treatment of the plaintiff. The dissent took issue with this assertion in concluding that the defendant's violation of the statute was, at the least, some evidence of negligence: "The prohibition against practicing medicine without a license was for the very purpose of protecting the public from just what happened in this case."

The result in *Brown v. Shyne* is questionable. If the case is analyzed by asking whether evidence of the violation of the statute could tend to prove an increased risk to those in the plaintiff's position, the issue becomes more clear. It is true that having a license in and of itself confers no additional skill on its holder. But as a group, those who do not have a license to practice medicine surely are less capable of following applicable medical standards than those who are licensed to practice. Consequently, it can be plausibly argued that the absence of a license is at least some evidence that the defendant did not comply with the applicable medical standard in treating the plaintiff, since the absence of a license is some evidence that the defendant did not have the skill and knowledge that would have enabled him to comply. Of course, not everyone without a license is incapable of complying with the applicable standard. Perhaps the defendant had lost his license the day before treating the plaintiff because his renewal form had been lost in the mail. But these are matters of evidence, to be taken into account by the jury.

---

[25] 242 N.Y. 176, 151 N.E. 197 (1926).

One could go even further and argue that the purpose of the statute was to prevent unlicensed practitioners from putting patients at risk of being treated by those who are not capable of complying with medical standards. It would then follow that the defendant was negligent per se, although the plaintiff's claim would not be for malpractice, but for negligent violation of the licensing statute. In any event, this analysis suggests that the argument that evidence of the statutory violation should play a role in *Brown* is grounded not only on intuition but also on logic.

VII. Negligence as a Matter of Law: The Roles of Judge and Jury

Thus far we have been exploring the ways that the law pours meaning into the concept of negligence, largely in order to assist the jury in making the negligence determination. This exploration has assumed that the jury ordinarily makes that determination. But that is not always the case. In certain situations—for example, in the case of the violation of statutes—that decision is kept from the jury and made by the court "as a matter of law." But there is also a general rule about whether an issue is or is not "a jury question." Issues are submitted for decision by the jury if "reasonable people could disagree" about the resolution of the issue. And issues are decided as a matter of law if "reasonable people could not disagree." This rule applies both to pure questions of fact (i.e., entirely empirical issues) and to mixed questions of fact and law, such as whether the defendant was negligent.

The decision whether a particular issue poses a jury question is made at trial through rulings on motions for a directed verdict and, in more complicated situations, through jury instructions. For example, if there is uncontradicted evidence that I drove blindfolded down Main Street and collided with the plaintiff's vehicle, then whether I was negligent will not be a jury question. Rather, at the close of the evidence the court would grant the plaintiff's motion for a directed verdict on the issue of my negligence. Reasonable people could not disagree that I was negligent. But if the factual question whether I drove blindfolded is in dispute, then the court could not simply grant a directed verdict on the issue. Instead, the jury will be instructed that, if it finds that I drove blindfolded, then it *must* find that I was negligent, because driving blindfolded is negligent as a matter of law.

This is, in effect, lawmaking by the courts about what constitutes negligence. In granting a motion for a directed verdict on the negligence issue, a court is not ruling that a jury *would not* find for the defendant, but that the jury *should not* and therefore *may not* so find, because it would be unreasonable to do so. There is of course an element of judgment involved in the granting of directed verdicts on mixed questions of fact and law. The judgments of different trial courts on such questions involving the same or similar sets of facts are harmonized through the appellate process. Whether a directed verdict should have been granted is a question of law that can be decided on appeal and, over time, the trial courts can be given guidance through appellate decisions regarding the kinds of questions that should and should not be submitted to juries.

There is also considerable significance in a decision to deny a motion for a directed verdict. In holding that reasonable people could disagree about the negligence issue in a particular case, a court is necessarily implying that a decision for either the plaintiff or for the defendant would be acceptable. Since the only precedent set by such a holding is that the facts of the case pose a jury question, it follows further that if the same situation arose again, it would be acceptable for a different jury to decide the issue differently. This is hardly a prescription for deciding like cases alike, notwithstanding that such treatment is a core principle in our system. The only equal treatment that like negligence cases receive in this respect is that they are submitted to the jury for decision.

Over a century ago, writing in THE COMMON LAW, Holmes argued that this state of affairs was unacceptable:

> But supposing a state of facts often repeated in practice, is it to be imagined that the court is to go on leaving the standard to the jury forever? Is it not manifest, on the contrary, that if the jury is, on the whole, as fair a tribunal as it is represented to be, the lesson which can be got from that source will be learned? Either the court will find that the fair teaching of experience is that the conduct complained of usually is or is not blameworthy, and therefore, unless explained, is or is not a ground of liability; or it will find the jury oscillating to and fro, and will see the necessity of making up its mind for itself.[26]

---

[26] Oliver Wendell Holmes, Jr., THE COMMON LAW 98 (M.Howe ed. 1963).

Nearly four decades later, as a Justice of the U.S. Supreme Court, Holmes put his idea into practice in *Baltimore and Ohio R.R. v. Goodman*.[27] Goodman was killed when the truck he was driving was struck by the defendant railroad's train at a grade crossing. The railroad's defense was that Goodman was negligent as a matter of law and that since contributory (i.e., the plaintiff's) negligence was then a complete defense, the case could not go to the jury. The trial court denied the railroad's motion for a directed verdict in its favor, and submitted the issue (plus others) to the jury, which found for the plaintiff. The U.S. Supreme Court reversed, holding that "nothing is suggested by the evidence to relieve Goodman of responsibility for his own death" and that, if necessary, someone in Goodman's situation "must stop and get out of his vehicle, although obviously he will not often be required to do more than to stop and look." Thus, the Supreme Court held that a directed verdict should have been granted for the defendant because the plaintiff was negligent as a matter of law.

Seven years later, however, Holmes' ideal of a set rules that could be applied without the need for jury decisions and their accompanying variability was dealt what has turned out to be a fatal blow. In *Pokora v. Wabash Railway Co.*,[28] the U.S. Supreme Court was faced with a similar though not identical fact situation. The trial court directed a verdict for the defendant on the authority of *Goodman*. In an opinion by Justice Cardozo the Supreme Court reversed, noting that

> Standards of prudent conduct are declared at times by the courts, but they are taken over from the facts of life. To get out of a vehicle and reconnoitre is an uncommon precaution, as everyday experience informs us. * * * In default of the guide of customary conduct, what is suitable for the traveler caught in a mesh where the ordinary safeguards fail him is for the judgment of a jury.[29]

In effect, the Court said that the plaintiff in *Goodman* may have been contributorily negligent as a matter of law given the particular facts of his case, but that it does not follow that everyone who has not stopped, looked, listened and (if necessary) gotten out of his car is contributorily negligent. That depends on the circumstances.

---

[27] 275 U.S. 66, 48 S.Ct. 24, 72 L.Ed. 167 (1927).

[28] 292 U.S. 98, 54 S.Ct. 580, 78 L.Ed. 1149 (1934).

[29] 292 U.S. at 104–06, 54 S.Ct. at 582.

The move from *Goodman* to *Pokora* (both decided in the pre-*Erie* era when the Supreme Court had the authority to create federal common law) reflects the treatment that Holmes' view has received generally. There has not been a tendency over time for rules of law to develop regarding the kind of behavior that is and is not negligent. Rather, if anything, the courts' inclination has been to leave juries with even greater discretion and to grant fewer directed verdicts.

There are two reasons why things have developed this way. First, fact situations that are sufficiently similar to warrant the development of rules of law governing them have not recurred. Instead, the courts have usually concluded—as did Justice Cardozo in *Pokora*—that reasonable people could consider the factual variations between cases such as *Goodman* and *Pokora* to be sufficiently important to permit juries to decide them differently. Just as not every railroad grade-crossing accident is the same, so not every lane-changing automobile accident and not every slip-and-fall case is the same. Second, it is both less dangerous and less elitist for elected judges (and most state judges, who hear most tort cases, must stand for re-election) to leave tough decisions about norms of behavior to juries rather than deciding these issues themselves. In the long run such decisions probably have greater legitimacy and help to reduce the influence of politics on the outcome of tort claims.

However, the kinds of cases in which the position Holmes took is most satisfactory are precisely those that are constantly recurring because they arise out of precisely the same facts. These are the modern, "mass" tort cases in which the same product or behavior is alleged to have injured large numbers of people. If these cases are tried individually, then the question of the defendant's negligence must be submitted to different juries dozens or hundreds of times, and the same action or product design can be judged negligent or not negligent by many different juries. If, for example, a defendant failed to warn purchasers and other users of the dangers of exposure to asbestos in 1963, at some point that behavior should be judged either negligent or not once and for all, rather than permitting dozens of juries to "oscillate to and fro" on the issue, as Holmes put it. The courts have tried to find ways to give a definitive answer, but through such modern procedural devices as collateral estoppel and class actions, rather than through the rules of law that Holmes envisioned.

4

Proof of Negligence

Ordinarily there is nothing distinctive about proving negligence. The plaintiff introduces evidence of the defendant's behavior and contends that the defendant failed to take a precaution that it was reasonable to take. Sometimes, however, direct evidence of what the defendant did or did not do is unavailable. In such cases negligence is not proved directly, but by circumstantial evidence. This Chapter is about how negligence is proved in cases such as this, and about a doctrine that is sometimes used in aid of proving negligence—*res ipsa loquitur*, or literally "the thing speaks for itself." In order to understand proof of negligence by circumstantial evidence, as well as *res ipsa*, it is necessary first to understand the allocation of the burden of proof in negligence and other tort cases generally.

I. The Burden of Proof

A. *Burdens in the Ordinary Case*

The plaintiff in a tort suit bears the burden of proof on each element of his case. That burden is composed of two parts: the *burden of production* and the *burden of persuasion*. The burden of production is sometimes termed the burden of "going forward with the evidence." After all the plaintiff's evidence is introduced, that evidence must be capable of supporting an inference by the jury that (among other things) the defendant breached the applicable standard of care. In negligence cases, of course, the plaintiff must prove breach by showing that the defendant was negligent. This means that based on the evidence an inference of negligence must be permissible, not that such an inference is required. Satisfying the burden of production is sometimes referred to as making out a *prima facie* case.

The decision whether the plaintiff has satisfied the burden of production is made by the court, which makes this decision by ruling on the "legal sufficiency" of the evidence. In contrast, the jury actually

87

determines the "weight" of the evidence. Merely because the evidence is legally sufficient to permit an inference of negligence does not mean that the jury is required to draw that inference. When an inference of negligence is merely permissible then an inference of no negligence also is permissible.

Once the evidence goes to the jury, the plaintiff bears the burden of persuasion. The jury is instructed that the plaintiff has satisfied this burden only if it is persuaded by a preponderance of the evidence that (among other things) the defendant was negligent. If the jury finds that it is only as probable as not that the defendant was negligent, then the plaintiff's case fails. The jury must be persuaded that the defendant was "more probably than not negligent," or the plaintiff has not satisfied his burden of persuading the jury by a preponderance of the evidence.

Since negligence is the failure to exercise reasonable care, typically negligence is proved by showing 1) what the defendant did; and 2) that what the defendant did or failed to do did not constitute reasonable care. In addition, it is virtually always in the interest of the plaintiff also to show 3) what would have constituted reasonable care, though it is sometimes said that such proof is not required. In nearly every case, therefore, the plaintiff attempts to prove some untaken precaution that he or she contends would have constituted reasonable care on the part of the defendant and that would have avoided the injury at issue.

B. The Problem of Circumstantial Evidence

A difficulty arises, however, if the plaintiff does not have specific evidence of what the defendant did or did not do, or of all the potentially relevant facts associated with the cause of the plaintiff's injury. Then there is only circumstantial evidence that the defendant was negligent, if there is evidence at all. Sometimes proof of the circumstances is sufficient to permit an inference of negligence, but sometimes it is not. For example, suppose that you are walking in the fruit and vegetable aisle of the local supermarket when you suddenly slip and fall. Immediately after the fall you see a fresh yellow banana peel stuck to your foot. In your suit against the supermarket you prove only these facts, plus the scope of your injuries.

You have a problem. A jury would be permitted to infer that you had fallen because of the presence of the banana peel on the aisle. And a jury would be permitted to find that the defendant was required to use reasonable care to assure that there were no banana peels in its aisles. But, based on these facts alone, should a jury be permitted to find that the defendant had failed to exercise reasonable care?

I think not. In this case the plaintiff has not proved how long the banana peel had been on the floor, or who placed it there.[1] The defendant is not strictly liable for injuries resulting from slips on its floors, but only for injuries resulting from negligence. The defendant might be expected to conduct periodic, perhaps even frequent inspection of its aisles to remove dangerous material from them. But the evidence does not seem sufficient to permit any inference that such inspections were not conducted. For all anyone knows the banana peel had only been in the aisle a few seconds before the plaintiff slipped on it. Reasonable people could not find that the defendant should be constantly inspecting that very aisle. A simple Learned Hand calculus confirms this— people would not want to pay a price for fruit and vegetables that included the cost of constant guarding of the aisles where they are shelved. Note that this is not a conclusion that the defendant was *not* negligent; it is only a conclusion that a jury would not be warranted in drawing any inference, one way or another, about whether the defendant was negligent. The great mistake that students of this subject often make is to jump too quickly to the use of Latin phrase *res ipsa loquitur* in a situation such as this instead of engaging in hard-headed analysis. In this situation the thing does not speak for itself, one way or the other.

All this follows from the fact that the plaintiff bears the burden of production: the jury could not conclude based on the evidence that, more probably than not, the defendant did not conduct a reasonably frequent and competent inspection. Therefore, after the plaintiff has rested his case, the defendant would move for a directed verdict on that ground, and the court would—or should—grant that motion, without requiring the defendant to introduce any evidence at all. At first glance this may seem unfair, since we do not at this point know whether or not the defendant was negligent; we simply do not have enough evidence one way or the other to decide. But the very idea behind the burden of production is that the plaintiff must introduce evidence from which the jury could conclude that the defendant was negligent; the defendant need not prove that it was not negligent.

---

[1] See *Goddard v. Boston & Maine Railway Co.*, 179 Mass. 52, 60 N.E. 486 (1901).

Now let us change the hypothetical a bit. Suppose that all the facts are the same except that the banana peel on which the plaintiff slipped was brown and mushy rather than yellow and fresh. Can the plaintiff now survive the defendant's motion for a directed verdict? This is a much closer question. It is a matter of common knowledge, not really needing any proof, that banana peels tend to darken and become more mushy after they have been removed from bananas for a period of time. Consequently, the plaintiff has now introduced some evidence—though admittedly not very much—from which it could be inferred that the peel had been on the floor for more than just a moment when the plaintiff slipped on it. And based on the permissible (though not required) inference that the peel had been on the aisle for more than just a moment, it might be permissible for a jury to conclude that a reasonably frequent and competent inspection of the aisle would have discovered the peel and caused it to be removed during the period when the peel was on the floor.

Nonetheless, some courts still would grant the defendant's motion for a directed verdict, because the evidence of the banana peel's condition provides only a very slight basis for inferring that it had been in the aisle long enough to have been discovered by a reasonable inspection.[2] There are other alternatives, and the evidence gives the jury only a slight basis for choosing among them: the peel might have been removed from a very brown, ripe banana and dropped on the floor just a moment before the plaintiff slipped on it; or someone might have carried the peel into the store and dropped it on the floor just a moment before the plaintiff encountered it. Based on ordinary experience these seem to me to be less probable alternatives, however, and if I were the trial judge I probably would deny the defendant's motion for a directed verdict. But the point here is that, because the evidence now supports a finding that the peel had been lying in the aisle for some time, the facts of this revised hypothetical come much closer than do the facts of the first hypothetical to permitting an inference that the defendant did not conduct a reasonable inspection.

Notice that this analysis proceeded without any need for the use of the Latin phrase *res ipsa loquitur*, or reference to anything speaking "for itself." The question was simply whether there was enough evidence to support an inference that the defendant had not conducted an adequate inspection of the aisle in its supermarket. In the first hypothetical the answer clearly was that there was not enough evidence and

---

[2] See, e.g., *Joye v. Great Atlantic and Pacific Tea Company*, 405 F.2d 464 (4th Cir. 1968).

that the plaintiff therefore did not meet the burden of production. In the second hypothetical the question was closer. So one might plausibly wonder when, if ever, there is any need for a special doctrine regarding proof of negligence. Thus far, all we have seen is that in the absence of direct evidence of negligence, sometimes circumstantial evidence is sufficient to permit an inference of negligence, and that sometimes circumstantial evidence is not sufficient to permit such an inference.

II. *Res Ipsa Loquitur*

There is a class of cases in which something beyond the use of circumstantial evidence appears to going on, and the doctrine *res ipsa loquitur* is invoked. *Res ipsa loquitur* has long been so firmly established in tort doctrine that black-letter prerequisites to its application have been developed. It is always a condition of invoking the doctrine that the event causing the plaintiff's injury must be one that 1) ordinarily does not occur in the absence of negligence. But the way in which the other requirements are expressed varies. Some jurisdictions say that 2) the instrumentality causing the injury must be within the exclusive control of the defendant, and that 3) the injury must not be due to any voluntary action or contribution by the plaintiff. Others simply require that causes other than the defendant's negligence be sufficiently eliminated by the evidence. Both sets of requirements are ways of stating what it takes to establish a circumstantial case of negligence on the part of the defendant, though of course the latter may prove in certain cases to be considerably more flexible than the former.

A. *An Ordinary Rule of Circumstantial Evidence*

When the requirements of *res ipsa* are met, in most jurisdictions the effect is that the jury is permitted, though not required, to find that the defendant was negligent. This means at the least that the plaintiff survives the defendant's motion for a directed verdict at the close of the plaintiff's case. Ordinarily it also means that the case will go to the jury, although occasionally the evidence thereafter presented by the defendant shows as a matter of law that the defendant was not negligent and the defendant is granted a directed verdict at the close of his case. For example, suppose that the plaintiff shows that he was a passenger on the defendant's train when it derailed. Such accidents ordinarily do not happen in the absence of negligence. Therefore the plaintiff has made out a *prima facie* case on negligence. But then the defendant proves by undisputed evidence that moments before the train derailed the track had been sabotaged, without any warning or reason to expect sabotage. Probably the defendant would then be granted a directed verdict.[3] But in the absence of such a definitive, undisputed defense, the plaintiff's *res ipsa* case goes to the jury.

In *Byrne v. Boadle*,[4] one of the earliest cases to employ res ipsa loquitur expressly, the plaintiff was struck by a barrel of flour that fell out of a window of the defendant's warehouse. The plaintiff introduced no evidence of the manner in which the barrel came to fall or that the defendant's employees were responsible. The court held that the plaintiff had nonetheless made out a *prima facie* case, because there are some cases in which the mere fact of the accident having occurred is evidence of negligence. In these cases "the thing speaks for itself," and what it speaks of is negligence.

In my view there is no particular harm involved in labelling this kind of case with the term *res ipsa loquitur*, as long as one recognizes that the doctrine is doing no work other than labelling. That is, on the facts of *Byrne v. Boadle* the plaintiff has made out a *prima facie* case on the two issues that often figure in cases in which *res ipsa* is invoked: identification of the defendant as the party physically in control of what occurred, and negligence. First, on those facts it would be permissible to infer that the defendant's employees were responsible for the barrel's falling. After all, the barrel fell from the defendant's warehouse. It is of course possible that someone other than the defendant's employees was responsible (a customer supervising the lowering of the barrel out the warehouse window, for example), but in the absence of any other evidence on the issue, proof that the barrel fell from the defendant's warehouse satisfies the plaintiff's burden of production by identifying the defendant as the party responsible for the negligence in the case, if any. Second, based on this evidence it would be permissible for the jury to find that barrels do not ordinarily fall out of warehouse windows in the absence of negligence, and therefore that the defendant was negligent in having failed to take reasonable precautions to prevent the barrel from falling.

The case is therefore one in which the evidence on both issues satisfies the plaintiff's burden of production. What distinguishes the case from an ordinary negligence suit is that, because there is no direct evidence of what the defendant's employees were or were not doing at the time the barrel fell, the plaintiff cannot point to any particular untaken precaution that would have prevented the barrel from falling

---

[3] See *Kanter v. St. Louis, Springfield, & Peoria R.R.*, 218 Ill.App. 565 (1921).

[4] 159 Eng. 299 (Ex. 1863).

had that precaution been taken. Many cases in which *res ipsa loquitur* is invoked share this characteristic. They are simply cases in which there is only circumstantial evidence on the issues of identification and negligence, but that evidence is sufficient to satisfy the plaintiff's burden of production. In such cases *res ipsa* is merely a label for this class of cases. That is, the doctrine does not create any inference that is not already permissible anyway on the basis of evidentiary probabilities alone.

Another way to understand this point is to think of the decision that the plaintiff has met his burden of production as a way of minimizing the degree of error that would otherwise result. Suppose that in cases like *Byrne v. Boadle* the plaintiff were held not to have satisfied his burden of production, and that the defendant's motion for a directed verdict were granted at the close of the plaintiff's case. If it is in fact true that barrels do not ordinarily fall out of warehouse windows in the absence of negligence by the warehouser, then the probability is at least 51 percent that the defendant has been negligent when a barrel does fall. If the defendant's motion for a directed verdict is nonetheless granted in such cases when there is no direct evidence of negligence, then the defendant wins 100 percent of the time. The rate of error is therefore at least 51 percent, since ordinarily a barrel does not fall in the absence of negligence. On the other hand, if the plaintiff is held to have satisfied his burden of production, then even if there is no other evidence at all and even if the jury finds for the plaintiff 100 percent of the time, the error rate is 49 percent or less, because the defendant is in fact negligent at least 51 percent of the time. Thus, submitting the case to the jury produces a lower rate of error than granting the defendant's motion for a directed verdict.

B. "Smoking Out" the Evidence from the Defendant

All of this, of course, assumes that the defendant will not produce any evidence. If the defendant's motion for a directed verdict is denied, however, then unless the defendant presents some evidence in an effort to show affirmatively that he was not negligent, the case will go to the jury with only the plaintiff's evidence, and the jury will probably draw the inference it is permitted but not required to draw—that the defendant was in fact negligent. So denying the defendant's motion for a directed verdict on the ground that the plaintiff has satisfied his burden of production creates a strong incentive for the defendant to put on some kind of case. In *Byrne v. Boadle* this might have consisted of testimony (for example) by the defendant's employees indicating how careful they were being when the barrel fell, or indicating that the pulley holding the rope being used to lower the barrel unexpectedly broke. Because invoking *res ipsa loquitur* results in the denial of defendant's motion for a directed verdict at the close of the plaintiff's evidence, it is sometimes said that the great advantage in cases where *res ipsa* is invoked is that the defendant is then forced to present evidence—forced, that is, to defend himself rather than hide behind the difficulty the plaintiff faces in adducing direct evidence about the accident.

On this view, *res ipsa* is not merely a label, but actually performs the function of "smoking out" evidence in the possession of the defendant. When this is true and the ordinary rules of evidence would have dictated that the defendant's motion for a directed verdict at the close of the plaintiff's case be granted, *res ipsa* does real work: the doctrine creates an artificial inference of negligence, in order to give the defendant the incentive to explain what actually happened. The inference is "artificial" because, if the ordinary rules governing drawing an inference of negligence from circumstantial evidence would on their own have required that the defendant's motion for a directed verdict be denied, then there would be no need for *res ipsa*. Ironically, then, in this situation *res ipsa* actually does more than merely label what would have happened anyway, precisely because the thing does not speak for itself.

How often *res ipsa* is in fact needed in order to perform this function is open to question. In the days before modern discovery, it may well have been true that the only way to force the defendant to produce direct evidence about the accident was to wait until trial and then to deny his motion for a directed verdict at the close of the plaintiff's case. Indeed, the court in *Byrne v. Boadle* seemed to think that the plaintiff could not have made out his *prima facie* case by calling witnesses from the defendant's warehouse to prove that they were negligent. Perhaps this was because the court believed that the witnesses would not tell the truth, but it may also have been because in the absence of discovery the plaintiff would not have known in advance what they would have said. But with the aid of modern discovery procedure, today's plaintiff could depose under oath everyone who was involved in handling the barrel and everyone responsible for safety at the warehouse. Whatever the defendant's employees know about the accident, the plaintiff can force them to disclose. Any evidence generated in this manner that is favorable to the plaintiff can then be adduced as part of the plaintiff's *prima facie* case. Thus, it may be that *res ipsa* came into being partly in order to help smoke-out evidence that would not otherwise be available to the plaintiff. But it may equally be true today that because of modern discovery the doctrine is no longer needed to perform this function.

C. The Ybarra Problem

In light of modern discovery, then, do we even need *res ipsa*? Perhaps the most celebrated case in which the smoke-out argument can be made is *Ybarra v. Spangard*.[5] In that case the plaintiff sued several different health care providers, one of whom more probably than not committed malpractice while the plaintiff was unconscious. The plaintiff's case was permitted to go to the jury. Upon the jury finding for the plaintiff the defendants were held jointly liable. Admittedly, no single defendant was more probably than not negligent. But absent the application of *res ipsa* none of the defendants would have had an interest in telling what they knew. None of the defendants had any financial incentive to reveal what, if anything, he or she knew about the injury, because each would automatically be granted a directed verdict at the close of the plaintiff's case. The party who had actually caused the plaintiff's injury obviously had no incentive to do anything but stay silent, and none of the other defendants who happened to have witnessed the act of negligence of another (if any had been seen anything) had any incentive to do anything but stay silent either. Without evidence regarding which defendant was responsible for the injury, the plaintiff could not have survived the defendants' motions for a directed verdict at the close of his case, because each individual defendant was less likely than not to have been negligent.

Invoking *res ipsa* in *Ybarra* created the possibility of smoking-out evidence from one of the defendants who had witnessed another's malpractice, or from the defendant who had actually committed the malpractice in question, who might have preferred to admit his wrongdoing rather than see his or her colleagues held liable for something they did not do. But in order for *res ipsa* actually to be able to smoke-out the evidence, two factors must exist in situations such as *Ybarra*: 1) One or more of the defendants must actually have knowledge about the cause of the plaintiff's injury that would be useful as evidence. This will not necessary be the case, since sometimes no defendant will have witnessed anything—and even the defendant who did cause the injury may not know that he did. 2) Any defendant who does have evidence

---

[5] 25 Cal.2d 486, 154 P.2d 687 (1944).

that would be useful to the plaintiff must be willing to lie under oath in a deposition but willing to tell the truth under oath at trial. Otherwise *res ipsa* is not needed, since the defendant would reveal his evidence in a deposition that could then be used as part of the plaintiff's case at trial even if *res ipsa* were not available to get the plaintiff past a motion for a directed verdict. I suppose that sometimes both factors will exist, but how often is not at all clear. Just as often, I suspect, either no defendant will have any useful evidence, or the party who does have it will not be willing to reveal it at all, preferring to have his or her malpractice insurer pay his or her fraction of the judgment instead of "ratting" on a colleague. The price that must be paid in order to use *res ipsa* to smoke-out evidence when it is in fact capable of being smoked-out, therefore, is to permit the jury to impose liability on all the defendants, even when none has any evidence and even when all but one of them are, in all probability, entirely innocent.

The strength of the general argument for *res ipsa* thus depends in part on two empirical questions that are not really answerable: in cases in which there is no direct evidence of negligence and the circumstantial evidence alone is legally insufficient, how often there is any evidence to be smoked out, and how often would *res ipsa* smoke it out? If there were good reason to believe that often there is evidence to be smoked out and that *res ipsa* often could do the smoking, then that would explain the doctrine's separate existence. In light of the limited number of situations in which *res ipsa* is likely to be useful in this way, however, then what is its function? I think that *res ipsa* must be justified selectively on a case-by-case basis, for whatever specific reasons make it especially appropriate to force a particular defendant to put on a case of some sort rather than to grant his motion for a directed verdict at the close of the plaintiff's case. For instance, on occasion the defendant's testimony introduced as part of the plaintiff's case will lack credibility, and the court may conclude that if the defendant is forced to introduce evidence of his own he will "cook his own goose." Or there may be other cases in which, in light of the facts, the court simply has an intuition that there is evidence that will not be forthcoming unless the defendant is forced to put on a case. And it always is possible to force the defendant to put on a case but then to grant his motion for a directed verdict at the close of his case, unless something inculpatory has somehow materialized as part of his case. So conceived, *res ipsa* functions as a kind of exception to the ordinary rules governing drawing the inference of negligence from circumstantial evidence in cases where applying those rules is inappropriate.

96

Finally, for some observers the risk of error that results from invoking *res ipsa* even when the thing does not speak for itself is worth tolerating because, in their view, strict liability is preferable to negligence as a basis for liability. On this view, invoking *res ipsa* when the thing does not speak for itself and no evidence is smoked out simply permits the jury to impose strict liability through a verdict of negligence. *Res ipsa* under these circumstances is a way of obtaining under-the-table strict liability.

The trouble with this view is that there is nothing about the category of cases in which there is no direct evidence of taken or untaken precautions—that is, the category of cases in which *res ipsa* is potentially of value to the plaintiff—that warrants making them special candidates for strict liability. Why set things up so that the jury can most easily impose strict liability in the very cases in which there is the least evidence of negligence? For many there is no particular reason to do so. But perhaps for strong proponents of strict liability, half a loaf of strict liability, even if it is an illogically-chosen half, is better than none.

5

Cause–In–Fact

In any tort suit the plaintiff must prove not only that the defendant was negligent or otherwise breached the applicable standard of care, but also that the defendant's act or omission caused the injury or damage for which the plaintiff claims compensation. In many cases this is an utterly straightforward matter. If the defendant fails to stop his vehicle at a red light and collides with the plaintiff's vehicle proceeding with the green light, there is no question that the defendant's negligence caused the plaintiff's harm. But in other cases the issue is more difficult. In such cases understanding the purposes served by the causation requirement becomes more important, because these purposes help to inform application of the requirement to the facts at hand. And often in these problematic cases the complexity of the very idea of causation becomes evident.

I. The Conventional Tests: "But For" and "Substantial Factor"

The simplest and most widely accepted test for cause-in-fact is the "but-for" test. This test requires a determination whether, "but for" the defendant's negligence (or breach of another applicable standard of care), the plaintiff would have suffered injury or damage. If the answer is "no," then cause-in-fact is proved. But if the answer is "yes," then ordinarily the test is not satisfied and the defendant is not liable, because the plaintiff would have been injured even if the defendant had not been negligent. For example, suppose that a person falls off a boat that negligently carries no life buoys to throw to those in the water. That person sinks immediately below the surface and drowns.[1] Although the defendant was negligent, that negligence was not a but-for cause of the drowning. Even if there had been a buoy to throw, there

---

[1] For a case whose facts are highly similar to this hypothetical, see *New York Central R.R. v. Grimstad*, 264 F. 334 (2d Cir. 1920).

would have been no way for the buoy to reach the person drowning, because he sank beneath the surface immediately. On the other hand, if the decedent had bobbed onto the surface several times before drowning, it might be a jury question whether a properly placed buoy could have been thrown to him and would have saved him. But some courts would require testimony about the likely placement of each omitted buoy, and the throwing ability of those who were on board at the time, before permitting the causation issue to go to the jury.

There are many causes in fact—but-for causes—of any event. In an automobile collision case, if the defendant's parents had not met, if the defendant had not travelled to work on the day of the collision, if the defendant had not gone to college, bought a car, or run the red light, he would not have collided with the plaintiff. The key is whether one of these many but-for causes was negligent. If so, then the act or omission of the party responsible for this negligence is "a" cause in fact. A but-for cause is not necessarily what we would call "the" cause of the plaintiff's harm. Being a negligent but-for cause makes a defendant "eligible" for liability, so to speak, but the defendant is not liable unless his negligence was also a "proximate cause"—a concept examined in the next Chapter. To put it another way, if the defendant's negligence was not a but-for cause of the plaintiff's harm then there can be no liability, because the defendant's negligence was not even "a" cause of the plaintiff's harm. To be a negligent but-for cause is a necessary, but not a sufficient, condition of liability.

Instead of the but-for test, some courts ask whether the defendant's negligence was a "substantial factor" in bringing about the plaintiff's injury or damage. In theory the difference between the two tests might be great. The "but-for" test requires a firm finding that the defendant's negligence was an absolute prerequisite to what happened, whereas the "substantial factor" test could merely require a finding that the defendant's negligence was a major contributor. In practice, however, the difference between the two tests is largely a matter of emphasis. Both require the jury to determine what *would have happened* had the defendant not been negligent. Once the causation issue is submitted to the jury, it has mainly its own experience to draw upon and substantial leeway in making this counterfactual decision, whether the but-for or substantial-factor test is used.

Indeed, this "counterfactual" nature of the causation issue sometimes requires assuming that the jury has firm knowledge about the way the world works that none of us actually has. For example, in

Reynolds v. Texas & Pacific Ry. Co.,[2] the plaintiff weighed 250 pounds and was warned to hurry up to catch a train. Hastening down unlighted steps, she fell and was injured. In the plaintiff's suit alleging negligence on the part of the railroad in hurrying her down an unlighted stairway, the defendant railroad contended that she might just as easily have fallen in broad daylight while moving at a regular pace. But the court held that if the plaintiff proves that the negligence of the defendant "greatly multiplied" the chances of the accident, the plaintiff has made out a jury question on the causation issue. Whether the "but for" or "substantial factor" test is used in a case like this, the problem is the same: it is impossible to go back to the moment before the accident, "remove" the negligence of the defendant, and see what would have happened. We can never really know whether the plaintiff would have fallen if the stairs had been lighted and she was not hurrying.

Instead, all we can do is ask the jury to make a judgment, based on the evidence and its own experience, about what would have happened if the defendant had not been negligent. The more strictly we require that there be an evidentiary basis for making that judgment before submitting the case to the jury, the more often we will say that the plaintiff has not made out a *prima facie* case on the causation issue. In this sense, cause-in-fact is a bit like *res ipsa loquitur*. In *res ipsa* a case goes to the jury only if an inference of negligence *in this situation* is permissible because of what in general happens *in situations like this*. Similarly, in cause-in-fact disputes a court must decide whether an inference about what would have happened *in this situation* if the defendant had not been negligent is permissible, because of what ordinarily happens *in situations like this* when the defendant has not been negligent.

Typically that is all we ever really do in making causal attributions: decide what ordinarily happens in the absence of the factor that we think may have been a cause of the event in question. In *Reynolds*, for example, the jury knows that more often than not people don't fall down stairs, even if they are overweight. So if Mrs. Reynolds fell, other factors may well have caused her to fall. In her case two other factors—the fact that the stairs were not lighted and that she was told to hurry—were arguably the result of the defendant's negligence. Since there was no evidence that Mrs. Reynolds frequently fell on

---

[2] 37 La. Ann. 694 (1885).

lighted stairs when she was not hurrying, what the defendant did or did not do is the most probable explanation for what caused her to fall. In the absence of evidence of other probable causes, the defendant's negligence is the probable cause (or at least so the jury is permitted to find). Thus, sometimes the most effective way to prove that the defendant's negligence caused the plaintiff's harm is to eliminate a series of other possible causes. That leaves the defendant's negligence as a cause.

II. Multiple Causes, Indeterminate Causes, and the Conventional Tests

The but-for and substantial-factor tests work in straightforward, if not always entirely easy, fashion in cases involving only one defendant. On the other hand, when multiple possible causes are involved, the causation requirement is sometimes held to be satisfied even when the defendant's negligence is not a but-for cause (or substantial factor) of the plaintiff's harm. The exceptions to the conventional tests are a mixed bag that do not all fall into a single category. To understand these exceptions, it is helpful first to step back from the two conventional tests for causation to look at the theory underlying the causation requirement.

A. *The Theory Underlying the Causation Requirement*

Why is causation, however defined, always an element of a cause of action in tort? At first glance the answer may seem utterly obvious: if the defendant did not injure the plaintiff then there is no causation, no one injured, no damages, and no plaintiff to bring suit. But of course that answer is only half-right whenever the question matters. In any case in which causation is disputed, there *is* a plaintiff with an injury and damages or there would have been no suit to begin with. In such a case at least part of the reason we require that there be a causal connection between what the defendant did and what happened to the plaintiff is concern for corrective justice. If the defendant did not cause the plaintiff's loss, then it seems obvious that corrective justice does not require the defendant to compensate the plaintiff for that loss. Since the defendant did not wrong the plaintiff, there is no injustice for him to correct.

But this conclusion is not so obviously correct as it may seem to be. If the plaintiff has proved that the defendant was negligent in risking harm to the plaintiff—which of course he must do to prove breach of duty—then the defendant has in fact wronged the plaintiff. The defendant has risked harm to the plaintiff, even if that risk did not materialize in harm. If I exceed the speed limit on Main Street I am no less at fault when I finally stop the car without having caused a collision than if I injure you as a result of speeding. My wrong consists of risking the harm that may result from what I have done.

Now let us take the analysis a step further. If the wrong in such a situation was risking harm to those I might have injured, then perhaps the measure of damages payable to someone I do injure should not be that plaintiff's actual loss, but a sum equal to the probability that he would suffer harm, multiplied by the amount of harm that could be expected if harm did result. This, after all, is the "amount" of the risk that I took, and taking that risk was the wrong I committed. If I were held liable for that amount to everyone I risked harming on each occasion I did so, over time I would pay out the same sum in damages (though in smaller amounts to more people) as I would if I were only liable to those whom I injured.

Under such a system people would be compensated for the real wrong I committed—risking harm to them. Why don't we do it that way? One of the reasons we do not have such a system is that the people whose harm is risked but who are not injured have no immediate need for the money, and those who are injured do. That problem could only be solved if risk-based damages were always awarded, and uninjured plaintiffs who received compensation saved it for the time they were injured. For practical purposes that would be a an impossible system to operate, since everyone whose harm was risked could sue, and in every such suit the precise degree of risk posed by the defendant's acts toward each possible victim would be at issue. Consequently, under this theory, although the real wrong committed by negligent defendants is unreasonably *risking* harm to others, we have a causation requirement for reasons of expediency. But it would make at least theoretical sense to dispense with the causation requirement and impose liability for risk-based damages whenever there was negligence.

On this view, the "mere" expediency of the causation requirement becomes even more clear upon considering the issue from the standpoint of deterrence rather than corrective justice. For deterrence purposes the fact that the defendant *risked* harm to others is the relevant consideration. The whole point of imposing tort liability in order to deter unreasonable behavior is to give potential injurers the incentive to compare the amount of liability that they *anticipate* they will incur from taking a particular risk with the cost of reducing that risk by taking safety precautions. But the amount of liability they will incur from any given risky act is utterly variable, because the amount of damages suffered by any given victim is almost random. Insurance companies and repeat-player defendants may be able to predict with a fair amount of reliability how frequently they will be held liable, but the severity of the injury that any given victim is likely to suffer is in fact much harder to predict. Designing a truck without extra strength in its doors risks greater injury in side-collisions, but a collision under a particular set of circumstances may cause no harm, a sprained ankle, or death. The best that potential injurers (or their insurers) threatened with liability can do is to anticipate that, if a risk they take materializes in harm, they will incur liability equal to the average amount of damages that a potential victim will suffer.

From a deterrence standpoint, therefore, requiring proof of causation is not a moral imperative, but simply a way of communicating to the defendant in advance the scope of the liability it will face. If we had another way of threatening potential defendants with liability for the cost of the risks they take without requiring proof of causation, and then charging defendants with this amount of liability—for example, by imposing liability for average damages rather than those actually caused in any given case—then this alternative approach could serve the aim of deterrence just as well, if not better. Usually there is no reliable and accurate way of threatening liability so as to achieve optimal deterrence without requiring proof of causation. On the rare occasions when alternatives to the conventional tests for causation are available, however, the law sometimes carves out exceptions to the conventional tests. The availability of a suitable alternative test is not the entire explanation for the way the law deals with the sometimes quirky cases that are discussed in the following pages, but that availability explains many of what otherwise may seem to be arbitrary exceptions to the conventional rules.

B. Injury Caused by Multiple Sufficient Causes

The first set of problems involves cases in which two forces converge on the plaintiff, and either one alone would have been sufficient to cause all of the plaintiff's harm. Sometimes these forces converge simultaneously, sometimes sequentially but only a short time apart. Sometimes only one of these causes is negligent, sometimes both are negligent. To assure that the differences between these situations is clear, I will use the classic illustration of two fires reaching the plaintiff's house, either one of which is sufficient to destroy the house. But of course the point of the illustrations is that the fires represent forces set in motion by different parties and that these might be defendants causing injury not involving fires, but products, drivers, trains, or other forces.

1. Two Simultaneous Forces: Both Negligent

Suppose that two independently and negligently-set fires are burning toward the plaintiff's house. Either alone would be sufficient to destroy the house, and they both reach the house at the same time, destroying it together. In a suit against those who set the fires, the plaintiff cannot satisfy the but-for test: but-for either defendant's negligence, the house would have been destroyed anyway. Nonetheless, neither defendant can escape liability on this ground. Both are held to have caused the plaintiff's loss.

One way to explain this result is to say that, although neither defendant was a but-for cause of the plaintiff's harm, each was a substantial factor. I think that a more fruitful and candid way of explaining this result, however, is to understand that both the but-for and substantial-factor tests are not definitions of the concept of causation, but merely useful proxies for the concept. Most of the time these tests are perfectly acceptable ways of making operational what we mean by "cause," but not always. Here the tests don't capture what we mean by "cause." Picture each fire reaching a different portion of the house at the same time and starting to burn the walls. Everyone would say that each fire was an actual physical cause of the harm. It would be absurd to say that neither was a cause of the harm, when in fact both were, and doubly absurd to deny the plaintiff recovery because his house happened to be destroyed by two defendants rather than one. Moreover, here the choice is between overdeterrence (since the harm will occur anyway even when one of the defendants is careful) through the imposition of liability and underdeterrence through the failure to impose liability. The law chooses the former, threatening "too much" liability rather than too little.

2. Simultaneous Forces: One Negligent, One Not

Next suppose the same facts, except that only one of the two fires is negligently set. The facts in *Kingston v. Chicago & N.W. Ry.*[3] are virtually identical to this hypothetical, except that in *Kingston* one fire

---

[3] 191 Wis. 610, 211 N.W. 913 (1927).

was of unknown origin and therefore was not demonstrably innocent. Again, the but-for test is not satisfied, though here too one might say that the substantial-factor test is satisfied. Whether the negligent party should be liable even though the but-for test is not satisfied is a close question. Clearly that party's fire was a physical cause of some of the damage; it would be peculiar to say that it was not. On the other hand, the house would have been destroyed even absent that party's negligence, and if that party is held liable it will be liable for the entire amount of the loss, since the other party's fire was not negligently set. Imposing liability on the negligent party will slightly overdeter, since it will give such parties the incentive to take precautions against harms that will occasionally occur anyway because of a simultaneous non-negligent cause. And the plaintiff has much less basis for objection here than in the first hypothetical if there is no liability, because his house would have been destroyed regardless of what the negligent party did. Nonetheless, the tendency of the courts is to hold the negligent defendant liable in this situation, but not all courts do so. And as discussion of the following hypothetical demonstrates, it is essential to the courts that do impose liability in such cases that the negligent fire arrive no later than the non-negligent fire.

3. Sequential Forces

Next suppose that two fires arrive sequentially. The first totally destroys the plaintiff's house, very shortly after which the second arrives. Neither fire is a but-for cause of the harm, but the first fire was the actual physical cause of the harm. Probably this is enough to explain why the party responsible for the first fire is liable if the fire was negligently set, and why the party responsible for the second fire is not responsible, even if that fire was negligently set. Sometimes one party is negligent but lucky enough not to cause harm, either because no one is harmed or because some other earlier force has already caused harm that one's own negligence would have caused, but for that force.[4] Here there is no alternative to the but-for or substantial-factor tests that will work. The first fire was not a but-for cause, but physically did the damage. The second fire risked harm, but simply was not a cause of the harm, no matter how one defines that concept. The party responsible for the first fire, and only that party, can be held liable.

---

[4] Compare *City of Piqua v. Morris*, 98 Ohio St. 42, 120 N.E. 300 (1918). In that case the defendant was negligent but an unprecedented flood caused damage that probably would otherwise have resulted from the defendant's negligence. Because the flood, like the first fire, was the actual physical cause, the defendant was not liable.

C. Joint and Several Liability

When, for whatever reason, two or more defendants are liable to the plaintiff for the the same harm, the law typically treats them as "jointly and severally liable." In the first fire hypothetical discussed above, for example, the parties responsible for each negligently set fire would have been held jointly and severally liable to the plaintiff. This means that each is liable to the plaintiff as if he were the sole wrongdoer, responsible for the entirety of the plaintiff's damages. The plaintiff is therefore entitled to recover the full amount of his damages from either defendant. However, the plaintiff cannot ever recover more than the amount of his damages; if he has recovered the entire amount from one defendant, he can recover nothing in addition from the other defendant. And if he has recovered some from one defendant, then he can recover only the remainder from the other defendant.

At common law that was the end of the matter. When one defendant paid the plaintiff in full the second defendant who paid nothing to the plaintiff got a windfall, and when each defendant paid only a portion that was the way things stayed. This obviously unfair result has long since been remedied in every state by statutes that create rights of *contribution* among multiple tortfeasors in such situations. A right of contribution is essentially a right to be reimbursed by another defendant for a share of the amount paid to the plaintiff. Ordinarily such rights operate on a straight fractional-share basis. Thus, if there are two jointly and severally liable defendants, a defendant paying the plaintiff in full is entitled to contribution from the other defendant equal to one-half of the amount paid; if there are three jointly and severally liable defendants, the defendant paying the plaintiff in full is entitled to contribution from each of the other defendants equal to one-third of the amount paid, and so on.

Since the net effect of these rights of contribution is to allocate fractional-share responsibility to each defendant, one might then ask why this complicated method of allocating responsibility among multiple defendants is followed. Why not simply hold each defendant liable to the plaintiff for its fractional share in the first instance? The answer is that one or more of the defendants may be insolvent or otherwise impossible to collect from. Imposing joint and several liability places the risk of any defendant's insolvency on the other defendant or defendants rather than on the plaintiff. As between an innocent plaintiff and a group of negligent or otherwise-liable defendants, it is preferable for the defendants to bear the risk that one of their number cannot pay its share.[5]

Joint and several liability is imposed in three main situations. First, the defendants may be *joint tortfeasors*. If you and I together engage in a joint enterprise (e.g., a business partnership) and one of us is negligent, then we are jointly and severally liable for harm that results. Second, *independent tortfeasors* are jointly and severally liable for a *single, theoretically indivisible harm*. For example, suppose that one defendant speeds through an intersection and another fails to stop at a red light. The two vehicles collide and one runs onto the sidewalk, injuring a pedestrian. Under the but-for test for causation each defendant is a cause in fact of the pedestrian's injuries, because neither alone would have been sufficient to cause the injury. But because there is no way, even theoretically, to pinpoint the extent of either defendant's causal responsibility for the pedestrian's harm, each is jointly and severally liable for that harm. Finally, independent tortfeasors are jointly and severally liable for a *single, theoretically divisible but practically indivisible harm*. For example, in *Maddux v. Donaldson*,[6] one defendant's negligence caused a collision with the plaintiff's vehicle, and then a second defendant's negligence caused a second collision. In theory each defendant caused a certain portion of the plaintiff's harm, but for practical purposes the harm was indivisible—because the evidence did not support an inference as to the amount of injury caused by each defendant. At early common law the plaintiff could not recover because he could not prove the amount of harm each defendant caused, but the modern rule is that each defendant will be held jointly and severally liable for all the plaintiff's harm.

D. The Indeterminate Defendant

One class of cases that is especially troublesome under the conventional rules governing proof of causation is comprised of those in which a plaintiff clearly injured by tortious conduct cannot prove

---

[5] When this approach was introduced, the successful plaintiff was always "innocent" because contributory negligence was a complete bar to recovery. The matter has become more complicated in a world of comparative negligence, where the plaintiff is not necessarily "innocent," and may be entitled to recover even when he or she was as negligent (or more) than the defendants. Comparative negligence is discussed in Chapter Seven.

[6] 362 Mich. 425, 108 N.W.2d 33 (1961).

which of several possible causes was more probably than not the actual cause of his or her injury. This problem has generated a number of classic cases, and several different approaches to the problem.

1. Alternative Liability: *Summers v. Tice*

In *Summers*[7] two different hunters negligently shot in the direction of the plaintiff, a third hunter. One shot struck the eye of the plaintiff, who sued both hunters. Each defendant was *as probably as not* the but-for cause of injury to the plaintiff, but not more probably than not the cause. The court held that under these circumstances the burden shifted to each of the defendants to disprove that he had caused the harm. But in practice *Summers* is ordinarily understood to involve more than a mere shift of the burden of proof on the causation issue. It is the classic case of "alternative" liability, imposing liability on two negligent defendants, each of whom is equally likely to have harmed the plaintiff.

The rationale for the decision is not easy to find in *Summers*. The court apparently sought to justify its decision by saying that applying the conventional but-for approach would exonerate the defendants, even though both were negligent and the injury resulted from the negligence of one of them. This is not a reason for dispensing with the but-for test, however, but just an assertion of the obvious: that applying the but-for test sometimes relieves a negligent defendant of liability. Making that point does not explain or justify departing from it. Interestingly, alternative liability is rare, and appears to be applied only in cases involving two defendants. This limitation suggests that a good deal of the explanation for the result in *Summers* and the rare other cases in which the doctrine of alternative liability is applied is that each defendant is so nearly "more probably than not" the cause of the harm that the courts are unwilling to immunize them from liability. Add a third defendant and this dramatically ceases to be true: the per defendant probability drops from 50 percent to 33 and 1/3 percent. In such cases the courts show no willingness to hold the defendants liable in the absence of proof of causation.

---

[7] 33 Cal. 2d 80, 199 P.2d 1 (1948).

2. Industry-Wide Liability: *Hall v. E.I. Du Pont De Nemours Co., Inc.*

In *Hall*,[8] six manufacturers of blasting caps were sued by thirteen children injured in separate accidents. The court held that if a child could establish that it was more likely than not that any of the six defendants manufactured the particular cap that caused that child's injury, then the burden shifted to each defendant to prove that a cap it manufactured did not cause the injury in question. The theory behind the decision in *Hall* has never been entirely clear, but it seems to rest on two factors: a) the fact that the defendants acted consciously in parallel to produce caps in a fashion that made their manufacturer difficult to identify after they exploded, plus b) the comparatively small number of defendants. The flavor of the opinion suggests that, although the defendants may not have acted together to cause the injuries at issue, the threat of liability in similar situations in the future might encourage industries with a small number of companies to act together either to prevent injury, or at least to take steps that would enable victims to identify the individual company responsible when a product did cause injury.

3. Loss of a Chance to Survive: *Herskovits v. Group Health Cooperative*

Herskovits[9] is the best known of a series of decisions that usually involve an already-injured or ill plaintiff, whose chances of recovery or survival are reduced by the negligent actions of the defendant. The defendant in this case failed to diagnose the plaintiff's cancer until his chances of survival were only 25 percent. There was testimony, however, that even absent the defendant's malpractice (i.e, but for the malpractice), Herskovits' chances of survival would have been only 39 percent and his chances of dying therefore 61 percent. Notice that it could not be said in this case that, but for the defendant's malpractice, Herskovits more probably than not would have survived. This was because he would still have had a 61 percent chance of dying from the cancer had it been properly diagnosed. The court nonetheless held that there could be a recovery, though not for all of the damages resulting from Herskovits' death. The majority opinion did not specify how damages were to be calculated, but a concurrence suggested a method

---

[8] 345 F. Supp. 353 (E.D.N.Y. 1972).

[9] 99 Wash. 2d 609, 664 P.2d 474 (1983).

that the case has come to stand for: the plaintiff should recover 14 percent (the difference between 39 and 25 percent) of the damages resulting from Herskovits' death.

Probably the best way to describe this result is to say that the defendant is held liable for the reduction in the decedent's chances of surviving. This description can be squared with the traditional statement of the plaintiff's burden of proving causation, since in a sense the defendant was more probably than not the but-for cause of this *reduction* in decedent's chances. Indeed, the defendant was 100 percent responsible for this 14 percent reduction. Another way of describing the result is to say that *Herskovits* held the defendant liable for 14 percent of the damages at issue, because there was a 14 percent probability that the defendant's malpractice caused the plaintiff's death.

This latter description may be more realistic, but also articulates a less confining rule. Describing the rule as awarding 14 percent of the damages that the defendant might have caused makes loss-of-a-chance cases seem to be just one example of a more general problem: the defendant who can never be proved more probably than not to have caused any particular individual's injuries, but whose behavior over time is likely to injure 14 percent of the individuals whose harm his actions risk. In this sense the general problem is no longer the indeterminate defendant, but the indeterminate plaintiff. So understood, the *Herskovits* approach seems simply to impose proportional liability when the defendant is less probably than not the cause of the plaintiff's harm. But that is not generally done. The question, then, is how the courts imposing liability in lost-chance cases can distinguish in principle between these cases (in which there is liability) and the general problem of the defendant who is never liable because he is recurringly negligent but his negligence is never more probably than not the cause of the plaintiff's harm. The answer, I think, is that it is hard to see any such distinction in principle, but that somehow lost-chance cases appear on the surface to be sufficiently different from the general problem that the courts are satisfied that this class of cases can stand on its own. Moreover, because it is rare in any kind of case to have reliable quantitative data on the precise probability that the defendant's action caused the plaintiff harm, the issue usually can simply be sidestepped on this ground.

4. Market-Share Liability: *Sindell v. Abbott Laboratories*

The defendants in *Sindell*[10] were manufacturers of the drug DES. The class of plaintiffs consisted of women whose mothers had taken the drug while they were pregnant. The plaintiffs/daughters alleged that they suffered injury as a result of exposure to DES *in utero*. The problem was that no individual plaintiff could identify which manufacturer or manufacturers had made the DES that her mother had taken. The court circumvented this problem by holding that the plaintiffs need not prove individual causation. Rather, each plaintiff could recover from each defendant a portion of her damages equal to the defendant's share of the market for DES.

The theory behind *Sindell* is that, once it is clear that each defendant's DES injured some of the plaintiffs, the defendants should not escape liability merely because the plaintiffs cannot show which defendant injured which plaintiff. Because the DES made by the defendants was chemically identical, market share was a very accurate surrogate for the amount of harm each defendant caused. Consequently, imposing liability on defendants in proportion to market share forces each defendant to pay compensation for the amount of injury it caused, although not necessarily to those particular persons harmed by any given manufacturer's DES. In terms of deterrence this approach is optimal, because each defendant pays what it should. Corrective justice is less well served by market-share liability, however, because there is no matching up of each plaintiff with the defendant whose DES injured her. Under market-share liability the wrong done to each plaintiff is corrected, but it is not necessarily corrected by the party who wronged that plaintiff.

Although market-share liability might seem at first glance to be a solution to the general problem of proving causation in toxic exposure cases, a number of practical considerations have limited this approach to DES cases and a very few other claims. First, in the DES cases the plaintiffs alleged that their disease—vaginal adenocarcinoma—could be caused *only* by exposure to DES *in utero*. This was in effect a "signature disease": if the plaintiff had that disease, then it was caused by DES. But there are very few signature diseases—diseases that have only one cause. Market-share liability will work in cases of signature disease, because 100 percent of the market caused 100 percent of the disease. But when there are also other causes of the disease suffered by

---

[10] 26 Cal.3d 588, 607 P.2d 924, 163 Cal. Rptr. 132 (1980).

the plaintiffs, market-share is not an accurate surrogate for the total amount of the disease caused by any given defendant, because the cause of the disease in some people cannot be traced to any of the defendants.

Second, even when the plaintiffs do suffer from a signature disease, the relevant market-share data is not always available, especially when the relevant time period for determining market share—as in the case of DES—is twenty or more years before suit. And in any event, it is not clear which is the relevant market: national, state, or local. This choice would not only affect the relative shares of each defendant, but conceivably who was liable in the first instance: a particular defendant might be able to show, for example, that it did not market its product in the state where the plaintiff lived when she was exposed to the risk of harm.

Finally, usually it is not feasible to sue all possible defendants. Some have gone out of business, others may not be subject to the jurisdiction of the court where suit is brought. The result is that less than 100 percent of the relevant market is before the court. What is the scope of the liability to be shouldered by the defendants who are before the court in such a situation? A *relative-market-share* approach (which seemed to have been taken by *Sindell* itself, and only later set aside[11]) is to require that a substantial share of the market be joined as defendants in the suit, and then to hold those defendants liable (in proportion to their market shares) for 100 percent of the plaintiff's damages. Thus, if defendants who held 80 percent of the relevant market were joined in the suit, a defendant who had held 20 percent of the market would pay 25 percent (20/80) of the plaintiff's damages. This approach has the obvious disadvantage of imposing "excessive" liability on the defendants who are liable, much as does joint and several liability when some defendants are judgment-proof. The alternative, *absolute-market-share* approach is to hold defendants liable only for their actual market share, and to leave the plaintiff uncompensated for the missing share of the market. One disadvantage of this approach is that the plaintiff is incompletely compensated for his or her losses. Another is that a multiplicity of suits may result unless there is a requirement that a substantial share of the market be joined in any suit, even though liability will be based on absolute rather than relative market shares.

---

[11] See *Brown v. Superior Court (Abbott Laboratories)*, 44 Cal.3d 1049, 751 P.2d 470, 245 Cal.Rptr. 412 (1988).

These concerns reflect more than merely practical problems to be solved. Each concern suggests how market-share liability in practice may fail to achieve the theory behind this form of liability: there are so few signature diseases that market-share liability may be useful only occasionally; the limitations of market-share information may render accurate imposition of liability difficult; and in most cases there will either be over-imposition of liability or under-compensation of the plaintiff. This combination of difficulties has prompted many courts to reject market-share liability outright, and others to accept it only under very limited circumstances.

E. The Indeterminate Plaintiff

Consider now the class of cases in which a defendant has caused injury, but it is not possible to prove which individuals the defendant has injured. For example, suppose that exposure to a substance made by a single manufacturer causes some, but not all of a particular type of cancer—say, 60 percent. With respect to any given plaintiff suffering that form of cancer, the defendant is more probably than not the but-for cause of the plaintiff's harm. For some courts this would be enough proof of causation. For other courts, however, this form of statistical or epidemiological evidence would be insufficient standing alone to prove causation, because no plaintiff is able to prove anything about causation in his or her particular situation, but only about similarly situated plaintiffs in general.

Why is "naked" statistical evidence of this sort not sufficient proof for some courts? After all, statistical evidence is simply quantitative proof of probability, and probability is really all that anyone ever proves about causation. For example, suppose that a plaintiff introduces evidence sufficient to support a jury inference that, but for the defendant's having exceeded the speed limit, he would have been able to control his vehicle and would not have struck the plaintiff's vehicle. The plaintiff really has done nothing more than prove facts from which a jury could conclude that in more than half of the instances in which the two drivers act as the defendant and plaintiff act did, the defendant's negligence will cause the plaintiff injury. That evidence at its core is neither different from nor superior to statistics. If anything, when there is actual statistical data on the causation issue the plaintiff's evidence is entitled to more weight than in the collision case, because statistical data actually quantifies the probability of causation based on something more than casual experience. In the ordinary case such as the collision accident there is no such data, but only general experience on which to base a conclusion. The unwillingness of some courts to rely on statistical or epidemiological proof may therefore reflect their misconception of what goes on in the ordinary case.

On the other hand, many courts probably understand full well what they are doing when they hold that proof based on naked statistical evidence alone is insufficient. They may be reluctant to encourage litigants to gather supposedly objective data about the probability of causation that will tend to be reflected in a battle of experts whose data often will conflict. Or they may be content to live with the all-or-nothing rule that imposes liability on the defendant for 100 percent of the plaintiff's damages when the defendant is at least 51 percent likely to be the cause of the plaintiff's harm, as long as this "discrepancy" is not too obvious. Statistics bring the discrepancy right out into the open. Moreover, the aims of deterrence are perfectly well served in ordinary cases by threatening the same defendants with liability for 100 percent of the plaintiff's damages in some cases and no liability in others, even when in each case there is only a probability of causation, higher than 50 percent when there is liability and lower than 50 percent when there is not.

In the long run pretty much the right amount of liability probably is threatened and imposed by this all-or-nothing approach in ordinary cases. Potential defendants who risk injuring others typically cannot know in advance whether they will be advantaged or disadvantaged by the all-or-nothing approach to liability. Consequently, the threat of full liability when they have more probably not caused the plaintiff's harm, and no liability when they have less probably than not caused such harm, is just as likely to create optimal incentives as a more complicated approach that would award proportional damages, and without the higher transaction costs that would inevitably be associated with a more complicated approach.

What is true in the ordinary case, however, often is not true in the extraordinary case. Suppose, for example, that in the cancer hypothetical the substance manufactured by the defendant causes only 30 percent of all the cancers of a particular type. In that scenario the defendant is less probably than not a but-for cause of any given plaintiff's harm. The manufacturer therefore knows in advance that under the conventional approach to causation it will *never* be held liable for any of the harm that its product causes. The conventional approach therefore cannot create its normal incentive effect in this situation, because the defendant does not face the prospect of "too much" liability in some cases and "too little" in others. Instead there is always too little liability (i.e., none) threatened. The theoretically ideal alternative to denying liability in such cases would be to charge the defendant with liability proportional to every plaintiff's damages. Thus, if the defendant were proved to have caused 30 percent of the cancers in question, it would be liable for 30 percent of each plaintiff's damages. A number of commentators have proposed various versions of this approach.[12]

Yet this approach has not been adopted, for at least two reasons. First, there are few cases in which there is reliable quantitative data to support taking such an approach. Until there are a sufficient number of such cases, making such a radical change seems unwarranted. Second, if it were possible to identify the cases in which the defendant is systematically underdeterred because of its advance knowledge that it will never be a more-probable-than-not cause, then imposing proportional liability in these cases alone could make sense. But in the absence of the capacity to identify these cases, the logic of such "proportional liability" would be difficult to contain. If we were to adopt proportional liability in order to prevent underdeterrence in cases in which the defendant is definitely a cause of some harm but less probably than not the cause of any particular plaintiff's harm, then why not be consistent and also adopt proportional liability when the defendant is more probably than not, but only more *probably* than not, the cause of a plaintiff's harm? If proportional liability is designed to remedy underdeterrence, then why not also use it to remedy overdeterrence? The answer, of course, is that adopting this approach would require so radical shift in the way causation is determined and damages are calculated that no one even imagines that we would do this across-the-board. For both reasons, I think, there has been no real move to adopt proportional liability in cases involving the indeterminate plaintiff.

---

[12] See, e.g., David Rosenberg, *The Causal Connection in Mass Exposure Cases: A "Public Law" Vision of the Tort System*, 97 Harv. L.Rev. 849 (1984).

6

Proximate Cause

Even after the plaintiff has proved that the defendant was negligent or engaged in an activity that is subject to strict liability, that the plaintiff suffered injury, and that the defendant's actions were a cause in fact of the plaintiff's injury or damage, liability is not imposed unless the defendant's actions also were a proximate cause of the plaintiff's injury. Thus, after the other prerequisites to liability are satisfied, the doctrine of proximate cause operates as a limitation on liability.

This requirement has long generated unnecessary confusion. In most cases the proximate cause issue is simple and straightforward. The difficulties posed by the doctrine arise, I think, mainly because the rare cases in which proximate cause is contested tend to involve complex, unusual, or even bizarre sets of facts. In addition, no single formulation of the concept of proximate cause can fully describe how it is applied, because it is often used as a "fudge-factor" that permits judges and juries to decide that there ought not to be liability even when the other prerequisites to liability have already been satisfied. Nonetheless, the rudiments of proximate cause can be easily understood, especially if one takes care to distinguish the cases in which application of the doctrine is unremarkable from the rare, celebrated cases that have made proximate cause seem so perplexing. The following Sections therefore deal first with the basics; then with the exceptional cases that tend to pose difficulties; and finally step back from the details of proximate cause to try to understand what the doctrine really is designed to do.

I. The Basics

Most cases posing the issue of proximate cause can be resolved by the foreseeability test or by a closely related elaboration, the harm-within-the-risk test. The key to both these tests is to understand that proximate cause actually has as much to do with the negligence issue as with causation.

A. *Foreseeability*

The touchstone of proximate cause is foreseeability. The defendant's negligence is a proximate cause of the plaintiff's harm if that harm was a foreseeable result of acting as the defendant did. In ordinary cases there is no question at all that if the defendant was in fact negligent and that negligence was a cause in fact of the plaintiff's harm, then the proximate cause requirement also is satisfied. Suppose that the defendant fails to stop at a red light and collides with the plaintiff's vehicle. The defendant is negligent, the plaintiff suffered damage, and the defendant's negligence caused that damage. But is the defendant's negligence a "proximate" cause of the plaintiff's harm? Of course it is. It was highly foreseeable that someone passing through the intersection would be harmed if the defendant did not stop at the red light. Indeed, the risk that this kind of harm would result from running the red light is the principal reason for saying that the defendant was negligent. It is negligent to run a red light precisely because it is foreseeable that running a red light will cause an intersection collision. This is so indisputable that there is no proximate cause issue in such a case. If the defendant was negligent and that negligence was a cause in fact of the plaintiff's injury, then as a matter of law the negligence of the defendant also was a proximate cause of the plaintiff's harm. The jury will not even be instructed as to proximate cause.

What does this have to do with causation? Not much. Use of the term "proximate cause" is unfortunate and misleading. The determination that is made under the rubric of proximate cause has more to do with negligence than with causation. The first phase of the negligence issue is whether the defendant was negligent at all. That issue is decided under the rubric of negligence. The second phase of the negligence issue is whether the harm to the plaintiff was a foreseeable result of the defendant's negligence. That issue is decided under the rubric of

118

proximate cause. The first inquiry asks a general, all-risks-considered question. The second inquiry asks a particular question about what actually happened to this plaintiff.

B. The Harm-Within-The-Risk Test

The foreseeability test for proximate cause is sometimes clarified and sharpened by the harm-within-the-risk test. The run-of-the-mill negligence case almost always automatically satisfies the proximate cause requirement if the defendant was negligent. Conversely, there are occasional freak cases in which everyone would agree that, as a matter of law, the defendant's negligence was not a proximate cause of the plaintiff's injury, because injury to the plaintiff was not a harm-within-the-risk that made the defendant's action negligent.

For example, suppose that the defendant negligently parks his car next to a fire hydrant. The principal risk posed by this act is that blocked access to the hydrant will result in the destruction of property or injury to people, by fire. Suppose now that the plaintiff, driving by the hydrant where the defendant parked, skids on the road and collides with the defendant's parked vehicle. The plaintiff proves that, but for the defendant's negligence in being parked where he was, the plaintiff would have been able to bring his vehicle safely to a stop in the few extra feet of road space that would have been available. Thus, the plaintiff has proved that the defendant was negligent, that the plaintiff suffered injury, and that but for the defendant's negligence, the plaintiff would not have been injured. But that is not enough. What about proximate cause?

The question can be answered by applying the harm-within-the-risk test. Is the risk of the injury the plaintiff suffered one of the risks that makes the defendant negligent for blocking access to the fire hydrant? Almost certainly not. This answer can be given so confidently because the act of parking by the hydrant instead of a dozen feet further down the street simply does not increase the risk of the harm that materialized. A motorist passing by that spot is no more likely to skid into a car parked negligently than into a car parked a legal distance away from the hydrant. Negligence is the taking of unreasonable risks, whereas the act of negligence in this case did not at all increase the risk of what happened. In this sense what happened was not foreseeable. That is, the defendant's negligence did not foreseeably increase the risk of the harm that the plaintiff actually suffered. Note this use of the term "foreseeable." Of course what happened was "foreseeable" in the sense of being "imaginable." But what happened was not foreseeable in the sense that it is not one of the risks we would want the defendant to take into account in deciding whether to park by the hydrant, because parking by the hydrant did not increase the risk that the plaintiff would be harmed in that manner.

A number of well-known cases fall into this category. For example, in *Berry v. The Borough of Sugar Notch*,[1] the question was whether the negligence of operating a trolley above the speed limit was a proximate cause of harm that resulted when a tree fell on the speeding trolley as it passed by. Speeding did not at all increase this risk. Rather, it was simply a coincidence that the trolley was where it was when the tree fell, even though the trolley would not have been at that precise point had it not been speeding. Therefore, as a matter of law, the negligence at issue was not a proximate cause of the damage that occurred. Similarly, in *Gorris v. Scott*,[2] sheep were washed overboard from a ship as a result of negligent violation of a regulation requiring that they be kept in pens. But the regulation was promulgated under a statute designed to protect the sheep from contagious disease, not to keep them from being washed overboard. In both *Berry* and *Gorris*, the harm in question was not even arguably within the risk that had rendered the action causing the harm negligent. Therefore, in both cases, the courts held that the necessary element of proximate cause was absent.

Thus far we have examined the ordinary cases in which there is proximate cause as a matter of law, and the easy cases at the opposite extreme lie in which, as a matter of law, there is no proximate cause. In between lie cases that are a bit more difficult. Many of these are difficult largely because the harm-within-the-risk test does not easily resolve them. These are cases in which the risk that the plaintiff would suffer the harm that actually materialized was not the *principal* risk that rendered the defendant's action negligent, but that risk was a *secondary* foreseeable and relevant risk. For example, suppose that the defendant violates a statute requiring railroads to fence their rights of way and as a result injures a two-year old who has wandered onto the tracks. The legislative history of the statute reflects concern for injury to livestock from unfenced rights of way. Nonetheless, many courts

---

[1] 191 Pa. 345, 43 A. 240 (1899).

[2] 9 L.R.-Ex. 125 (1874).

would hold that a secondary purpose of such a statute is to reduce the risk of injury to people as well as livestock.[3] These courts would send the proximate cause issue to the jury.

Similar issues arise even when a statute is not involved. Then the question is whether, although the risk that materialized in harm was not the principal risk that made the defendant's action negligent, that risk was sufficiently significant to be a factor in the negligence determination. This is simply another way of posing the question, "Was the defendant's negligence a proximate cause of the plaintiff's harm?" For example, in *Wagner v. International Railway Co.*,[4] the defendant had been negligent in failing to close the door to one of its cars, thereby permitting the plaintiff's cousin to be thrown out as the car rounded a curve. The plaintiff was injured while attempting, with others, to rescue his cousin. Clearly the principal negligence of the defendant was in risking harm to someone who might fall out through the unclosed door. The question was whether the defendant's negligence was also a proximate cause of the plaintiff/rescuer's harm. Writing for the court, Judge Cardozo held that the defendant's negligence was a proximate cause of the plaintiff's harm, explaining this result with the famous phrase, "danger invites rescue." In effect the court held that one of the risks that makes it negligent to risk harm to another (when it is in fact negligent to do so) is the risk that a different individual will be injured while attempting to rescue him from the consequences of the defendant's actions. That others will attempt to rescue someone whose safety the defendant's actions put at risk is foreseeable; therefore harm to the rescuer is within the cluster of risks that makes the defendant's actions negligent—or so the jury may find.

The foreseeability and harm-within-the-risk tests, then, are a fairly straightforward way of attempting to understand the basic features of the doctrine of proximate cause. One cannot stop there, however, for two reasons. First, when the tests are satisfied, there is virtually always proximate cause. But when the tests are not satisfied, occasionally there is nonetheless proximate cause. Second, the cases that pose difficult proximate cause issues come in enough varieties that further examination of proximate cause is necessary to gain a complete appreciation of the doctrine's operation.

---

[3] For a case that nonetheless denies recovery on similar facts, see *Di Caprio v. New York Central Railway*, 231 N.Y. 94, 131 N.E. 746 (1921).

[4] 232 N.Y. 176, 133 N.E. 437 (1921).

II. Advanced Issues: The Difficult and the Unusual

Most of the issues that are not resolved by the basic tests for proximate cause fall into one of three categories: 1) cases involving the issue of what must be foreseeable; 2) cases involving the distinction between "intervening" and "superseding" cause; and 3) cases creating exceptions to the basic test.

A. What Must be Foreseeable?

Many of the more difficult and celebrated cases raising proximate cause issues can be analyzed by distinguishing between those involving unforeseeable plaintiffs, unforeseeable types of harm,[5] and unforeseeable extents of harm. It turns out that foreseeability is most often required in the first set of cases and least often required in the last set. The middle set of cases tend to be decided in ways that make generalization about their results more difficult.

1. Unforeseeability of Plaintiff

The most famous of all torts cases, *Palsgraf v. Long Island Railway*,[6] involved an unforeseeable plaintiff. A railroad employee helped a passenger onto a train that was pulling out of a station, dislodging a package the passenger was carrying. The package contained fireworks, which fell on the tracks and exploded, causing scales on the platform where other passengers stood to topple onto Mrs. Palsgraf. She sued the railroad for negligence. But the negligence of the railroad's employee—if there was any at all—consisted of his failure to exercise reasonable care toward the passenger and his package. Injury to anyone standing down the platform from this action was so unlikely that it was, for practical purposes, unforeseeable. It has often been observed that in all probability the scales were not dislodged by the concussion from the explosion, as the plaintiff contended, but by people on the platform running away from the explosion. The risk of injury caused by someone on the platform bumping into the scales probably was reasonably foreseeable. But the plaintiff apparently failed to make this much more straightforward contention.

---

[5] See Guido Calabresi, *Concerning Cause and the Law of Torts: An Essay for Harry Kalven, Jr.*, 43 U. Chi. L. Rev. 69 (1975).

[6] 248 N.Y. 339, 162 N.E. 99 (1928).

The issue, therefore, was whether the case could even go to the jury under these circumstances. Injury to someone in Mrs. Palsgraf's position was not even remotely one of the risks that should be taken into account by the railroad in deciding how to conduct itself toward the passenger getting on the train, because injury to such a person was unforeseeable—that is, highly improbable. Writing for the majority, Cardozo held that the case could not go to the jury. He put the point in terms of "duty," holding that the defendant had not breached a duty to Mrs. Palsgraf, because harm to her was not a foreseeable risk of what the defendant had done. In dissent, Judge Andrews rejected Cardozo's duty analysis. Employing the language of proximate cause, Andrews argued that foreseeability was a more malleable concept than Cardozo believed, and that the question whether the defendant's negligence was a proximate cause of the plaintiff's injury was properly for the jury.

The opinions thus disagreed on two grounds: whether the issue was duty or proximate cause, and whether the issue (whichever it was) should go to the jury. As to the first ground of disagreement, Cardozo said that before the question of proximate cause could even be reached, it was necessary to find that the defendant had breached a duty to exercise reasonable care toward the plaintiff. In contrast, Andrews said that the issue did in fact concern proximate cause. With respect to this first disagreement there probably was less difference between the two judges than they thought. Whether the explanation given is that there was no breach of duty to Mrs. Palsgraf, or that the defendant's negligence was not a proximate cause of the plaintiff's injury, the basis for the result the majority reached would be the same: Mrs. Palsgraf was an unforeseeable plaintiff.

The second ground of disagreement—whether the duty or proximate cause issue should have gone to the jury under the circumstances of the case—was more significant. If Cardozo had concluded that injury to Mrs. Palsgraf was even a remotely foreseeable result of what the defendant did, then he might have concluded that the question whether the defendant had breached a duty to her was for the jury to decide. But Cardozo did not think that reasonable people could disagree about that issue, because he did not think that injury to Mrs. Palsgraf was even remotely foreseeable. On the other hand, because Andrews did think that such injury was remotely foreseeable, he considered the proximate cause question to be appropriate for the jury. Cardozo thought that Mrs. Palsgraf was an unforeseeable plaintiff as a matter of law, whereas Andrews did not.

Now it is true that there is a good deal of language in Andrews' dissent suggesting that what I have identified as the first ground of his disagreement with Cardozo (duty versus proximate cause as the issue) was important to him. Andrews contended that negligence is not a relative concept in the way that Cardozo analyzed it. In Andrews' view, once a defendant is negligent in some way toward someone, then whether that negligence is a proximate cause of the harm that actually results is "all a question of expediency." But then Andrews recited a series of factors to take into account in making the proximate cause decision, most of which in one way or another relate to foreseeability—the very factor that Cardozo considered dispositive. So the difference between the Cardozo and Andrews approaches in any case in which injury to the plaintiff is not utterly unforeseeable probably is minimal.

Admittedly, it may be that in close cases, Andrews' proximate cause analysis would occasionally permit the question to go to the jury when Cardozo's approach would not, but typically the first, or "conceptual," difference between the two approaches is likely to be much less important than the second difference—whether or not the court thinks that reasonable people could disagree about the foreseeability of what actually happened. To put the same point another way, Cardozo could have employed Andrews' proximate cause approach to support keeping the case from the jury, just as Andrews could have employed Cardozo's breach of duty analysis to support sending the case to the jury.

Should it ever matter, however, whether injury to a plaintiff is or is not wholly unforeseeable, if the defendant was in fact negligent toward a different plaintiff? Why not hold the defendant liable for the injuries it caused to the unforeseeable plaintiff? After all, the defendant was already taking an unreasonable risk of harm to some foreseeable plaintiff or plaintiffs, or it could not be said that the defendant was negligent at all. Imposing liability for harm suffered by unforeseeable plaintiffs may deter such risk taking toward foreseeable plaintiffs. In response, it can be argued that imposing liability for harm suffered by the unforeseeable plaintiff is a bit like imposing liability without fault. The defendant will not take the risk of harming unforeseeable plaintiffs into account in any precise way, because they are unforeseeable—the defendant therefore cannot know of the risk to these plaintiffs, and is not at fault for having failed to consider their safety. The courts have never fully reconciled these two points of view. Sometimes courts employ Cardozo's approach, somtimes Andrews' approach. In whatever way this issue of the utterly unforeseeable plaintiff is resolved, however, once some harm to the plaintiff is even remotely foreseeable, the analysis changes, as in the following two categories of cases.

2. Unforeseeability of Extent of Harm

In contrast to the cases involving utterly unforeseeable plaintiffs are those in which the virtually universal "thin-skull" rule applies. The thin-skull rule governs the rights of foreseeable plaintiffs who suffer an unforeseeable extent of harm. Under this rule it is no defense that the plaintiff had an unforeseeable weakness or infirmity that caused his or her injury, or caused injury of much greater severity than would have been suffered in the absence of this weakness. As the courts say repeatedly, the defendant "takes his victim as he finds him." Thus, whereas under *Palsgraf* the defendant is not liable to a plaintiff who was unforeseeable, under the thin-skull rule unforeseeability is irrelevant. How can this difference between the treatment of unforeseeable plaintiffs and an unforeseeable extent of harm be explained?

Two different kinds of explanations can be given. The first explanation for the thin-skull rule is that rejection of the rule would create so many practical problems that the rule is a necessity. For example, suppose that even a foreseeable plaintiff could not recover compensation for injuries of unforeseeable severity. The plaintiff would then always be required to prove that the extent of his injuries was foreseeable. To prove that the severity of his injuries were foreseeable, the plaintiff would have to prove what a "normal" amount of injury under the circumstances would have been. But of course in any population of individuals a substantial percentage of them are not in perfect health; indeed, virtually everyone probably has some weakness or other that might qualify as analogous to a thin skull. People are born with some of these weaknesses, they acquire others, and sometimes they are temporarily injured and have their injuries aggravated by tortious conduct. If the thin-skull rule were not in force, in every case the jury would have to address which of these weaknesses, infirmities, and injuries, physical and mental, are "normal," or at least foreseeable. Expert testimony might be required on the question, and certainly would be admissible even if not required. The thin-skull rule avoids these complications entirely.

A second explanation for the thin-skull rule is that the rule imposes a desirable kind of strict liability. Because individuals vary enormously in the degree to which they are weak or strong, the defendant who can foresee the risk of injury to a particular plaintiff or class of plaintiffs must know that there is a distribution of the probable severity of the injury risked by any given action, from slight injury to severe injury. Even a light touch risks the low probability of causing severe injury. Consequently, any potential defendant can always foresee a thin-skulled plaintiff, at least in the statistical sense. For this reason, the threat of liability for an unforeseeable extent of harm can in fact promote optimal deterrence, because potential defendants can make at least rough calculations of the scope of the risk that their actions will result in such liability.

The exceptions to the thin-skull rule tend to confirm this explanation for it. There are whole classes of cases—decided under other doctrines altogether—in which the rule conceivably could be applied but is not, precisely because it makes more sense for the plaintiff to bear the risk in question than for the defendant to be held "strictly" liable for it. For example, the defendant does not take a negligent plaintiff as he finds him; rather, the plaintiff is either barred from recovering at all by contributory negligence, or under comparative negligence the award is reduced in proportion to the amount of negligence attributable to the plaintiff (for discussion of these doctrines, see Chapter Seven). Similarly, even a non-negligent plaintiff is obliged to take reasonable steps after injury to mitigate the extent of the losses he suffers. In these cases the defendant does not have to take his victim as he finds him; rather, some weakness of the plaintiff is taken into account in deciding whether and for how much the defendant is liable to the plaintiff.

Of course, one might say that it is not unforeseeable that a plaintiff will be contributorily negligent or fail to mitigate his damages after injury. But that would be all the more reason to apply the rule that the defendant takes his victim as he finds him in these situations. Yet the rule is not applied to these cases. The explanation is that it makes more sense for the negligent plaintiff to bear these costs than for the defendant to do so. As to these cases, the defendant's negligence is not a proximate cause of the losses resulting from the plaintiff's negligence or failure to mitigate. In each case, for substantive reasons that typically are not even discussed under the rubric of proximate cause or duty, tort liability does not follow the thin-skull rule. In short, when it makes substantive sense to hold the defendant liable for an unforeseeable extent of harm, the thin-skull rule applies. But in seemingly analogous cases in which the policy underlying the thin-skull rule would not be well-served by applying it, other tort-law doctrines do not require that the defendant take his victim as he finds him.

3. Unforeseeability of Type of Harm

Between the extremes of the utterly unforeseeable plaintiff and the foreseeable plaintiff with an unforeseeably thin skull lie cases involving what might be called an unforeseeable "type" of harm to a foreseeable plaintiff. Cardozo himself envisioned such cases toward the end of his opinion in *Palsgraf*:

There is room for argument that a distinction is to be drawn according to the diversity of interests invaded by the act, as where conduct negligent in that it threatens an insignificant invasion of an interest in property results in an unforeseeable invasion of an interest of another order, as e.g., one of bodily security.[7]

A number of classic cases and hypotheticals fall into this category. Suppose that the defendant negligently leaves a container of nitroglycerine on a shelf, and the container is accidentally knocked off the shelf. The nitroglycerine does not explode, though it lands on and injures the plaintiff's foot. May the jury find the defendant liable, or is there no liability as a matter of law? Commentators differ, and probably courts would as well.

At least one reason for the uncertainty of outcome in cases such as this is that the policies that underlie the distinction between the *Palsgraf* and thin-skull rules do not strongly dictate a general result either way. Some cases involving an unforeseeable type of harm to a foreseeable plaintiff resemble *Palsgraf*, in that the defendant is unlikely to be able to predict the scope of liability it may face for unforeseeable types of harm. But other cases resemble thin-skull claims in that a somewhat calculable range of harms might result from the defendant's negligence, even if some types of harm, realistically, are not even remotely part of what enters the determination of whether the defendant was negligent in the first instance.

Thus, in *In re Polemis & Furniss, Withy & Co.*,[8] a plank fell into the hold of a ship in which petrol was stored and caused an explosion that destroyed the ship. There were findings of fact that the defendant's employees were negligent in causing the plank to fall; that the explosion was caused by a spark resulting from the falling of the plank; and that the spark could not reasonably have been anticipated from the falling of the plank, though some damage to the ship might reasonably

---

[7] 248 N.Y. 339, 346-47, 162 N.E. 99, 101 (1928).

[8] 3 K.B. 560 (1921).

have been anticipated. The question was whether the defendant's negligence was a proximate cause of the unforeseeable harm. The defendant proposed a distinction between an unanticipated extent of harm and an unanticipated type of harm, which the court rejected. The court held instead that the defendant's negligence was a proximate cause of even unforeseeable harm, so long as the harm was a "direct" consequence of the defendant's negligence. By its terms, then, *Polemis* is a thin-skull case with the added caveat that the thin-skull rule applies only where an unforeseeable extent of harm is the *direct* consequence of the defendant's negligence.

Years later, however, *Polemis* was overruled in the British Commonwealth by *The Wagon Mound.* ! 9 • In that case the defendant negligently flushed oil from its ship while in Sydney harbor. The oil eventually caught fire and destroyed the plaintiff's dock. It was foreseeable that the oil would foul the dock, but not that it would ignite and burn the dock. The court held that the defendant could not be held liable for the fire damage to the dock, precisely because that damage was not foreseeable. The court's rationale seemed not only to overrule *Polemis*, but the thin-skull rule altogether, since the basis for the decision was that there is no point in holding a defendant liable for anything unforeseeable, even to a foreseeable plaintiff. Yet that has not been how the case has been read by subsequent courts. Rather, the courts have concluded that the thin-skull rule survives after *The Wagon Mound*. Therefore, the case must stand for the proposition that there can be no liability when an unforeseeable *type* of harm results from the defendant's negligence, even if that harm is a direct consequence of such negligence, but that there is still liability to a foreseeable plaintiff for an unforeseeable *extent* of harm.

Even under this limiting interpretation, *The Wagon Mound* states a rule that is more extreme than most courts in this country would accept. Faced with cases involving an unforeseeable type of harm to a foreseeable plaintiff, most American courts will make the proximate cause determination—or decide whether to permit the jury to make it—on a case-by-case basis. They are likely to take into account a variety of factors, including the directness of the harm, the degree to which it more closely resembles an unforeseeable type of harm than an unforeseeable extent of the same type of harm that was foreseeable, and whether the defendant's negligence caused other damage for

---

[9] *Overseas Tankship (U.K.) Ltd v. Morts Dock & Engineering Co. Ltd.*, [1961] A.C. 388 (P.C. Aust.) (*The Wagon Mound, No.1*).

which it is already being held liable and therefore not being totally exonerated from liability.[10] In short, as to unforeseeable types of harm to foreseeable plaintiffs, no general rule can be confidently stated other than that many such cases will be permitted to go to the jury on the proximate cause issue.

B. Intervening and Superseding Cause

Another problem that is not entirely solved by the foreseeability and harm-within-the risk tests involves intervening and superseding cause. In such cases the subsequent acts of independent third-parties or forces are the immediate cause of harm that results from the original negligence of the defendant. Then the question is whether the "original" defendant is or is not relieved of liability because of the subsequent acts of the third-party or subsequent force. For example, the defendant bartender serves a visibly intoxicated patron who then leaves the bar by car and negligently injures the plaintiff.[11] Or the defendant service station negligently leaves keys in the ignition of a car parked on its lot for servicing, and a thief who takes the car collides with the plaintiff.[12]

Standard terminology describes these cases as involving only "intervening" cause when the possibility of injury to the plaintiff is one of the risks that is taken into account in deciding whether the defendant's actions were negligent. In this situation the defendant's negligence is a proximate cause of the plaintiff's injury, or at least the issue is submitted to the jury. In this situation, the intervening act does not break the "chain" of causation leading from the defendant's act to the plaintiff's injury. On the other hand, when the risk of injury to one in the plaintiff's position is so remote that it is not a factor to be taken into account at all in deciding whether the defendant's actions were negligent, then the subsequent act of a third-party or operation of a new force is described as a "superseding" cause, and the negligence of the defendant is not a proximate cause of the plaintiff's injury. The subsequent act of negligence supersedes the defendant's act, and breaks the "chain" of causation.

---

[10] For the classic statement of this point of view, see Judge Friendly's opinion in *Petition of Kinsman Transit Company*, 338 F.2d 708 (2d Cir. 1964).

[11] See, e.g., *Vesely v. Sager*, 5 Cal.3d 153, 486 P.2d 151, 95 Cal.Rptr. 623 (1971).

[12] See, e.g., *Ross v. Hartman*, 139 F.2d 14 (D.C. Cir. 1943).

In keeping with this analytical structure, most courts would hold that the negligence of the bartender and the service station in the above hypotheticals were a proximate cause of the injuries at issue if the patron and thief had driven negligently themselves. The risk that an inebriated person or thief will drive negligently is sufficiently foreseeable that it is one of the things that makes it negligent to serve alcohol to someone who is already inebriated or to leave a car with keys in the ignition where it may be stolen, though the principal negligence entailed in the actions consists of risking injury to the patron and loss of the owner's car. Thus, the actions of the patron and thief would be described as "mere" intervening or subsequent causes, not superseding causes. To put the point in common sense terms, many actions are risky at least in part because, and sometimes precisely because, they subject the plaintiff to the risk that another person or force will later come along and injure the plaintiff.

As the service station hypothetical illustrates, sometimes subsequent third-party actions that are intentionally tortious and perhaps even criminal are sufficiently foreseeable to render the original actor's negligence a proximate cause of the harm immediately caused by the third-party. But since negligence often is more common than intentionally tortious or criminal actions, there will be cases in which subsequent third-party negligence is foreseeable, whereas more blameworthy third-party conduct is not. Then the original defendant's negligence will be held not to be a proximate cause of harm caused immediately by the intentional misconduct of a third party. In such situations the subsequent intentional misconduct breaks the "chain" of causation leading from the original defendant, because that misconduct was intentional rather than merely negligent. Of course, there are cases in which the original defendant is negligent precisely because his action risks intentional misconduct by a third party. Under these circumstances the chain of causation is not broken.

Conversely, sometimes the subsequent act of the third party which causes injury to the plaintiff is not even negligent. Is the original defendant's negligence then a proximate cause? For example, suppose the thief who stole a car with the keys left in the ignition is driving carefully when he collides with the plaintiff. Then the case is a lot like *Berry v. Borough of Sugar Notch.*[13] It is true that the negligence of the service station did slightly increase the risk to the plaintiff, since absent the theft there would have been one less car on the road with a chance

---

[13] See note 1, supra.

of non-negligently injuring the plaintiff. This is not a sufficient increase in risk, however, to make harm to the plaintiff foreseeable. On the other hand, sometimes injury at the hands of a subsequent, non-negligent third party is sufficiently foreseeable to make that risk one of the things that makes it negligent for the defendant to act as he did. For instance, if I negligently injure you and your injuries are aggravated by subsequent, non-negligent medical care, there is no question that my negligence is a proximate cause of the aggravation. Such aggravation is sufficiently common to make it foreseeable.

A variation on the intervening/superseding cause issue occurs when injury to the plaintiff is unquestionably foreseeable, but that injury occurs in a peculiar or bizarre manner. For example, in *Marshall v. Nugent*,[14] the defendant's driving forced a car in which the plaintiff was a passenger to run off the road. The plaintiff was at that point unharmed, but suffered injury after he had walked down the road and was struck by a third vehicle as he was attempting to warn oncoming traffic of the danger ahead. Despite the unusual way in which the plaintiff actually was injured, this did not preclude liability on the part of the defendant. As long as the plaintiff was injured at roughly the same time and in roughly the same place as was foreseeable, through the same general forces as were foreseeable, it is not necessary that the precise manner in which the injury took place have been foreseeable. If that were a requirement the defendant's negligence would rarely be a proximate cause of the plaintiff's harm, since there are an almost infinite number of detailed variations on the ways in which a foreseeable injury may occur.

All this is doctrinally straightforward. But an important non-doctrinal, practical consideration also helps to explain the increasing tendency of the courts to hold that subsequent forces are merely intervening rather than superseding causes. In all of the cases involving the subsequent act of a negligent third party, that party is of course liable to the plaintiff. The issue in the cases is whether the party (whom I have been calling the "original defendant") whose original negligence placed the plaintiff in a position to be injured by the third party also may be held liable. Holding that the original defendant's negligence also is a proximate cause of the plaintiff's harm (or that the jury is free to find that it is) thus renders a second defendant liable.

---

[14] 222 F.2d 604 (1st Cir. 1955).

The economic significance of this kind of development should be obvious: it adds a another pocket from which recovery may be obtained. And it is no surprise that in many of the cases, the original defendant is more likely to be solvent, or insured, or both, and therefore more able actually to pay compensation to the plaintiff, than the defendant whose negligence was the immediate cause of the plaintiff's injury. The bartender's employer and the service station are more likely to be able to pay, for example, than the patron and the thief, respectively. This does not mean that the courts decide these cases in an *ad hoc* manner depending on how solvent the original defendant happens to be. But the evolution of the case law to permit the imposition of liability on the original defendant probably has been influenced in a general way by the fact that in many of the cases the party who would otherwise be the sole defendant is unlikely to be able to pay a judgment entered against him.

III. Judge, Jury, and the Underlying Purpose of Proximate Cause

To round out our portrait of proximate cause, two points must be added. The first point concerns the significance of the relation between judge and jury in making determinations about proximate cause. The second, related point requires us to step back from the details of proximate cause and reflect about the underlying purpose of the doctrine.

A. *Judge and Jury*

Some of the complexity that appears to plague the law governing proximate cause can be reduced by attending to an important feature of the cases that often goes unrecognized. Many of the cases deal with a problem at the extreme end of the continuum: whether the defendant's negligence *was not a proximate cause* of the plaintiff's harm, as a matter of law. Thus, the question in these cases is whether the proximate cause issue can even go to the jury. Such famous cases as *Palsgraf* and *The Wagon Mound* fall into this category.

It is important to recognize, however, that the second category of proximate cause cases that raise difficult problems does not involve a situation at the opposite end of the continuum. Rather, these cases hold that the proximate cause issue was properly submitted to the jury, or was improperly kept from the jury. Few cases, that is, concern the situations in which the defendant's negligence *was a proximate cause* of the plaintiff's injury, as a matter of law. Aside from the thin-skull rule (which does fall into this category), there are few cases that address this problem, because it is unremarkable. If I run a red light and collide with another vehicle at the intersection controlled by the light, then of course my negligence is a proximate cause of the harm that results, as a matter of law. The very reason I am negligent in running the red light is that doing so risks causing precisely this kind of injury. If I am negligent in this situation, it is not a jury question whether that negligence was a proximate cause of what happened. In finding me negligent the jury necessarily has made that determination already.

The occasional opinions that do involve the second category of cases—which rule that the proximate cause issue is properly one for the jury—sometimes give the false impression that they are holding that the defendant's negligence was a proximate cause of the plaintiff's harm as a matter of law. In their understandable effort to justify rejection of the defendant's contention that, as a matter of law, its negligence was not a proximate cause of the plaintiff's harm, the courts in these cases sometimes seem to be suggesting the opposite. But of course the courts are not suggesting that the defendant's negligence was a proximate cause of the plaintiff's harm, as a matter of law. These decisions merely hold that, because reasonable people could disagree about whether the defendant's negligence was a proximate cause of the plaintiff's harm, the question was properly one to be left to the jury.

Thus, cases such as *Wagner v. International Railway*[15] and *Marshall v. Nugent*[16] are not the polar opposites of *Palsgraf* and *The Wagon Mound*. On the contrary, these cases occupy a middle point between the extreme cases in which as a matter of law there is no proximate cause and those in which as a matter of law the defendant's negligence is a proximate cause. It turns out that (to paraphrase Cardozo's famous line from *Wagner*) danger does not necessarily invite rescue. Rather, under *Wagner*, reasonable people could disagree about whether danger invited rescue under those circumstances, and that the question should therefore be submitted to the jury. Similarly, under *Marshall v. Nugent*, it is not true that as a matter of law the injury the plaintiff received by being struck by the defendant's car "was not remote, either in time or place, from the negligent conduct of defendant * * *". Rather (as the court took pains elsewhere in the opinion to note explicitly), it was for the jury to decide whether the injury to the plaintiff was or was not "remote."

---

[15] See note 4, supra.

[16] See note 14, supra.

The lesson to be learned from this distinction is that occasionally there are decisions holding on no-proximate-cause grounds that the plaintiff's case may not go to the jury (such as *Palsgraf* and *The Wagon Mound*). But more often the complex proximate-cause reasoning that one encounters in the opinions is verbal overkill, directed at explaining why the issue is simply one for the jury.

B. The Underlying Purpose of Proximate Cause

Proximate cause is a liability-limiting doctrine. The proximate cause requirement takes the universe of claims that are eligible for liability and designates those in which liability should not be imposed. Further, by distinguishing between cases that should and should not go to the jury, the doctrine expresses what lies behind its liability-limiting purpose in two different ways. First, decisions withholding a case from jury decision on proximate-cause grounds tend to do so in rule-based formulations that can never capture everything that enters into the decision that there is no proximate cause, as a matter of law. Indeed, in reading Judge Andrews' dissent in *Palsgraf,* I always get the sense that Andrews objects mainly to Cardozo's unwillingness to acknowledge the relevance of the many factors Andrews believes should be taken into account in making the proximate cause decision. His objection to the majority's decision to keep the case from the jury seems almost secondary. The majority opinion in *Palsgraf* gives helpful, but inevitably incomplete guidance to the courts as to the situations in which a case should not go to the jury.

Second, and in contrast, when a proximate cause issue does go to the jury, the very factors that are so difficult to articulate in a formal judicial opinion are likely nonetheless to be taken into by the jury. And it is in the jury room, I think, that the most significant and most frequently overlooked application of proximate cause doctrine actually takes place. In the jury room, the common-sense principle underlying proximate cause—that negligent defendants should not always bear liability to all the people or for all the harm they have caused, because at some point liability must stop—can be put into practice. Judgments about such matters as the degree of remoteness of the defendant's action from the plaintiff's harm, and whether the amount of liability that may be imposed on the defendant fits the tort it committed (something like what would be called "proportionality" in the field of criminal punishment), each of which fine-tune the negligence decision itself, can be made by the jury without the need to quantify or explain the weight given to each factor. The doctrine of proximate cause thus creates the need for a jury instruction that acquaints the jury with its responsibility not merely to make a mechanical decision applying the rules of tort law, but also to use its judgment in deciding whether the defendant was sufficiently blameworthy under all the circumstances to deserve to bear liability. Far from being the theoretical and conceptual construct that the appellate decisions sometimes make it seem to be, in this sense proximate cause is the most practical and realistic of doctrines, for it asks the jury to step back after it has applied the individual pieces of the liability puzzle and look at the whole picture before it makes its final decision.

7

Defenses Based on Plaintiff's Conduct

he defenses based on plaintiff's conduct—contributory and comparative negligence, as well as assumption of risk—form an important part of many personal injury and property damage suits. Each
is an "affirmative" defense. That is, the defendant bears the burden of
pleading and proving the facts necessary to support one of these defenses.
The defendant must prove that the plaintiff's conduct was negligent or
consisted of assumption of risk, that such conduct was a cause in fact of
the plaintiff's injury, and that such conduct was a proximate cause of this
injury. In the typical case involving a defense based on plaintiff's
conduct, then, each party tries to prove what amounts to a full tort claim
against the other. The difference is that the plaintiff attempts to prove
that the defendant breached a duty to him, whereas the defendant attempts
to prove that the plaintiff breached a duty to himself.

I. Contributory Negligence

Contributory negligence is the failure of the plaintiff to exercise
reasonable care to protect himself or his property from the risk of
harm. Almost as soon as negligence emerged in the early nineteenth
century as a distinct tort, the defense of contributory negligence began
to develop along with it. In *Butterfield v. Forrester*,[1] for example, the
court seemed to think it self-evident that a negligent plaintiff had no
right to recover from a negligent defendant. From the inception of the
doctrine until the 1970's, in most states the contributory negligence of
the plaintiff was a complete bar to recovery. Even a slightly negligent
plaintiff could recover nothing from a negligent defendant, if the plaintiff's negligence was both a cause in fact and a proximate cause of his
own injuries. At that point statutes in many jurisdictions and a few

---

[1] 103 Eng. Rep. 926 (K.B. 1809).

judicial decisions replaced this complete bar with comparative negligence, under which the negligence of the plaintiff does not bar recovery but reduces it.

Sometimes the conduct that constitutes contributory negligence also is primary negligence, so to speak. For example, almost every act of negligent driving risks harm to the driver and to others; whether the negligent driver or another party (or both) is injured is often just a matter of luck. On the other hand, some acts of contributory negligence are merely that—they create an unreasonable risk of harm to oneself but not to anyone else—using a defective chain saw unsafely when no one else is in the vicinity, for instance.

At the core of the defense of contributory negligence is the notion that it would be unfair to impose liability on the defendant when the plaintiff has negligently contributed to his own injury. The trouble with this notion is that its opposite is also true. It is unfair to completely relieve the defendant of liability merely because the plaintiff was also a cause of his own injury. Nor can causal reasoning explain the defense. There is nothing in the facts of the countless cases in which the defense of contributory negligence has been applied to suggest that the plaintiff is the sole cause in fact or proximate cause of his own harm. Rather, in these cases the defendant's negligence and the plaintiff's negligence are both causes in fact and both proximate causes of the plaintiff's harm. Finally, deterrence cannot explain the defense either. To whatever small extent the contributory negligence defense deters potential plaintiffs from being negligent, it fails to deter potential defendants, who can anticipate being relieved of liability in some cases even when they are negligent.

Despite considerable historical scholarship on contributory negligence, it is still not entirely clear why the defense developed in the way it did, as a complete bar to recovery. Part of the explanation may be that when negligence was first recognized as a separate tort, recovery on that basis was regarded as sufficiently unusual that it was thought appropriate to make compensation available only to plaintiffs with completely "clean hands." In addition, there has long been speculation by some commentators—though the matter is disputed—that the defense of contributory negligence was employed by the courts as a device to reign in the power of juries, which nineteenth century judges sometimes distrusted. The defense is only a fully effective device for achieving this aim, however, when it is possible to find contributory negligence as a matter of law and therefore to grant a directed verdict for the defendant notwithstanding the defendant's own negligence. Finally, though today we find comparative negligence to be more compatible with our sense of fairness, the nineteenth century courts may simply have been unable to see this approach as a coherent stopping point between the extremes of no-liability and full-liability when the plaintiff's negligence had contributed to his own injury.

Nevertheless, as time went on the courts recognized the harsh effect that sometimes resulted from the complete bar to recovery effectuated by the contributory negligence defense. A number of doctrinal exceptions and practices emerged at least in part in order to ameliorate this harsh effect. These are discussed in the following Sections.

A. The Safety Statute Exception

Many courts hold that when the defendant's negligence consists of the breach of a statute designed specifically to protect a class of persons unable to protect themselves against the defendant's negligence, the contributory negligence of a member of the protected class is not a bar to recovery. For example, if a statute requires ladders furnished to certain employees to have safety shoes, the negligence of an employee in using a ladder without safety shoes does not bar a negligence action against the party who was under a statutory duty to furnish the proper ladder.[2] The logic behind this rule is not particularly compelling, since much negligent conduct that is not a statutory violation is considered negligent precisely because those whose harm the conduct risks cannot adequately protect themselves against this risk. Otherwise the risk taken by the defendant might not be an unreasonable risk to take. The safety statute exception seems primarily to reflect a reaction to the harsh effect of the contributory negligence bar to recovery in a category of cases that seem on their surface to be conceptually distinct from those in which the defense is ordinarily available, but which on deeper analysis are difficult to distinguish from ordinary cases.

B. The Greater-Degree-of-Blame Exception

Contributory negligence is not a defense to an intentional tort. The justification for this rule lies in both deterrence and corrective justice. Acting with intent to harm another person is far more objectionable and worth deterring than the failure to take sufficient care to protect oneself from harm. For the same reason, as between an intentional tortfeasor and a contributorily negligent victim, corrective justice is

---

[2] See *Koenig v. Patrick Constr. Corp.*, 298 N.Y. 313, 83 N.E.2d 133 (1948).

more faithfully served by imposing liability on the tortfeasor than by denying recovery to the negligent victim. Both deterrence and corrective justice are served, then, through a rough comparison of the faults of the two parties.

The same reasoning is applied to situations in which the plaintiff was contributorily negligent but the defendant's conduct was more blameworthy than mere negligence, even if it was not intentional. The defendant's conduct may have constituted gross negligence, recklessness, or wanton and willful misconduct. The greater-degree-of-harm exception to the contributory negligence defense is generally applied in any of these situations—whenever the defendant's conduct consists at least of gross negligence. Just as interesting for our purposes, however, is the fact that the exception does not apply when the plaintiff's conduct is as blameworthy or more blameworthy than the defendant's conduct. For example, even if the defendant's conduct showed wanton and willful disregard for the safety of others, if the plaintiff showed wanton and willful disregard for his own safety, then the defendant is relieved of liability. In effect the same degrees of blame cancel each other out. Thus, something like a rough comparison of the faults of the parties not only determines when there is an exception to the contributory negligence defense, but also when there is no exception.

C. Last Clear Chance

A third example of the courts' effort to ameliorate the harsh effect of contributory negligence is the doctrine of last clear chance. I have never been certain whether last clear chance constitutes deliberate judicial obfuscation in the service of a desired result, or just plain confusion. Either way, last clear chance is a striking by-product of the contributory negligence defense. If the negligent defendant had the last clear chance to avoid harming the plaintiff, then the plaintiff's contributory negligence is not a bar to recovery. Last clear chance trumps the defense of contributory negligence.

Why would that be so? Being the last in time to have an opportunity to avoid injuring someone does not render the party who had the first chance to do so any less a proximate cause of the injury. The first and second negligent actors may both be proximate causes of what happens because of their negligence. Nor is there anything particularly more blameworthy about having the last chance to avoid injuring another person than in having the first chance to do so. On the other hand, when a defendant has a chance that is both last *and* clear, the failure to take that chance may well be more blameworthy than ordinary carelessness. A clear chance is one that is open and obvious. If that clear chance to avoid injury also is the last chance—because at that point the plaintiff cannot extricate himself from danger—and the defendant knows this, then the inference that the defendant knew that he or she alone could avoid the injury is also likely to be permissible. Under these circumstances, one might say that the defendant was an entire order of magnitude more blameworthy than he would have been had he simply failed to exercise reasonable care to avoid injury, at the same time that the plaintiff was also failing to exercise reasonable care. That is surely what was going on in the case in which the last clear chance doctrine seemed to originate, *Davies v. Mann*.[3] There the plaintiff was apparently negligent in tying the forefeet of his donkey together so that it could not move, but the defendant then drove his wagon right over the donkey. In cases such as this last clear chance might be understood as a another version of the greater-degree-of-blame exception to the contributory negligence defense.

I find all this plausible as an explanation of how the courts first came to think that last clear chance was an appropriate exception to the contributory negligence rule. But for several reasons the comparison of faults explanation of last clear chance tends to contain the seeds of its own demise. The defendant who had the last clear chance may not have been more blameworthy than a merely careless defendant—in fact, he may have been merely careless. This is because the case law makes it clear that in order to invoke last clear chance, the plaintiff need not prove that the defendant actually appreciated the position of danger in which he encountered the plaintiff and then failed to avoid injuring the plaintiff. Rather, last clear chance requires only that the defendant "had reason" to appreciate that danger. Having "reason to know" that one is about to injure the plaintiff is not the same as knowing. The requirements of last clear chance therefore can be met without proof that the defendant was any more than negligent in failing to appreciate the facts staring him in the face, and then failing to exercise the opportunity he would have had to avoid injuring the plaintiff if he had not been negligent in this manner. Sometimes, of course, the defendant will have been more than merely negligent, because he will have actually known of the plaintiff's danger. But sometimes not. So the attractiveness of the crude comparison of faults that helps to explain the different-degree-of-blame exception to contributory negli-

---

[3] 10 M. & W. 547, 152 Eng. Rep. 588 (Exchequer 1842).

gence can justify only a portion of the situations in which last clear chance may apply. Thus, over time, the courts have applied the doctrine not only when the defendant had the last clear chance, but also when the defendant's chance was last but not clear.

And the converse is also true. The doctrine is often applied when the defendant's chance was clear but not last. This occurs when the plaintiff could have extricated himself from his position of danger up until the moment of injury through the exercise of reasonable care, but has failed to do so. For example, the plaintiff may simply be negligently inattentive and just as capable as the defendant until the very moment of injury of avoiding harm to himself, simply by paying attention and getting out of the way. Something like a crude comparison of faults may help to explain the application of last clear chance to this situation, but not because the defendant's chance was last. The plaintiff could also have avoided injury up until the last moment. However, if in this situation the plaintiff is in a position of obvious peril and the defendant knows this but nonetheless injures him, the inference that the defendant did so intentionally is likely to be permissible. This is surely more blameworthy than the plaintiff's merely negligent inattentiveness. But since both the defendant and the plaintiff could have avoided injury to the plaintiff up until the instant before it occurred, the defendant did not have the last chance to avoid the injury. The timing of the defendant's chance, which the very name of the doctrine "last clear chance" proclaims to be decisive, is logically irrelevant to the doctrine's application in this situation.

Admittedly, if one is in fact simply comparing the faults of the parties, it makes sense to relieve the plaintiff of the effect of his contributory negligence when the defendant's chance is clear but not last. The party whose chance to avoid the injury is clear probably is more often more at fault than the party whose chance was last but not clear. If this is so, however, then the distinctiveness of last clear chance as an exception to the contributory negligence defense in cases involving sequential negligence has disappeared. Once sequence is logically irrelevant to the calculus, why purport to make sequential negligence by the parties a prerequisite to engaging in what amounts to the comparison of faults? Why not simply move to comparative negligence generally? The answer, of course, is that eventually that is exactly what happened. Last clear chance was a transitional doctrine that has tended to fade away with the advent of comparative negligence, because it was merely a way of ameliorating the harsh effect of contributory negligence in a set of situations that, as the set expanded, could no longer be satisfactorily distinguished from the mine-run of contributory negligence cases.

D. The Jury Question/General Verdict Approach

The last reflection of the way in which contributory negligence eventually fell into almost complete disfavor is not a doctrine, but a practice. Whether the plaintiff was contributorily negligent is a quintessential jury question. Indeed, although the rhetoric courts use in determining whether to submit the question of defendants' and plaintiffs' negligence to the jury is highly similar, in practice the courts often are more inclined to submit the latter issue to the jury than the former. Since juries themselves are known to favor plaintiffs, other things being equal, this practice itself helps to ameliorate the harsh effect of the contributory negligence defense.

A less obvious but just as important effect of this approach is that it permits what amounts to under-the-table comparative negligence. Although the jury in every case in which the contributory negligence defense is in force is instructed that such negligence is a complete defense, experienced lawyers virtually all agree that it is common for juries to disregard this instruction. Instead juries often return "quotient" verdicts in which they reduce the plaintiff's recovery through a rough comparison of the faults of the parties. Juries can most easily circumvent the complete-bar rule in this way when they are asked only for a general verdict. Typically the evidence regarding such items of loss as future medical expenses and lost wages, if any, and past and future pain and suffering, is sufficiently open-ended that awarding any sum within a very wide range of values is within the jury's discretion. Consequently, the jury may make a smaller award than the maximum that might be expected without necessarily revealing that it "split the difference." A smaller award than the maximum permitted by the evidence could just as easily reflect a finding that the plaintiff was not negligent at all, but suffered less damage than the plaintiff contended. The result in such cases is that everyone suspects the jury of having invoked comparative negligence, but no one can be sure whether this actually occurred.

II. Comparative Negligence

Over the last four decades a revolution of sorts has replaced the contributory negligence defense with a comparative negligence regime. All but a few states have now adopted comparative negligence, most by statute but a few by judicial decision.[4] As I have just noted, under-the-table comparative negligence probably was at work in many jury deliberations for a long time, though unsystematically and without control or instruction by the courts. With the formal adoption of comparative negligence, however, an entire system of rules implementing the basic concept had to be developed. By now there are hundreds of reported decisions addressing a variety of issues that arise in connection with the new defense. It is nonetheless a measure of the time it takes for a system of common law adjudication to do the backing and filling necessary to produce a mature body of doctrine that, even after several decades, many issues are still unsettled in many states.

A. *The Basics*

Although the verbal formulation setting out the comparative negligence defense varies, the core of the defense is the same. Under comparative negligence, the contributory negligence of the plaintiff does not necessarily bar recovery. Instead, the plaintiff's recovery is reduced "in proportion to the amount of negligence attributable to him," to quote the typical operative provision. Normally this occurs by assuming that, by definition, the total amount of negligence contributing to the plaintiff's injury or damage was 100 percent. The jury must divide (or compare) the negligence of the parties and attribute a percentage to each. The plaintiff's recovery is then reduced by his percentage. For example, suppose that the plaintiff's damages are $100,000 and that the jury finds the plaintiff to have been 40 percent negligent. Reducing the plaintiff's recovery by 40 percent yields $60,000. He therefore recovers $60,000, because his recovery is reduced in proportion to the amount of negligence attributable to him.

---

[4] See, e.g., *McIntyre v. Balentine*, 833 S.W.2d 52 (Tenn. S.Ct. 1992); *Li v. Yellow Cab Co. of California*, 13 Cal.3d 804, 532 P.2d 1226, 119 Cal.Rptr. 858 (1975).

1. Pure or Modified Comparative Negligence?

There are two forms of comparative negligence. Under the "pure" form, the plaintiff's negligence is never a complete bar to recovery. Rather, comparative negligence applies regardless of how much more negligent the plaintiff was than the defendant. In contrast, under the "modified" form of comparative negligence, if the plaintiff is found to be more negligent than the defendant (and under some versions, "as negligent" as the defendant), comparative negligence does not apply and the plaintiff's contributory negligence is a complete bar to recovery. Under modified comparative negligence, when the plaintiff is entitled to recover anything he recovers exactly what he would recover under pure comparative negligence. The difference is that the plaintiff can always recover something under pure comparative negligence except when he is 100 percent negligent, which is tantamount to saying that the defendant was not negligent at all and therefore not liable. In contrast, under modified comparative negligence a plaintiff who is more negligent than the defendant (and under some versions, as negligent as the defendant) recovers nothing.

Under modified comparative negligence a small variation in the amount of negligence attributed to the plaintiff can mean the difference between a substantial recovery and none at all. Probably the most common jury attribution of negligence is a finding that each party was 50 percent negligent. In a jurisdiction that applies modified comparative negligence as long as the plaintiff's negligence is "not greater than" the defendant's, the plaintiff recovers one-half of his damages under this scenario. In a jurisdiction that applies comparative negligence only if the plaintiff's negligence is "not as great as" the defendant's, however, the plaintiff will be completely barred from recovery when there is a 50–50 attribution. Juries that understand this possibility can take it into account, making sure that they do not attribute "too much" negligence to the plaintiff and thereby bar him from any recovery at all. But because the way in which comparative negligence is administered varies, this is not always possible. In some states the jury is instructed regarding the way in which comparative negligence operates and can make an "adjustment" in the amount of negligence attributed to the parties to assure some recovery for the plaintiff, if the jury so desires. In other states, however, the jury is simply asked to bring in a special verdict indicating the total amount of the plaintiff's damages and the amounts of negligence attributable to each party. The court then makes the calculations necessary to determine if the plaintiff is entitled to a recovery and, if so, in what amount.

2. The Basis for Comparison

Comparative negligence is just what its name implies—comparative *negligence*, not comparative causation. It is possible for a party to be slightly negligent and cause a great deal of harm, just as it is possible to be very negligent and yet cause little harm. Although the prospect of comparing causation rather than negligence is sometimes attractive, it would be difficult to operate a comparative causation system. The very notion of a causal comparison apart from the parties' negligence is far from clear. Suppose that the plaintiff drives 60 miles per hour in a 30 mile per hour zone and the defendant drives 90 miles per hour in the same zone. One view of the matter would be that the parties' causal contributions should be measured by the amount of their causal negligence. On this view the defendant's contribution is 66 and 2/3 percent and the plaintiff's 33 and 1/3 percent—60 miles per hour over the speed limit versus the plaintiff's 30 miles per hour over. Another view would be that the amount of each party's causal contribution is a matter separate from their negligence, once it is shown that they are negligent. On this view the defendant's causal contribution is 60 percent (9/15ths of the total amount of speed) and the plaintiff's was 40 percent (6/15ths). Both of these approaches, however, ignore other factors that may have contributed to the amount of damage that actually resulted from the parties' negligence—for example, the weight of each vehicle.

In theory, comparing negligence alone and not causation sidesteps these issues. Of course, instructing the jury that it is to take negligence only into account in making its comparative attribution is not the same as assuring that this is done. Moreover, comparing negligence is not always a simpler task than comparing causation, though it is admittedly a different operation. For instance, it not at all clear in the above example that the defendant was twice as negligent as the plaintiff. The defendant was exceeding the speed limit by twice the amount of the plaintiff's exceedence. But plaintiff was driving at a speed (60 miles per hour) at which he was undoubtedly able to control his vehicle. In contrast, at 90 miles per hour the defendant probably had much less ability to control his vehicle, and much less experience doing so at that speed as well. Perhaps, therefore, the defendant was more than twice as negligent as the plaintiff.

Nor is the comparison always between the same "kinds" of negligence. Suppose that the defendant was speeding and that the plaintiff failed to come to a complete halt at a stop-sign. The jury in this case must compare "apples and oranges," so to speak. At least, however, the comparison is between two different kinds of negligent driving. Sometimes the forms of negligence the jury must compare are even less like each other than this. Sometimes the jury must compare apples and waste baskets: suppose that the plaintiff negligently failed to trim a tree on his property and as a result the defendant, who was negligently speeding, did not see a stop-sign obscured by the tree. Braking at the last minute the defendant skids and injures the plaintiff. The negligence of the two parties adds up to 100 percent. How much negligence should be attributed to each?

The *law* of comparative negligence has nothing much to say about the problems entailed in making such comparisons. And I am not suggesting that it should. These are simply problems for a jury instructed to compare the negligence of each party. The jury must struggle, evaluate, and respond with a comparative attribution of the parties' negligence. But no one should assume that a jury's responsibility under comparative negligence is as simple and straightforward as comparing two quantities that are already in the same currency of exchange. The jury's task is more complicated than that, and sometimes far more complicated.

3. Assessment

There is considerable debate in the literature about the comparative effectiveness of contributory and comparative negligence in deterring accidents. The overall implication of this literature is that neither approach is likely to be a systematically superior method of deterring accidents. Intuitively this seems obvious: other things being equal, plaintiffs are likely marginally to exercise greater care under contributory negligence and defendants are likely marginally to exercise greater under comparative negligence. No one can say in general whether the loss of deterrence in the one respect will or will not be more than offset in the other respect. In any event, in practice other things usually are not equal. To take just one of many complicating factors as an example, whether potential victims know that a comparative negligence rule is in force may affect the relative deterrence capacity of comparative and contributory negligence rules. Yet some people will know about the comparative negligence rule and others will not. Consequently, one's assessment of the attractiveness of comparative negligence must depend mainly on considerations other than deterrence.

In my view the appeal of comparative negligence to the ordinary individual's sense of fairness is sufficiently great to render this factor alone virtually dispositive on the issue. The contributory negligence rule that completely barred recovery from a negligent injurer because the victim also was negligent, without regard to the degree of that negligence, is highly objectionable to most people's sense of fairness. Virtually every ordinary person's immediate reaction to the contributory negligence defense is that recovery should not be barred in this situation, but that the amount recovered should be reduced in some proportion that takes the victim's negligence into account. One might quibble about whether the proper approach should be pure or modified comparative negligence, and about the details of the scheme adopted. But the day when the contributory negligence defense meshed with the common sense morality of ordinary people—if it ever did—has long since passed. The enactment of comparative negligence legislation in all but a handful of states is a reflection of the now-dominant moral sense that some recovery should be permitted for negligent victims, though not as much as for those who were not at all negligent.

B. Applications

Legislative enactment or judicial adoption of comparative negligence creates the need for a whole new jurisprudence resolving the many issues that arise under a comparative negligence regime. Entire treatises are now devoted to these issues, few of which are resolved in the statutes or judicial decisions that initiate the new regime.

1. Multiple Defendants

Suppose that the plaintiff is 40 percent negligent and two defendants each are 35 and 25 percent negligent, respectively. In a modified comparative negligence jurisdiction, does the plaintiff recover anything? That depends on the underlying logic of modified comparative negligence. If this logic is that a plaintiff should be entitled to recover something unless she is principally responsible for her own harm, then recovery should be permitted. On the other hand, if the underlying logic of a modified system is that a defendant should not be held liable unless she is at least as responsible for the plaintiff's harm as the plaintiff, then there should be no recovery in this situation. Most courts have found the former answer preferable. The move from contributory to comparative negligence tends to be made more because of the unfairness of contributory negligence to plaintiffs than because of a desire to plug a loophole in the liability of defendants. A focus on the scope of the plaintiff's responsibility therefore seems most appropriate in the handling of multiple defendant cases.

2. Joint and Several Liability

Prior to the adoption of comparative negligence, multiple defendants were jointly and severally liable to the plaintiff. If the plaintiff and two defendants are 40, 35, and 25 percent negligent, respectively, is each defendant liable only for its share of the plaintiff's damages, or are the two defendants jointly and severally liable for 60 percent of the plaintiff's damages? Under contributory negligence, as between a negligent defendant and an innocent plaintiff (the only kind of plaintiff who could recover at all under contributory negligence), joint and several liability properly places the risk of one defendant's insolvency on the other negligent defendant. Under comparative negligence, however, the plaintiff is not entirely innocent, because he too was negligent.

Three approaches are possible. The first is to hold the defendants jointly and severally liable for the amount of the judgment (for 60 percent of the plaintiff's losses) even though the plaintiff also was negligent. If the defendants are merely concurrent but not joint tortfeasors, then there is no particular logic to this approach; it is simply a carryover of the prior rule. On the other hand, if the defendants are joint tortfeasors or otherwise acted in concert, the approach has some appeal. Second, at the other extreme is an approach that holds each defendant liable only for its own proportional share of the reduced judgment. Thus, the first defendant in the hypothetical would pay 35/60ths of the judgment. If the second defendant, whose proper share is 25/60ths were unable to pay, then the plaintiff would be left without recourse as to that share. This approach presupposes that, in effect, not only are the defendants injurers of the plaintiff, but that the plaintiff is an injurer of the plaintiff. Under this logic, each party is liable to the plaintiff in proportion to the amount of its negligence, and no party should be liable for more than its share.

The flaw in this logic leads to the third and, in my view, most sensible approach. If each party including the plaintiff is an injurer, then the injurers as a group should pay the injured party, and should bear the risk that one of their number is insolvent. On this view, the solvent defendant and the plaintiff should bear the risk of the other defendant's insolvency, in proportion to the amount of negligence attributable to them. In our example, the plaintiff is 40 percent negligent and the solvent defendant is 35 percent negligent. The insolvent defendant is 25 percent negligent and is unable to pay its share of the defendants' total share of 60 percent of the plaintiff's losses. Under the third approach, the plaintiff's and the solvent defendant's responsibility for the insolvent defendant's share would be apportioned by comparing the amount of negligence attributed to them. The total of their negligence is 75 percent. In addition to its own share, therefore, the solvent defendant would be liable to the plaintiff for 35/75ths of the insolvent defendant's share. The plaintiff would have to bear the remaining 40/75ths of the insolvent defendant's 25 percent share himself.

3. Effect on Other Common Law Doctrines

Skeletal comparative negligence statutes often make no reference to the new status, if any, of such common law doctrines as last clear chance, assumption of risk, and the greater-degree-of-blame exception to the contributory negligence defense. What should be the status of these doctrines under comparative negligence?

As a transitional doctrine designed largely to mitigate the harsh effect of the complete bar of the contributory negligence defense, last clear chance should have no role as a separate doctrine once comparative negligence is adopted. Most courts have so held. Of course, to the extent that failing to avoid injuring the plaintiff renders the defendant more negligent than the plaintiff, the jury is entitled to take into account the defendant's failure to use the last clear chance into the negligence comparison. But the jury also is entitled to take other factors into account. Having failed to take the last clear chance should no longer be dispositive on the question whether the plaintiff may recover, though that failure may be relevant.

It is especially important for last clear chance to be abolished entirely or not at all under a modified comparative negligence regime. Otherwise perverse results may ensue. Suppose that last clear chance were merely abolished when comparative negligence applies, but continued to be in force when the plaintiff was more negligent than the defendant. Then a plaintiff injured by a defendant who failed to take the last clear chance would be better off proving that he was more negligent than the defendant—because last clear chance would eliminate the effect of his contributory negligence and he would be entitled to a full recovery. In contrast, if the plaintiff proved that he was less negligent than the defendant, then (because last clear chance would not apply under comparative negligence) he would obtain only a partial recovery. Conceivably a 51 percent negligent plaintiff could recover in full, whereas a 49 percent negligent defendant would recover only 49 percent of his losses. To avoid this cockeyed kind of result, last clear chance must be entirely preserved or entirely abolished.

Treatment of the greater-degree-of-harm exception under comparative negligence varies. Once the jury is directed to compare the faults of the parties, there is little need to place their actions into categories of blame. Instead, degrees of fault can be compared directly. Nonetheless, some courts have interpreted their comparative negligence statutes to apply only to negligence actions and therefore to have no effect on the greater-degree-of-blame exception. In effect, these courts have held that the plaintiff's negligence is no defense at all to an intentional or similar tort, but that neither does comparative negligence abolish the same-degree-of-blame defenses to such torts.

Finally, in contributory negligence the defense of assumption of risk (discussed in the next Section of this Chapter) completely bars the plaintiff from recovery when he knowingly assumes the risk that the defendant will injure him. Usually this defense is available, however, only when the plaintiff's assumption of risk was unreasonable and therefore negligent. The majority of courts have concluded, therefore, that it would make little sense to preserve an independent assumption of risk defense within comparative negligence, since the plaintiff's unreasonable assumption of risk can simply be taken into account in making the comparative negligence attribution.

4. Strict Liability

Contributory negligence is a defense to a strict liability action in some jurisdictions and not in others. The availability of the defense also sometimes varies depending on the type of strict liability action at issue. How should the adoption of comparative negligence affect strict liability actions if the statute itself does not address the issue?

The most straightforward approach is simply to apply comparative negligence wherever contributory negligence previously applied. But it could be argued that contributory negligence ought to continue to be a complete defense to a strict liability claim wherever it was a complete defense prior to the adoption of comparative negligence, because the plaintiff is clearly more negligent than the defendant, who is held liable without fault. A fairly persuasive response to this argument is that when a defendant is held strictly liable it is not found to be free from negligence; rather, the issue is simply irrelevant. It is possible that the defendant was negligent, and therefore possible to compare that negligence with the negligence of the plaintiff, if any. Whether the defendant was negligent and, if so, how negligent, would then become issues at the trial of any strict liability action in which the defendant raised the defense of the plaintiff's negligence.

In some strict liability situations, however, contributory negligence was not a defense. Should comparative negligence be applied in these situations? The strength of the argument opposing introduction of this new defense depends on the reason contributory negligence was not a defense. If the point of denying the defense was that the defendant in the kinds of cases that are subject to strict liability is the best bearer of the risk that the kinds of accidents in question will occur, then that does not change with the enactment of comparative negligence. On the other hand, if contributory negligence was not a defense because it was viewed as excessively harsh, then a comparative negligence defense to strict liability might make sense. For example, it may be that in cases involving strict liability for abnormally dangerous activities comparative negligence should not be a defense for this reason, but that in strict products liability actions comparative negligence should be a defense. These forms of strict liability are discussed in Chapters Eight and Nine, respectively.

A final problem, relevant in both of the contexts just discussed, is how comparative negligence can possibly operate if the defendant was not in fact at fault but is held strictly liable nonetheless. What is the jury to compare with the plaintiff's negligence? The answer from the courts that have addressed this problem is not entirely coherent, and sometimes they have come close to admitting it. For example, in holding that comparative negligence does apply in strict products liability cases, the Supreme Court of California dismissed the argument that the jury in such cases would be required to compare "apples and oranges," and instead redescribed the jury's function. Comparing the fault of the parties, the Court said, was not what the jury was really being asked to do. Rather, the jury was to engage in an "equitable" apportionment of liability.[5] The Court's ultimate conclusion—and that of many courts

---

[5] *Daly v. General Motors Corp.*, 20 Cal.3d 725, 575 P.2d 1162, 144 Cal. Rptr. 380 (1978).

addressing the issue—was that regardless of whether it is conceptually coherent to employ comparative negligence in strict products liability cases, it will be done because it is fair to do so.

5. Setoffs?

Suppose that in an automobile accident in a pure comparative negligence jurisdiction, both the plaintiff and the defendant/counterclaimant are injured. A judgment is entered in favor of each party, specifying the amount of damages to be awarded to each. If neither were insured there would ordinarily be a setoff of the smaller award against the larger one, with the net amount remaining awarded to the party who had the larger judgment. For example, if the award to the plaintiff (in light of the amount of negligence attributed to him) were $100,000 and the award to the defendant/counterclaimant (again, in light of the amount of negligence attributed to him) were $50,000, then the plaintiff would be entitled to recover $50,000 from the defendant/counterclaimant, and the defendant/counterclaimant would be entitled to recover nothing from the plaintiff.

But suppose that both are covered by liability insurance. Should the result be the same? If there is no setoff, then the defendant/counterclaimant's insurer owes the plaintiff $100,000, and the plaintiff's insurer owes the defendant/counterclaimant $50,000. On the other hand, if there is a setoff, then the defendant/counterclaimant's insurer owes the plaintiff $50,000, and the plaintiff's insurer owes nothing: the parties' insurers save $50,000 each. The argument for a setoff is that liability insurance simply pays judgments that are owing, and only after a setoff can the amount actually owed be calculated. The response to this argument, which has prevailed whenever the issue has arisen, is that a major function of liability insurance, especially in the auto-accident setting, is not merely to protect injurers against liability, but also to assure victims a recovery from negligent parties who cannot afford to pay judgments themselves. A setoff would further deprive victims of compensation, after they have already been awarded only partial compensation in the first instance because of their negligence. It follows that no setoff should be allowed, and that each party's liability insurer must pay his or her adversary's judgment.

III. Assumption of Risk

The notion of "assumption of risk" is used in four different contexts in tort law, often without the clarity necessary to distinguish these contexts from each other. It probably would be most beneficial to abolish the phrase "assumption of risk" entirely and use different terms for each of the four situations in which the phrase is now used. But obviously that is not possible. Consequently, we must live with the multi-faceted concept of assumption of risk, taking care to recognize that the concept has different meanings, and different legal consequences, in different situations.

A. Express Assumption of Risk

Sometimes an individual contractually agrees in advance to waive his or her right to bring a tort action against a potential injurer. This often happens, for example, in residential leases containing disclaimers of the landlord's liability to the tenant for negligence, or when a skier buys a lift ticket. Often these waivers are valid when entered knowingly, voluntarily, and with appreciation of their significance, although waivers that do not satisfy these requirements may be invalid. This form of assumption of risk, when valid, is simply a contractual surrender in advance of the right to sue. The party surrendering this right is in fact assuming a risk, in the sense that she may be tortiously injured but uncompensated. Note that this form of assumption of risk does not hinge in any way on the nature of the plaintiff's conduct, aside from her express agreement to waive her tort rights.

The remaining three forms of assumption of risk are often said to be "implied," in order to distinguish them from an express agreement waiving the right to sue. Because these other three forms of assumption of risk otherwise are very different from each other, however, they must be considered separately.

B. No Duty of Care Breached by the Defendant

Suppose you go to a baseball game and sit behind first base. The third baseman fields a ground ball and throws high to the first baseman. The ball flies into the stands and injures you. In your suit against the owner of the stadium, you allege that it was negligent of the defendant to fail to erect a net behind first base to protect fans from the risk of this kind of injury. This theory of liability will be rejected on the ground that it was not negligent for the defendant to have failed to erect a net behind first base. This is not a defense based on the plaintiff's conduct, and indeed not a defense at all. Rather, the defendant prevails because of the failure of the plaintiff to satisfy his or her burden of showing that the defendant was negligent.

Another way of saying the same thing is to say that you "assumed the risk" that you would be injured by a high throw to first base. But this way of putting the point is simply the logical corollary of the finding that the defendant was not negligent. Indeed, except in connection with activities that involve strict liability for the injuries they cause, a victim/plaintiff always and necessarily "assumes" the risk that he will be non-negligently injured. "Assumption of risk" in this sense is simply another way of saying that there is no liability because the defendant did not breach a duty of care to the plaintiff. In an unfortunate turn of phrase this form of assumption of risk is sometimes referred to as "primary" assumption of risk, to distinguish it from what is sometimes called "secondary" assumption of risk (discussed immediately below). However, there is nothing at all "primary" about this usage or the situation to which it is applied, aside from the fact that it is a way of talking about failure of the plaintiff's *prima facie* case rather than about a defense. But the usage, though far from universal, is sometimes employed by the courts.

This does not mean that the name "assumption of risk" is applied in such situations for no reason at all. On the contrary, often the reason that the defendant is held not to be negligent turns on factors that involve the openness of the risk in question and the voluntariness of the plaintiff's participation in the activity in question, in addition to the reasonableness of the risks posed by the activity in light of its benefits. That is why the phrase assumption of risk is more likely to be applied to attending a baseball game than, say, to walking down the street. Note, however, that in walking down the street I "assume the risk" that I will be injured by non-negligent driving. The logical structure of the law applying to these situations is the same, even if the phrase "assumption of risk" seems to apply more comfortably to the baseball game.

C. A Subset of Contributory Negligence

There are two general ways in which a plaintiff may unreasonably risk suffering harm. The first involves the plaintiff's careless failure to recognize or appreciate a risk. The second is the plaintiff's conscious

155

taking of an unreasonable risk. Each is contributory negligence. But the second form of contributory negligence is typically called "assumption of risk." Unlike the two forms of assumption of risk discussed above, this form of assumption of risk is in fact a defense, and it is based on the plaintiff's conduct in taking a risk. This defense is sometimes called "secondary" assumption of risk. But of course it is secondary only in the sense that it is a true defense, available as a way for the defendant to avoid liability even if proved negligent.

The problem with use of the term assumption of risk to describe this form of contributory negligence is not that the use is inaccurate, but that it is potentially misleading to juries. Only the conscious taking of an *unreasonable* risk—negligent assumption of risk—is a defense. If I am walking carefully down the street and you injure me by driving negligently onto the sidewalk, you do not have a defense that I assumed the risk of injury because I knew that some people drive negligently. On the contrary, it was entirely reasonable for me to be walking on the sidewalk, and you are liable. Referring to assumption of risk separately in a jury instruction, however, may give the jury the impression that non-negligent assumption of risk is a defense to a negligence claim. A jury instruction that it is a defense (complete or partial depending on whether contributory or comparative negligence applies) if the plaintiff was contributorily negligent *or* assumed the risk of harm would imply that assumption of risk is something different from contributory negligence. Such an instruction would imply (or at least could easily be understood to imply) that non-negligent assumption of risk is a defense, separate and apart from contributory negligence.

Now it possible to avoid misleading the jury, by employing an instruction indicating that assumption of risk is simply one of the two kinds of contributory negligence that may constitute a defense based on the plaintiff's conduct: unreasonable careless risk taking, and unreasonable conscious risk taking. The trouble with this approach is that we do not really have a technical term for the former category, other than "negligence by the plaintiff." For this reason, the very use of the technical-sounding phrase "assumption of risk" to refer to the latter category still runs the risk that the phrase will stand out in the jury's mind and be perceived as something separate from ordinary contributory negligence. This does not mean that the concept should not be used by lawyers and judges analyzing available defenses—this is in fact the one situation in which the term "assumption of risk" seems appropriate and useful. But the potentially misleading character of the phrase "assumption of risk" when used in conjunction with "contributory negligence" suggests that it may be prudent not to use the phrase "assumption of risk" in jury instructions that also refer to contributory negligence.

D. Conscious, Reasonable Risk-Taking

The last situation which is sometimes describing as "assumption of risk" involves non-negligent risk-taking. For example, in the *Eckert*[6] case described in Chapter Three, the plaintiff's decedent was killed rescuing a child from being struck by a train. The court held (among other things) that this was not contributory negligence—i.e., assumption of risk—because the decedent's behavior was not unreasonable under the circumstances.

There is no question that as a matter of fact in this and similar situations the plaintiff took a risk—i.e., knew that he might be injured and went forward despite this risk. But that does not mean that he "assumed the risk" in the legal sense. Although the case law by no means provides a uniform answer, the decided trend, especially in the modern cases, is to side with *Eckert* and to hold the fact that the plaintiff consciously but non-negligently took a risk is not a defense. After all, why should the plaintiff who does not know of a risk negligently created by the defendant be better off than the plaintiff who is aware of the risk and decides reasonably to take it? In most cases it makes normative sense to treat both plaintiffs in the same way, though perhaps room for an occasional exception ought to be preserved. For example, there may well be cases in which one would want to say that the plaintiff's actions, in context, amount to a waiver that very much resembles an express assumption of risk, even in the absence of the plaintiff's use of words to that effect. Such matters as the availability of a choice between alternatives that are offered by the defendant at different prices, together with the plaintiff's clear understanding of the risks posed by the more dangerous but cheaper alternative, would be relevant in determining whether there had been an implied waiver in that situation.

Moreover, sometimes the plaintiff's reasonable assumption of risk will by curious analogy resemble the actions of those defendants who fail to exercise the last clear chance to avoid accidents. Suppose that the defendant has acted negligently and is not in a position to undo that negligence. The plaintiff then consciously takes the risk that he will be

---

[6] *Eckert v. Long Island R.R.*, 43 N.Y. 502 (1871).

injured by the defendant's negligence. The plaintiff's risk-taking is both last and, in the sense that it was not inadvertent, clear. This recognition makes it easier to understand how some courts in this situation might say that, although the plaintiff's action was not unreasonable and there was no explicitly verbal waiver on the plaintiff's part, the timing, clarity, and voluntariness of the plaintiff's informed decision to take the risk in question yield the conclusion that the plaintiff may not recover because he had "assumed" the risk of the defendant's negligence.

8

Strict Liability and Nuisance

T his Chapter concerns liability for what have come to be called
"abnormally dangerous" activities, for "nuisance", and "vicarious"
liability. These forms of liability are imposed without regard to the
negligence of the defendant and are therefore referred to as "strict"
liability. It is important to recognize at the outset, however, that these
liabilities are strict, but not absolute. That is, liability is imposed in the
absence of negligence by the defendant only when a dangerous activity
is "abnormally" so, only when an activity rises to the level of a "nuisance," or (in the case of vicarious liability) only when one party is
responsible for the actions of another. The key to understanding strict
liability, therefore, is to be able to identify the criteria that must be
satisfied to render an actor strictly liable—i.e., liable without regard to
negligence. To put it another way, the critical question is what characterizes the activities for which the negligence requirement is dropped. To
address this question, we turn first to the general theory behind strict
liability, and then to the three main forms that it takes.

I. The Theory Behind Strict Liability

Strict liability does not replace negligence liability—it is imposed
in addition to negligence liability. What strict liability does, therefore,
is impose liability for an additional category of injuries—those caused
non-negligently. The theory supporting the imposition of liability for
negligence is that such liability is designed to promote optimal deterrence of accidents and to achieve corrective justice. So the theory we
seek must explain what is gained by imposing liability for the additional increment of injuries that is made subject to liability without
regard to negligence.

One's initial inclination is to suppose that imposing strict liability
will achieve additional safety and therefore additional accident reduction beyond what negligence liability alone can achieve. After all, this

159

line of thinking goes, strict liability threatens potential injurers with liability for a greater range of activities and therefore ought to generate more deterrence. In fact, however, this is unlikely to be true as a general matter. Assuming that negligence liability is accurately imposed (a key assumption that is relaxed below), strict liability will not cause any particular activity to be conducted with greater safety than negligence liability. Recall from the discussion in Chapter Three that the threat of liability for negligence deters all the accidents worth deterring—those whose costs outweigh the costs of avoiding them—because liability for negligence is imposed when accident costs do outweigh avoidance costs, and is not imposed when accident costs do not outweigh avoidance costs.

Strict liability goes farther and imposes liability even in the latter cases, when avoidance costs outweigh accident costs. But imposing liability in these cases will not change the level of safety at which potential defendants engage in the activity in question: in these cases it is cheaper to go on having accidents than to invest in the additional safety necessary to avoid them. Because, in these cases, avoidance costs outweigh accident costs, and potential defendants are threatened with liability only for accident costs, it is cheaper to continue causing these accidents than to avoid them, even though one is strictly liable for their costs.

This conclusion does not depend on accepting the Learned Hand calculus as the basis of negligence liability, or on an economic theory of tort liability. Indeed, the conclusion does not even depend on any particular conception of what it means to be negligent. The conclusion depends only on the assumption that potential defendants will tend to act in their own self interest. Setting litigation costs aside, when defendants are held liable, they pay accident costs only—damages suffered by victims. Potential defendants will only avoid paying accident costs by acting more safely when acting more safely is less expensive than taking safety precautions. Consequently, holding defendants liable even when they have not been negligent will not cause them to act any more safely than it is already in their self interest to act.

The same is true of plaintiffs. Denying a plaintiff recovery when neither the plaintiff nor the defendant was negligent cannot make plaintiffs behave more safely. In fact, the underlying inquiry really is not whether there should be strict liability for defendants or only negligence liability. Rather, the real question is who should bear strict liability: potential injurers or potential victims. To see this, focus on what happens in a system in which there is only liability for negligence. Under such a system there still are non-negligently-caused injuries. Because there is no strict liability for these injuries, those who suffer the injuries have no cause of action against those who caused the injuries. This setup can be accurately understood as "no strict liability for injurers." But it is just as accurate to understand a negligence regime as "strict liability for victims." This kind of strict liability system is implemented not by lawsuits, but by the absence of lawsuits— i.e., by declining to impose strict liability on injurers. The operative effect of this denial of strict liability recovery by victims is that victims bear the cost of their own non-negligently-caused injuries—they are "strictly liable" for them, to themselves.

And because victims must bear the cost of these injuries, they have the same incentives that any potentially liable party has to compare the costs and benefits of engaging in the activity that causes them or engaging in some less risky substitute. Thus, the real choice is between strict liability for injurers on the one hand, and negligence liability for injurers plus strict liability for victims, on the other hand. The choice, therefore, is not whether to shift from negligence liability to strict liability, but under what circumstances to shift from strict liability for victims to strict liability for injurers.[1] In making this choice, whatever it is that can make strict liability superior to negligence liability must be considered, because the question is not whether there will be strict liability at all, but which kind of strict liability—on the part of victims or on the part of injurers—will maximize these benefits.

If all this is so and strict liability does not create higher levels of safety than negligence liability, then what *can* strict liability achieve that negligence is not already achieving? There are five ways in which strict liability *potentially* can be superior to negligence. Strict liability, however, cannot always secure these benefits. That, in fact, is the whole point: when imposing strict liability for injuries caused by a particular activity can achieve one or more of these benefits, this serves as an argument for the imposition of strict liability on injurers. The difference between the cases in which strict liability is imposed on injurers and those in which liability is imposed only for negligence is, or at least ought to be, the difference between activities with respect to which such strict liability can and cannot generate these benefits.

---

[1] See Guido Calabresi and Jon T. Hirschoff, *Toward A Test for Strict Liability in Torts*, 81 Yale L.J. 1055 (1972).

A. *Greater Accuracy*

It is useful to begin by relaxing the assumption that negligence liability is always accurately imposed. The purpose of imposing negligence liability is to deter negligence and to correct the injustice resulting from negligently caused injuries. Suppose then that juries sometimes make mistakes in determining whether defendants are negligent—as of course juries do. Shifting from negligence to strict liability in the class of cases in which such inaccuracy is likely to be most prevalent might, under these circumstances, more effectively achieve the goals of negligence liability than can negligence liability itself.

The key is to identify the cases in which this would be true. Two hypotheticals can illustrate the problem. Suppose that in a class of cases involving one activity—call them Class A cases—juries impose liability for negligence 40 percent of the time, whereas in fact defendants are negligent 60 percent of the time. The rate of error in these cases is 20 percent under-imposition of liability. But the imposition of strict liability in Class A cases would not reduce the rate of error; strict liability would increase error. Under strict liability defendants would be liable 100 percent of the time, whereas they are in fact negligent only 60 percent of the time. The rate of error would therefore be 40 percent over-imposition of liability, as compared to 20 percent under-imposition of liability under negligence. Some readers may still want to argue that the former is preferable to the latter (and certain of the notions discussed later in this section may support them), but their argument cannot be based on a reduction in the error rate, since strict liability increases the error rate in Class A cases.

Consider now Class B cases, in which the defendant is negligent 60 percent of the time but juries impose liability only 10 percent of the time. The error rate is 50 percent under-imposition of liability. Under strict liability the error rate would be reduced from 50 percent under-imposition of liability to 40 percent over-imposition of liability. What kinds of cases might these be? The best candidate is the class of cases in which evidence of the defendant's negligence is either not available or very difficult to obtain—perhaps because the kinds of accidents that characterize these cases tend to destroy the relevant evidence—but defendants often are in fact negligent. The courts sometimes find the transportation of highly flammable material that is likely to destroy evidence of negligence when it explodes to fall into this category. This may sound a lot like the kind of analysis that leads to *res ipsa loquitur*, which of course is a negligence doctrine. Recall, however, that one of the functions of that doctrine also is to reduce the error rate, and that some *res ipsa* cases closely resemble strict liability. It should come as no surprise, therefore, that *res ipsa* and strict liability have in common their potential capacity to reduce the error rate of the conventional negligence system.

B. Administrative Cost Savings and the Level-of-Generality Issue

Negligence cases require a determination that is not necessary under strict liability—whether the defendant was negligent. Making the negligence determination costs the time and money of judges, juries, the parties, and their attorneys. A shift to strict liability saves these costs, but this is a gross, not a net saving. Because strict liability does not require proof of negligence, in general it is likely that there will be more claims when an activity is subject to strict liability than when there is liability only for injuries that result from conducting the activity negligently. Thus, although per case administrative costs are likely to be lower under strict liability than under negligence, the cost of litigating additional cases under strict liability must be figured in if one is making a total-cost calculation.

This interaction between per-case and total costs depends in part on the level of generality at which a strict liability standard is established. The per case cost of adjudication under a strict liability standard set at a "high level of generality" is very likely to be lower than the per case cost of adjudication under a standard set at a "low level of generality." For example, whether an activity is "abnormally dangerous" can be determined in accordance with a per se rule that admits of few exceptions and is almost cost-free to apply—a rule such as "all use of explosives is abnormally dangerous and results in strict liability." This is a rule set at a very high level of generality. On the other hand, whether there is strict liability might be made to depend on a series of factors that distinguish some uses of explosives from others—for example, how common the use of explosives is in a particular area and how useful it is in that community. This kind of context-dependent rule that is formulated at a lower level of generality will result in case-by-case adjudication that is likely to be more expensive and complicated than litigation under a rule operating at a high level of generality.

In short, strict liability has the potential to generate administrative cost savings as compared to negligence, but whether those savings actually occur depends heavily on the level of generality of the strict liability rules in question.

C. Activity-Level Effects

Although strict liability cannot create additional incentives to conduct any *particular* activity more safely, the shift to strict liability can create an incentives for potential defendants to engage in safer activities. The operative distinction here is between safety-level effects and activity-level effects. Strict liability can generate the latter in ways that negligence liability cannot.[2]

Suppose that I manufacture a product that is sold up and down the East Coast. I deliver the product to purchasers on trucks that I own and operate. Naturally these trucks are involved in a certain number of accidents. Of course I face liability only for *negligent* maintenance or operation of my trucks. In theory, there could be liability for the "negligent" decision to ship always by truck, on the ground that it would be safer, all things considered, for me to ship via some alternative method. But in practice this never happens, because of the difficulty of demonstrating that it is negligent to have engaged in a particular activity (such as shipping by truck) at all. And shifting to strict liability will not cause me to assure that my trucks are more carefully maintained or operated. For example, imposing strict liability for all injuries caused by transportation accidents, rather than only for those caused by negligence, simply imposes on me and other transporters the cost of accidents that are not worth avoiding through the exercise of additional care.

Nonetheless, a shift to strict liability would give me more reason to consider alternative methods of delivering my products. As long as I am liable only for negligence it was cheaper, all things considered, for me to ship by truck. Once there is strict liability, however, it may turn out that, in fact, other methods of delivery are cheaper, because they are inherently safer—that is, they involve fewer non-negligently-caused accidents. For this reason, shipping by train or air may prove to be less expensive after, but not before, the shift to strict liability. And of course it may be that a partial rather than a complete substitution of

---

[2] See Steven Shavell, *Strict Liability versus Negligence*, 9 J. Legal Stud. 1 (1980).

one activity for another is the cost-minimizing approach. Thus, strict liability may produce activity-level effects that negligence liability cannot.

Another way of putting this point is to say that under strict liability potential injurers are threatened with liability for the full cost of their risky activities, whereas under negligence liability they are not forced to fully "internalize" these costs. Under strict liability, therefore, potential injurers have the incentive not only to consider whether to conduct their activities more safely (an incentive they already have under negligence), but also whether to shift to safer activities. The result is a potentially more efficient allocation of resources among possible activity levels and activities.

The reader might quickly suppose that strict liability is therefore categorically preferable to negligence. For two reasons, however, the choice is more problematic. First, there may be activities for which there are no readily available substitutes. Imposing strict liability for injuries caused by these activities could result in more disadvantages than advantages—more claims, no greater safety, and little or no change in activity level. Second, and more significantly, remember that in a sense there is always strict liability and therefore there are always activity-level effects. The real question is whether there should be injurer strict liability, or only injurer negligence liability plus victim strict liability. In some cases, depending on a host of factors, including the parties' knowledge of and control over alternatives, superior activity-level effects can be expected from injurer strict liability, but in other cases such effects can be more effectively obtained from injurer negligence liability with victim strict liability. This will occur when the most safety can be obtained by influencing potential victims' activity levels. Consequently, the choice often is not an easy one. And it is this kind of difficulty that, of course, tends to explain why we do not have universal injurer strict liability, but a mixed system in which negligence liability predominates but there are pockets of strict liability.

D. Additional Research Incentives

The threat of liability for negligence creates what might be called "research" incentives. It may be that I do not at present have a fully effective method of avoiding negligent behavior. The fact that I am threatened with liability for negligence, however, creates an incentive on my part to search for such methods. To continue the hypothetical from the preceding section, the threat of liability for negligence may cause me to investigate better methods of training my truck drivers and safer routes to travel, or to study the qualities that enable my safer drivers to avoid accidents and then to hire with these qualities in mind.

But strict liability creates additional research incentives, because under strict liability there is more to be gained by avoiding liability. Under negligence, injurers are not liable for accidents that are not worth avoiding. Consequently, injurers have no incentive to attempt to discover cost-effective methods of avoiding these injuries. In contrast, under strict liability, at any given time there is a class of accidents that produces injuries not worth avoiding. But because injurers are liable for these injuries anyway, discovering a cost-effective method of reducing or eliminating the injuries they cause will redound to their benefit. This research may run from the very formal, such as laboratory investigation of new ingredients or designs, to the very informal, such as simple investigation of alternative methods of transportation of the sort I described earlier. Indeed, the informal end of this continuum reflects the connection between the potential activity-level effects of strict liability and research incentives. In a sense the research incentives that strict liability may create are incentives to discover activities or activity levels that may substitute for those that currently generate strict liability, in order to reduce net costs.

Like the other potential benefits of strict liability, this matter of research incentives does not admit of easy generalization. Some parties are more likely than others to be in a position to perform formal research; and some activities are more likely than others to be susceptible to change through cost-effective research. Moreover, research itself entails certain costs but uncertain benefits. The payoff from research cannot be known in advance. Investment in research therefore is not investment in accident reduction, but in potential accident reduction. How much research is worth doing can never be known with certainty. Thus, while it is generally true that imposing strict liability can create greater research incentives than negligence alone, it will not necessarily produce additional research in any given situation.

E. More Extensive Loss Distribution

The last difference between strict liability and negligence is that strict liability is likely to involve more extensive loss distribution than negligence. As I indicated in my discussion of the goals of tort liability in Chapter One, this justification for the imposition of liability is the subject of debate, whatever the standard of liability that is in force. To the extent that loss distribution is regarded as an appropriate goal, however, strict liability probably is superior to negligence in this regard. In general, injurers are more likely than victims to be large institutions that can spread the cost of liability directly in their prices or services, or to purchase liability insurance whose cost is included in these prices or services. And in automobile liability, the one major area in which injurers are predominately ordinary individuals, access to liability insurance, with the broad loss distribution that such access entails, is virtually automatic.

Even in the domain of loss distribution, however, injurers are not necessarily always superior to victims as loss bearers. For example, consider health care costs resulting from a tortious injury—one of the principal components of damages that personal injury victims recover from tortfeasors. More than three-quarters of the population is covered by health insurance. To be sure, such insurance does not always cover every dollar's worth of health care expenses incurred by personal injury victims. But the insurance provides substantial protection. The cost of the health-care component of the vast majority of personal injury victims' losses is already spread in broad channels of loss distribution. The choice, therefore, is not between broad loss distribution through injurer strict liability or narrow distribution by declining to adopt such strict liability. Rather, the choice is between two different channels of broad distribution.

* * *

Having examined the potential advantages of strict liability over negligence at a general level, we are now prepared to look at specific doctrines. But it is important to understand the significance of the foregoing analysis. Our task up to now has been to understand what strict liability has the *potential* to do that negligence cannot. Whether and when strict liability actually can do these things is a separate question that is resolved by the specific doctrines to which we now turn out attention.

II. Traditional Strict Liability

What the law of torts terms "traditional" strict liability involves liability for injuries caused by activities—ordinarily uses of land—that were first termed "ultrahazardous" and that are now termed "abnormally dangerous." This Section traces the development of this form of liability and of the limitations on its scope.

A. The Rise of Liability for "Ultrahazardous" Activities

Aside from some pre-existing rules governing liability for escaping animals, "traditional" strict liability begins with the English case of *Rylands v. Fletcher*.[3] The defendant in *Rylands* had a reservoir constructed at a point on his property that he did not know lay above, or at least was contiguous with, a former coal mine. The water in the reservoir escaped through the mine, flooding the plaintiff's property. The plaintiff could not show any negligence for which the defendant was responsible, although conceivably the independent contractors whom the defendant had hired to construct the reservoir were negligent in failing to discover the danger in question. The case went to trial and was then appealed through several layers of appellate courts. Ultimately the House of Lords held that the defendant was strictly liable.

Rylands was decided against the background nineteenth-century rule that there was liability only upon proof that the defendant was negligent. Consequently, the key question in the case is under what circumstances an exception to this general rule will be made. The court purported to answer the question by holding that there would be strict liability for damage caused by what it called the "non-natural use" of the defendant's land. What exactly the court meant, however, was unclear. At the extreme this might mean that the escape of anything brought onto land that was "not naturally there" (to use the language of Justice Blackburn in one of the lower appellate courts in the case) would automatically result in liability for the damage caused by the escape. But such an "exception" to the rule that in general there is liability only for negligence would have threatened to swallow up the negligence rule as it applied to land use, since virtually all damage caused by land use results from activities that are not "natural" to the land in this sense.

The American courts thought that the *Rylands* exception did swallow up the liability-only-for-negligence rule, and understood the case to be rejecting much of negligence law. More wedded to the negligence requirement in the late nineteenth century than the English courts, most American courts therefore rejected *Rylands*, sometimes vehemently. For example, in *Brown v. Collins*,[4] the defendant was sued for damage caused by the non-negligent escape of his horses. The

---

[3] L.R. 3 H.L. 330 (1868).

[4] 53 N.H. 442 (1873).

court held for the defendant, stating that "[e]verything that a man can bring on his land is capable of escaping * * *." The court rejected the plaintiff's claim that the defendant should bear strict liability, stating that it is "impossible that legal principle can throw so serious an obstacle in the way of progress and improvement."

Thus the American courts at first took the opposite extreme, rejecting virtually all strict liability. Over the next half-century on both sides of the Atlantic, however, the courts moved away from their seemingly extreme positions and adopted an increasingly intermediate view of the scope of strict liability. In England the courts clarified the meaning of a "non-natural use," explaining that a "natural" use was one that was ordinary or common to the area in which it took place. And in the United States, although the courts often still rejected *Rylands* by name, they began to create a series of specific and at first limited exceptions to the general rule that there was no liability in the absence of negligence. In the beginning only the most dangerous and unusual activities, such as the use of explosives where this was not to be expected, resulted in strict liability. But as time went on the kinds of cases made subject to the exception expanded to include the operation of oil wells and even the storage of unusual quantities of water. Interestingly, the decision whether to include an activity in a strict liability category came to be one for the court, not for the jury.

Sometimes the courts called the doctrine under which strict liability was imposed for damage caused by these and other activities "absolute nuisance." But by the 1920's there were enough decisions following a similar pattern for them to be recognized as involving strict liability for conducting an "ultrahazardous activity."[5] The two factors that determined whether an activity was ultrahazardous were the degree of danger it posed and how common it was in the area. The more dangerous and the less common the activity, the more likely it was to qualify as ultrahazardous.

These factors tend to mesh in a rough and ready way with the theory of strict liability set out in the preceding Section. Remember that the choice is not between strict liability and no liability, but between strict liability for injurers and negligence liability for injurers with victims being "strictly liable" for injuries not caused by another's negligence. The two factors that qualify an activity as ultrahazardous identify the situations in which imposing liability on potential injurers

---

[5] See Restatement (Second) of Torts § 520.

will maximize strict liability's benefits. First, the more dangerous an activity is, the more violent it is likely to be, and therefore the more likely it is to destroy evidence that would enable the plaintiff the prove that the defendant conducted the activity negligently. Second, the more uncommon an activity is in a particular area, the more likely it is that the activity-level and research incentives created by the threat of strict liability will be most effective operating on potential injurers rather than on potential victims.

This latter point is true for several reasons. To the extent that an activity or land use is uncommon, those who are its potential victims are unlikely to know much about it and therefore unlikely to be in a position to do much to protect themselves against the risk the activity poses. In addition, land uses tend to involve capital investments and therefore to be comparatively costly to alter. And potential victims of an uncommon land use tend already to be engaged in common uses when the potential injurer makes the decision whether to engage in an uncommon use. If you are already operating a coal mine on your land you cannot very well pick up and go when a reservoir is built nearby. The potential injurer is therefore likely to be in a better position to fix optimal activity-levels at the outset, when the cost of doing so is at its lowest, because this does not involve sacrificing already-made investments.

In contrast, when a particular activity is neither especially dangerous nor uncommon in an area, potential injurers probably are not superior to potential victims in their ability to control the risk of injury through activity-level adjustments or research. In fact, to the extent that the activity in question is characteristic in an area—maintaining mill dams in certain New England counties or oil wells in certain Texas counties, for example—then many potential victims are also potential injurers, because they too engage in the activity. So these kinds of activities are unlikely to be considered ultrahazardous. Certainly a potential victim considering locating in the area is on notice of the risk to which he is subjecting himself and can look to the behavior of existing land owners for guidance as to the best mix of protections to adopt against a risk that is not uncommon. In short, strict liability for engaging in ultrahazardous activities is something like common law zoning, designed to encourage similar land uses in a particular area and to impose the cost of engaging in a dangerous and uncommon use on the party who decides not to comply with the "zoning" implications of the strict liability rule.

B. The Modern Conception: Strict Liability for "Abnormally Dangerous" Activities

By the time the Second Restatement of Torts was prepared in the 1960's, there had been a sufficient number of strict liability cases that the factors comprising the test for strict liability appeared to be more nuanced than the two blunt criteria figuring in the test for ultrahazardousness. The new test included three different factors affecting dangerousness (degree of risk, probability of harm, and inability to eliminate the risk by the exercise of reasonable care), two factors affecting commonness (the extent to which the activity is uncommon and its "inappropriateness" to the area), plus a new consideration: the extent to which the value of the activity to the community is outweighed by its dangerousness. To distinguish this new test from the one it replaced, it was termed strict liability for damage caused by "abnormally dangerous" activities.[6] This modern test meshes with the theory of strict liability in roughly the same way as did the earlier test, except that the last factor—value to the community—occasionally functions as a trump, saving from strict liability the rare activity that warrants protection from this regime even when it is dangerous and unusual.

The new test both reflects the tendency of the courts in the modern period to engage in case-by-case analysis of strict liability claims and encourages this practice. The advantage of this approach is that it has the capacity to draw fine distinctions between activities in light of the weight of the six factors that comprise the new test. But the approach also has disadvantages. The great advantage of the earlier ultrahazardous activity approach was not only that it was simpler, but also that, for precisely this reason, it encouraged the formulation of strict liability rules at a comparatively high level of generality. The fact that the question whether to impose strict liability was typically for the court (as it still is) rather than for the jury underscored the importance of the level-of-generality feature of the strict liability decision. The modern tendency to fine-tune through the use of a multi-factored test inevitably pushes decisionmaking to a lower level of generality.

For example, in *Indiana Harbor Belt R.R. Co. v. American Cyanamid Co.*,[7] the defendant was a manufacturer that had shipped 20,000 gallons of a toxic and flammable chemical in a leased railroad

---

[6] See Restatement of Torts § 520.

[7] 916 F.2d 1174 (7th Cir. 1990).

tank car. The plaintiff was a company in the business of switching cars from one railroad line to another. The car leaked while in a railroad yard at which it was to be switched. As a consequence the plaintiff was forced to undertake decontamination and other measures to prevent injury and further property damage, including evacuating nearby homes.

The court declined to impose strict liability on the defendant, focusing heavily on two considerations. The first was the probability that the leak could have been prevented through the exercise of reasonable care in the inspection and maintenance of the tank car in question. The court distinguished cases holding transporters of gasoline strictly liable for explosions, on the ground that explosions typically destroy evidence of negligence, whereas leaks do not. The second consideration was the impossibility, in the court's view, of strict liability's having an activity-level effect in this kind of case, because of the difficulty of routing rail-transported material away from the metropolitan areas that serve as railroad hubs.

The court's reasoning may well be correct on the merits. But note the low level of generality at which this application of the criteria for determining whether an activity was abnormally dangerous took place. The court did not ask whether, in general, the transportation of flammable toxic material is abnormally dangerous. Rather, the questions the court considered were whether there is strict liability when the particular means of escape of such material from the railroad tank car in this case could ordinarily be prevented through reasonable care, and whether the adoption of particular alternative routes of railroad transportation would result from the imposition of strict liability. These are highly fact-sensitive and context-dependent questions. As a consequence, the decision in *Indiana Harbor Belt* provides incomplete guidance, at best, as to the proper result when the next tank-car accident involves an explosion rather than a leak, or a smaller quantity of the same substance that could have been shipped by truck or air instead of rail. That is unfortunate. But given the multi-factored test that has now emerged in the case law, that is the point at which traditional strict liability has now arrived: in each case, consideration of a series of factors is required, with the almost inevitable result that context-dependent and therefore comparatively specific rather than general rules characterize the field.

C. Limitations and Defenses

The limitations on and defenses to traditional strict liability confirm what this form of liability is all about. There is strict liability only for the kind of harm whose risk makes the activity abnormally dangerous. This is a complicated way of saying that there is only strict liability if engaging in the relevant activity is not only the cause in fact, but also the proximate cause of the harm the plaintiff suffered. That requirement is not remarkable, except that of course the whole point of proximate cause—to assure that a defendant is held liable only for those consequences of his acts which the law wishes to be actionable—underscores that strict liability is not absolute liability for engaging in a particular activity, but liability only for those consequences that the law is designed to influence.

Perhaps the most celebrated example of this limitation on liability is *Madsen v. East Jordan Irrigation Co.*,[8] in which the plaintiff's mother mink ate their young after being frightened by blasting. The defendant was held not to be strictly liable, precisely because the possibility that this would occur is not even one of the secondary risks that enters into the decision to impose strict liability for blasting. One way to understand this point is to say that the risk that mother mink will eat their young is not highly foreseeable to blasters; a second way is to say that the purposes of strict liability are best served by holding the plaintiff strictly liable for this kind of harm, because the risk is much more foreseeable to mink owners. With respect to the risk that blasting will frighten nervous animals, mink owners are in a better position than blasters to make the activity-level and research calculations that strict liability induces.

For the same reason, from early on it was established that the defendant is not strictly liable if the harm in question results from an Act of God, or the unforeseeable intervention of a third party, or from the plaintiff's knowing and unreasonable assumption of the risk of harm. For example, the harm at issue may result from a flood of utterly unprecedented magnitude, or vandalism, or the plaintiff's own recklessness. In these situations the purpose behind strict liability—creating incentives beyond those flowing from the threat of liability for negligence—is less easily served. The cause of the harm in such cases is only remotely foreseeable. Because the saving available to the de-

---

[8] 101 Utah 552, 125 P.2d 794 (1942).

fendant from adjusting its activity levels in anticipation of liability for that kind of harm is therefore likely to be speculative, the threat of liability would affect the defendant only marginally at most, and not much is to be gained from imposing strict liability.

III. Nuisance

A nuisance is a substantial and unreasonable interference with the right of an owner or occupier of land to the *use and enjoyment* of the land. Nuisance is distinct from trespass, which involves interference with the right of *possession and occupancy* land. In general, nuisances tend to be pollution of one sort of another—contamination of water or air, excessive noise, or other activities that affect use of another's property. There is a sense, however, in which virtually any use of land affects use of a neighboring parcel. The presence of a perfectly tasteful building three hundred feet from my house may affect my view, my ability to live without any noise at all, the number birds that fly over my land, and so forth. If every such affect were a nuisance, compatible land ownership could never exist: thus the requirement that a nuisance be both substantial and unreasonable to be actionable.

There is some dispute in the commentary and treatises as to the standard of care that applies in nuisance. In the view of some authorities, the standard of care is intention to interfere with the plaintiff's rights. But it turns out that this means only that the defendant must be aware of the effect that its activities have on the plaintiff and then continue to conduct the activities. Other authorities suggest that a nuisance also may be actionable on the basis of negligence or strict liability. I doubt that the accurate answer matters for most purposes. Though it is worth recognizing that in particular jurisdictions certain technicalities may make all the difference, a useful working definition is that a nuisance is an activity resulting in a particular kind of harm—interference with the use or enjoyment of land—and that this interference may be actionable on a strict liability basis (as well as on negligence or intent grounds) if the other preconditions to liability are met.

What makes nuisance both interesting and distinctive, therefore, is what sets it apart from ordinary torts involving intention, negligence, or strict liability. Two things stand out: what makes an activity a nuisance to begin with, and the remedies that are available once an activity is determined to be a nuisance.

A. When Is an Activity a Nuisance?

The hornbook definition of a nuisance as a substantial and unreasonable interference with the use or enjoyment of land reflects the notion that land uses tend to affect each other. For this reason, minor "interference" by one landowner with certain uses and enjoyments of other landowners is virtually inevitable. Even on a peaceful suburban street I cannot expect complete quiet or a backyard totally free of the smell of barbecued hot dogs. Nor can the owner of a business located in an industrial area expect to avoid the smells and fumes of ordinary manufacturing. Up to a point the rule is that modestly incompatible uses must "live and let live." To constitute an actionable nuisance, therefore, an interfering use must be both substantial and unreasonable in the particular context in which it occurs.

Once a particular use is more than modestly incompatible with another use, a judgment-call by the courts is required. The need for such a judgment-call is expressed in the rule that in determining whether an activity is a nuisance, the courts "balance the equities." What counts as a "substantial" interference depends on all the circumstances, including the nature of the neighborhood or area in which the plaintiff and defendant occupy or use their properties. And what counts as an "unreasonable" interference (which does not necessarily not mean an unreasonable activity) depends on the same factors.

Nowhere is the fact that the courts balance the equities more evident than in the "coming-to-the-nuisance" problem. Suppose that a particular use—for instance, a factory that emits particulate matter from a smoke stack—has been operating in an area surrounded by a woods. The plaintiff then erects a home in the woods and contends that the factory's emissions constitute a nuisance. Suppose further that if the plaintiff's home had existed when the factory began operation, the factory's emissions would have constituted a nuisance.

On first consideration one might want to say that the plaintiff has only himself to blame and should not be able to recover. Certainly the plaintiff's awareness of what he was getting into is one of the equities to be considered, but further consideration shows why this cannot always be dispositive. First, a rule that the first party to make an active use of property gets the right to do so without fear of liability in nuisance would encourage a race to make active use of land even if such use was otherwise premature. That would cause an undesirable "development race." Second, the "first" use really is not operation of the factory, but maintenance of the nearby property in an unimproved condition. The plaintiff was not failing to use the property at all when the factory began operation. On the contrary, he was "using" the property as woods. To permit the defendant *automatically* to insulate himself from the law of nuisance by building a factory is in effect to give him a right to restrict the plaintiff's potential use and enjoyment simply by being the first in the area to do something more with his land than enjoy its natural condition.

Moreover, inevitably there must come a point at which, if the factory is otherwise a nuisance, the factory must yield to its neighbors regardless of whose active use was first. For example, once the entire area surrounding the factory is developed with single family homes, the emission of particulate matter is certain to constitute a substantial and unreasonable interference with the plaintiffs' use and enjoyment of their land. The factory owner is not necessarily behaving unreasonably; but his interference with the plaintiffs' use is nonetheless "unreasonable" in the sense of being a greater interference than they should have to tolerate under the circumstances.

A finding that the factory is a nuisance, however, is only the first step in a two-step process of decision that takes place in nuisance actions. The second step requires determination of the remedy that is available once a particular use is held to constitute a nuisance.

B. *The Remedial Alternatives*

Most tortious activity has long since concluded by the time an action seeking compensation for the losses the activity has caused reaches a courtroom. As a consequence, the only practical remedy is the payment of damages to the plaintiff. In nuisance, however, often this is not the case. It is common for the nuisance to be continuing at the time a suit alleging its existence comes to trial. Therefore, two remedies are available. The defendant may be ordered to pay the plaintiff damages for all past and future losses, but may be permitted to continue the activity that constitutes the nuisance. Or the defendant may be ordered to pay the plaintiff damages for all past losses, and enjoined from continuing the nuisance thereafter.

Traditionally the law of nuisance has been that the court balances the equities not only at the liability stage in determining whether the defendant has engaged in a nuisance at all, but also at the remedial stage in determining whether to enjoin the defendant from continuing the nuisance or to permit the nuisance to continue and to hold the defendant liable in damages only for the plaintiff's future losses. In making their remedial decisions the courts take a variety of factors into account, including the parties' respective faults, if any, the hardship to the parties in respect of the continuance or discontinuance of the nuisance, and the value of the activity that constitutes the nuisance to the surrounding community. Thus, in *Boomer v. Atlantic Cement Co., Inc.*,[9] the court declined to enjoin the operation of a cement plant that was important to the economy of the area in which it was located, in part on the ground that the cost of discontinuing the nuisance—in both dollars and loss of employment—was grossly disproportionate to the amount of harm the nuisance was causing. This does not mean, however, that a strict cost-benefit analysis occurs in every case. Many courts balance the equities in the plaintiff's favor and grant a request for an injunction unless the equities weigh decidedly in the defendant's favor.

Appreciating the nature of this kind of equity-balancing is probably all that is necessary to understand the rudiments of nuisance remedies. For some time now, however, commentators have been investigating the structure of nuisance remedies by uncovering some of the assumptions that underlie the choice among remedies.[10] The commentators' insights reveal a side of tort liability that often remains hidden, because already-completed harms figure in most tort actions. The starting point for the analysis is the simple point that the plaintiff may be successful or fail in seeking either of two remedies: damages or an injunction. As a consequence, there are in fact four possible remedial alternatives to be considered when a plaintiff sues for nuisance.

1. No Nuisance: Defendant "Enjoins" Plaintiff

In the first situation the plaintiff is completely unsuccessful in his nuisance suit. The simplest way to understand this situation is to say that the court has held that the defendant has not engaged in a nuisance and has therefore denied the plaintiff any remedy. Although such a ruling means that the defendant's activity is not a substantial and unreasonable interference with the plaintiff's use and enjoyment of his land, it means something else as well. In fact, the defendant's activity almost always does interfere in some way with the plaintiff's use and

---

[9] 26 N.Y.2d 219, 257 N.E.2d 870, 309 N.Y.S.2d 312 (1970).

[10] See, e.g., Guido Calabresi & Douglas A. Melamed, *Property Rules, Liability Rules, and Inalienability: One View of the Cathedral*, 85 Harv. L. Rev.1089 (1972); A. Mitchell Polinsky, *Resolving Nuisance Disputes: The Simple Economics of Injunctive an Damage Remedies*, 32 Stan. L. Rev. 1075 (1980).

enjoyment, even if not in a substantial and unreasonable way. Consequently, although the legal effect of the failure of the plaintiff's suit is merely to permit the defendant's activity to continue, the practical significance of this permission is that the defendant's activity limits the scope of the plaintiff's use and enjoyment of his land. In effect, then, when a plaintiff's nuisance suit completely fails, the defendant enjoins the plaintiff—i.e., limits the plaintiff's future use and enjoyment of his land. Thus, suppose that you live near me and play rock music on Friday evenings in the spring. If my nuisance suit against you fails, then you have enjoined me by limiting my quiet enjoyment of my land.

This ruling need not end the matter, however. You now have what amounts to property right to play rock music on Friday evenings. But if my quiet enjoyment of my land is worth more to me than your music is to you, after I lose my suit (or even before if I know I will lose) I may want to try to buy your right to interfere with my enjoyment. A decision that you have not committed a nuisance merely allocates to you the right to decide whether to use that right or to sell it to me. Of course, like the owner of any property right, you are entitled to place whatever value you wish on it, including deciding that you will not sell at any price.

2. Nuisance: Plaintiff Enjoins Defendant

The traditional remedy when the defendant's interference is substantial and unreasonable is for the court to enjoin—i.e., prohibit—the defendant from continuing the nuisance, and to award the plaintiff damages for past losses resulting from the nuisance. For example, if my neighbor's playing of music is so loud and so continuing that I cannot hear myself talk inside my own house, my nuisance suit may succeed. I will then be entitled to damages for my past losses, and perhaps to an injunction from the court directing the neighbor to cease playing music that can be heard outside his home.

Notice however that, like the "remedy" that results when there is a finding of no nuisance at all, the issuance of an injunction need not end the matter. Rather, a holding that the plaintiff is entitled to enjoin the defendant means that the plaintiff has what amounts to a property right to be free from the nuisance being committed by the defendant. But at least in theory the plaintiff may sell that right to the defendant and thereby permit the defendant to continue his activity, at whatever price the plaintiff wishes to charge and the defendant is willing to pay. If the plaintiff sells, in effect he will have substituted his right to an injunction for the payment in advance of future damages, but damages as measured by the plaintiff rather than by a jury.

Unfortunately, however, the matter usually is not as simple in practice as it is in theory. Sometimes hundreds of people are affected by the nuisance and may be named as plaintiffs in the nuisance suit. The defendant in such a situation is unlikely to be able to succeed in a buyout of an injunction, because of the practical difficulty of dealing with multiple plaintiffs or because the last plaintiff to sell his right has a very valuable asset—with the result that there are multiple "hold-outs" seeking to be the last plaintiff to sell. Therefore, whereas a single-plaintiff injunction may well be bought-off by the defendant, a multiple-plaintiff injunction is likely to be enforced.

This prospect leads to an important insight. In the single-plaintiff situation the law can afford, so to speak, to make a mistake. If the benefit to the defendant of continuing the nuisance is wholly out of proportion to the benefit to the plaintiff of discontinuing the nuisance, it is likely that the plaintiff will have his price and that the plaintiff's right to an injunction will be purchased by the defendant. No real harm is done, though some money must change hands to correct the law's "mistake." In contrast, in the multiple-plaintiff situation the law cannot afford to make a mistake, because the "market" in nuisance rights is unlikely to be able to correct that mistake through the sale of the plaintiffs' right to an injunction back to the defendant. For this reason, in the multiple-plaintiff situation a high degree of confidence that an injunction rather than an award of damages is the proper remedy is even more desirable than in the single-plaintiff situation.

3. Nuisance: Defendant Compensates Plaintiff

In view of the above analysis, the first two remedies—defendant enjoins plaintiff and plaintiff enjoins defendant—will need to reflect a high degree of confidence on the part of the court that the proper solution to any particular conflict between land uses is that one should dominate the other. The next two remedies involve an award of damages rather than the issuance of an injunction. The significance of the decision to employ one of these remedies is more complicated.

Suppose that plaintiffs sue for an injunction or, in the event that the request for an injunction is denied, an award of future damages resulting from the continuation of the nuisance. For either of two reasons, the court might decline to issue the injunction and award damages instead. On the one hand, having balanced the equities the court might decide that the social and economic costs of discontinuing the nuisance are greater than the cost that will result from permitting it to continue. An award of future damages rather an injunction would therefore be the correct solution to the conflict between land uses reflected by the plaintiffs' suit. This was the solution reached in *Boomer v. Atlantic Cement*, discussed above. On the other hand, the court might be uncertain as to the proper solution. As I noted above, when there is reason to believe that the plaintiffs and the defendant can bargain to a solution, then issuing an injunction still permits them to do this. But if a bargained-for solution is unlikely to result because of the large number of plaintiffs involved, the issuance of an injunction could produce the wrong result. An award of damages permits the nuisance to continue if it can pay its way—that is, if the benefit to the defendant of continuing the nuisance is greater than the amount of damages awarded—which is of course the harm that the jury predicts will result from continuation of the nuisance. Otherwise the defendant will simply discontinue the nuisance instead of paying future damages. One critical difference, then, between issuing an injunction and awarding damages only, is that the former remedy has the potential to permit the plaintiffs to decide whether the nuisance should be continued and, if so, at what price, whereas the latter remedy permits the defendant to decide.

4. Nuisance: Plaintiff Compensates Defendant

At first glance this fourth possible remedy seems nonsensical and the result only of a desire for symmetry with the previous one. How could a plaintiff bring suit but end up paying the defendant? In fact, however, the remedy has both a logic of its own and a limited basis in the case law.

The logic of the remedy starts from the premise that the correct solution of the conflict between the plaintiffs' and the defendant's land uses is uncertain. An injunction is therefore not the preferable remedy, at least not where multiple parties are involved and the "wrong" remedy cannot be bought off. But suppose that, after balancing the equities, the court concludes that the plaintiffs should be entitled to cause discontinuance of the nuisance only if doing so is worth it to them. The proper remedy would then be to permit the plaintiffs to compensate the defendant for the cost of discontinuing the nuisance. If the benefit to the plaintiffs of discontinuing the nuisance is greater than the cost of doing so—as measured by the jury—then the plaintiffs will pay. And if that cost is not worth it, they will decline to do so and continue to suffer the nuisance.

It is rarely better to have the plaintiffs rather than the defendant decide whether continuing the nuisance is worth its costs, but occasionally the situation does arise. For example, in *Spur Industries v. Del E. Webb Development Co., Inc.*,[11] the plaintiff developer came to the nuisance, a cattle feed-lot. Smells and flies emanating from the lot constituted a nuisance to the owners of the developed properties. But the court concluded that, because the developer had come to the nuisance, it should bear the cost of relocating the feed-lot. In effect, the developer, as plaintiff, was entitled to purchase an injunction by compensating the defendant for discontinuing the nuisance.

5. A Synthesis

In the case of each of the four possible nuisance remedies, either the plaintiff or the defendant is found to have an entitlement to use his or her land in the manner that is contested, and the other party must tolerate that use. The successful party's entitlement may be protected strongly, in the manner of a property right by an injunction, or more weakly, in the manner of a tort right, by the payment of damages only.

Thus, the decision that there is no nuisance protects the defendant with a property right, which he can decide to sell or not sell, at his price. Similarly, a decision enjoining the defendant from continuing a nuisance protects the plaintiff with a property right, which she can decide to sell or not, at her price. In contrast, an award of future damages to the plaintiff protects the plaintiff with a "liability right" or "liability rule" only. In this situation the value of the plaintiff's entitlement as set by the jury, rather than by the plaintiff, prevails. Finally, an award of future damages to the defendant protects the defendant with a liability right or liability rule only. And in this situation the value of the defendant's entitlement as set by the jury, rather than by the defendant, prevails.

In short, when an entitlement is protected strongly, as a property right, the party holding the entitlement cannot be forced to sell it. But when an entitlement is protected weakly, as a liability right, another party can force the holder of the entitlement to "sell" it, and the price of sale is set by the jury rather than by the holder of the entitlement.

---

[11] 108 Ariz. 178, 494 P.2d 700 (1972).

Typically a tort right can only be protected weakly, by a liability rule, because the conduct interfering with a plaintiff's entitlement has already occurred. There is no choice but to permit a jury to place a "price" on the lost or damaged entitlement through an award of damages. But in nuisance, because the defendant's conduct often is continuing, the choice between the strong protection afforded by a property right and the weaker protection afforded by a liability right must be made.

IV. Vicarious Liability

The principal example of vicarious liability—liability for injury caused by the conduct of another party—is the doctrine known as *respondeat superior* ("let the superior answer"). Under this doctrine an employer is liable under some circumstances for the torts committed by an employee. An employer whose employee commits a tort may of course be liable in his own right for negligence in hiring or supervising the employee. If in my business I hire a truck driver who has a record of drunk driving and on whom one day I detect the smell of bourbon, I (along with my employee) may be held liable for negligence if his driving causes injury. But that is not "vicarious" liability—I am held liable for my own negligence in hiring that employee or letting him drive after I know he has been drinking.

It has long been settled, in addition, that employers are liable even absent their own negligence, for torts committed by their employees "within the scope of employment." The theory behind this form of liability is similar to the theory behind strict liability generally. As between the employer and the victim, the employer probably is in a better position to make the activity level and research decisions that can affect accident levels. Moreover, it will often be difficult to prove that a particular employee was negligent, because identifying the employee in question is not possible even when it is clear whose employee he is. So *respondeat superior* may generate greater accuracy than negligence liability alone. Finally, note that this form of liability does not substitute the employee's liability for the employer's liability. Rather, the employee continues to be liable, but *respondeat superior* adds the employer as an additional defendant. Given that employees as a group are more likely to be judgment-proof than employers, the cost-spreading function of strict liability clearly seems to play a role in supporting the doctrine.

Two questions then arise. First, who is an "employee?" Second, when is a tort committed "within the scope of employment?" The requirement that the agent of the defendant be an employee is an effort to distinguish at a fairly high level of generality between those situations in which strict liability is likely to have the desired incentive and cost-spreading effects and those in which is not. The principal situation in which the party committing a tort is an agent but not an employee involves independent contractors. If I hire an electrician to do work in my apartment, he contracts with me but is not my employee. I do not and could not control the manner in which he works to any great degree. Indeed, if I told an electrician how to perform his work he would probably tell me to get lost. And of course electricians and other independent contractors work for many parties, not just one. The possibility of control by an individual—other than the electrician's own employer—is therefore minimal. Finally, the electrician's employer is just as likely to have a "deep pocket" and therefore to be in a position to spread the cost of liability as is the party who hires him. All this may not be true in every instance, but it is often enough true to make it worthwhile to draw a bright-line distinction (i.e., a rule at a high level of generality) between employees and independent contractors in applying *respondeat superior.*

The second requirement of *respondeat superior* is that the tort at issue be committed within the scope of employment. The idea behind this requirement is that the incentive effects of strict liability can operate through employers only so far. At some point the employer's capacity to control the conduct of employees, and consequently the strength of the argument for imposing strict liability, both diminish. The phrase that captures this point is the distinction between a "detour" and a "frolic." The employer is liable for torts committed on a "mere" detour by the employee, but not for torts committed while the employee is on a frolic of his own. This is an easy enough point to see in the simplest of cases. If I tell my truck driver to deliver a package across town and instead he drives a thousand miles west, I am not liable for the accidents he causes while on that frolic. But if he goes three blocks out of his way to visit his girlfriend, I am liable for accidents that result while he is on that detour. Obviously, it is not always possible to draw a bright line between mere detours and frolics.

In addition, a number of hard cases arise when the employee clearly is on a frolic, but it happens that the employer actually is in a pretty good position to influence the conduct in question. The classic case on this point is *Ira S. Bushey & Sons, Inc. v. United States*,[12] in which a drunken seaman returning from shore leave opened the valve on a drydock and thereby caused severe damage to the ship then in the dock for service. There is no way to describe this as a "mere" detour. But drunken sailors are not only predictable; at least in the case of employees in the military, such conduct is also somewhat subject to control by the employer. And of course the employer in that case—the U.S. government—had the deepest pocket of all. Strict liability could therefore serve loss distribution purposes as well. So perhaps it is not surprising that the court pushed out the envelope of liability a bit farther than it had been in the past and held that the tort was committed within the scope of employment. The decision in *Bushey* is not typical, but its overall flavor is not wholly extraordinary either. What counts as conduct "within the scope of employment" will depend on how effectively imposing liability on the employer for injuries caused by that conduct will serve the purposes of strict liability.

---

[12] 398 F.2d 167 (2d Cir. 1968).

9

Products Liability

This Chapter concerns liability for injury and damage caused by defective products. A substantial portion of products liability law employs rules governing negligence and strict liability that closely resemble the standards of care that have been covered in earlier Chapters. This area of the law is nonetheless distinctive for two reasons. First, applying the concepts of negligence and strict liability to products liability has proved more difficult than might be supposed. Second, unlike most of the other areas of tort liability covered in earlier Chapters, the parties in a product liability lawsuit often are in an indirect (or sometimes even direct) contractual relationship with each other. The law of products liability is therefore in a position to take the actual and potential terms of this relationship into account in fashioning the tort law rules that apply to product-related injuries.

Most products today are sold in a chain of distribution that begins with the manufacturer, and sometimes even before, with the maker of component parts that are supplied to the manufacturer. The manufacturer sells to an intermediary such as a wholesaler, distributor, or dealer. There may be more than one such intermediary before the product finally reaches a retailer, who eventually sells it to a purchaser. The product may then injure the purchaser, another user of the product, or a bystander. Early on in the history of products liability there was very little basis for recovery against anyone other than the retailer—the "immediate" seller of the product. The right to recover from a "remote" seller such as a wholesaler or manufacturer who sold to the retailer was largely unknown. The "privity of contract" requirement made such recoveries impossible.

The history of products liability, however, is the story of the progressive creation and addition of causes of action for injuries caused by defective products. Each new cause of cause of action has complemented rather than replaced a previous basis for liability. Consequently, in a very real sense any study of the history and development of products liability law is at the same time the study of products liability law as it now stands. That history is comprised of four eras: the era of contract privity; the era of negligence; the era of warranty, in which the courts made the transition from negligence to strict liability; and the modern era of strict liability. Although any division of an important field of law into four such simple categories automatically oversimplifies, this categorization is a useful way to clarify and organize one's understanding of the field.

I. The Era of Contract Privity

Prior to the twentieth century there was no general law of products liability, and certainly no tort law of products liability. Rather, what liability there was for injuries caused by products arose within the law of contracts. It was therefore accurate to say that there was no products liability in the absence of privity of contract—i.e., unless the person injured was a party to a contract that was breached. And even if there was privity of contract and the product sold pursuant to the contract caused injury, there might not be liability. That depended on what the contract provided, or was interpreted to provide. And in the nineteenth century era of *caveat emptor*—"let the buyer beware"—the courts were unlikely to be sympathetic to the injured purchaser whose contract provided nothing about his rights in the event that he was injured by the product in question.

The leading case reflecting the privity rule is *Winterbottom v. Wright*,[1] an English decision involving a plaintiff who was injured by a defective stagecoach that had been supplied to his employer. In his suit against the maker of the stagecoach, with whom he had no contract, the plaintiff was denied recovery because of the absence of privity. Some commentators say that the case has been misinterpreted and that *Winterbottom* neither stated nor reflected a general rule that a product maker was immune from tort liability in the absence of privity. Be that as it may, *Winterbottom* certainly came to stand for such a rule.

To the modern mind the privity requirement seems unfair. It does not seem sensible to insulate a negligent manufacturer from liability to the very people whom its product is most likely to injure if the product is unsafe, on the ground that there is no contract between the manufacturer and the victim. Nonetheless, it is useful to try to imagine what a liability regime based on the privity limitation could have come to look

---

[1] 10 M. & W. 109, 152 Eng. Rep. 402 (1842).

like over time. The privity limitation may still be rejected as inappropriate even in the modern context, but the assumptions that lie behind the limitation may not seem nearly so absurd as the modern view of *Winterbottom* makes them appear to be.

Suppose that even today the purchaser injured by a product had no cause of action against any remote seller, but was limited to a suit against the party who had sold him the product. It is nonetheless plausible to suppose that there would have developed a series of contractual undertakings creating some liability on the part of remote sellers such as manufacturers. For example, immediate sellers of certain products probably would find it in their interest to compete for business by offering to compensate purchasers and members of their families injured by the products sold. Intermediate sellers such as wholesalers probably would then find it in their interest to compete for the business of retailers by offering to reimburse them for some or all of the injury-liability costs that the retailers had undertaken by contract. In turn, manufacturers probably would find it in their interest to compete with each other for the business of wholesalers by offering to reimburse them for the costs of reimbursing retailers. In this way the cost of injuries suffered by product purchasers and their families could ultimately be passed up the chain of distribution. The cost of providing this protection would be shouldered first by manufacturers. But in one way or another this cost would be passed down the chain of distribution, since the price of the product at each stage would include either the cost of compensation or the cost of making the product safer so as to avoid the need for compensation, whichever were less.

It is difficult to say exactly what the scope of these various contractual undertakings would be in the absence of any tort liability. Some products might carry no contractual right to compensation; some might carry a right to full compensation on the model of tort damages regardless of the fault of anyone in the chain of distribution; and others might come with a more limited right to compensation—for example, only in the event that the injury resulted from the sellers' negligence and only for medical expenses and lost wages resulting from the injury. The difficulty of predicting the precise contours of a privity-of-contract liability regime is not a weakness, however, but part of the argument in favor of such a regime. The reason it is difficult to predict the particular liability rule or rules that would have developed is that different people probably would want to contract for different packages of product price and safety, and compensation for product-related injuries. Similarly, different products might come with different combinations of these features because of differences between the products. Of course, in an age of mass produced products not everyone could have her own liability contract customized with each purchase. But just as today's purchasers of motor vehicles are offered the choice between regular and extended warranties covering the engine of their vehicles, so there might have developed a series of different liability packages available at different prices. If it is plausible to suppose that, even in the absence of tort liability for product injuries, consumer preferences could have caused contract-based product liability to develop with at least some of this diversity, then there is also some plausibility to the argument that the uniform tort-based product liability law that has actually developed is sub-optimal.

That this argument is plausible, however, does not necessarily make it correct. First, totally missing from the analysis is any treatment of product injuries suffered by bystanders. Under modern tort-based product liability law a pedestrian (for example) injured by a bus that goes out of control because of defective brakes has a cause of action against the manufacturer of the bus (and possibly the manufacturer of the brakes). A contract-based liability regime could never have developed in a way that would have adequately protected such bystanders, because by definition a bystander has no contract with any party in the chain of product distribution. Tort law rules would have been required to provide such bystanders with a cause of action that *Winterbottom* denied them. Second, just because a contract-based liability regime of some sort probably would have developed if *Winterbottom* had not eventually been overruled, it does not follow that such a regime would have been more suitable than the tort law regime that now prevails. Various imperfections in the product markets might have generated a sub-optimal body of contract-based product liability law. In short, markets that afford consumers choice and legal rules that do not afford choice both tend to be imperfect. The real question is not which approach could operate with high effectiveness, but which approach or combination of approaches has the potential to be less imperfect than the other.

All this has simply been a mental exercise designed to help us see what might have been. The contract-based approach embodied in *Winterbottom v. Wright* was long ago rejected, and the tort-based approach has been dominant for more than eighty years. But even today the differences between the contract and tort-based approaches are not entirely academic. At many points in the law of product liability the preferences of consumers for a particular mix of product price, safety, and compensation for product-related injuries can help to inform the choice among possible tort-based rules of liability. For this reason, although the 19th-century contract privity rule has been long been dead, the idea behind that approach—consumer sovereignty—may still aid in the evaluation of modern tort-based rules governing product liability.

II. The Era of Negligence

As so often happens in the development of the law, almost from the very moment that the contract privity rule became firmly established the courts began to create exceptions to it. Perhaps the most prominent exception was the rule in *Thomas v. Winchester*,[2] which eliminated the privity requirement when the plaintiff's injury was caused by an "imminently" or "inherently" dangerous product. In such cases the plaintiff could sue the manufacturer of the product for negligence, despite the absence of privity. In the beginning the number of products found to be inherently dangerous was small, and included only such obviously hazardous things as poison. But slowly the members of the category expanded to include coffee urns, scaffolds, and bottles of aerated water. For all practical purposes at this point the exceptions had swallowed up the rule.

The demise of the privity requirement was not formally recognized, however, until Judge Cardozo's opinion in *MacPherson v. Buick Motor Co.*[3] in 1916. The defendant there had manufactured an automobile which was sold by a dealer to the plaintiff, who was injured when a wheel made of defective wood collapsed. The plaintiff sued for negligence, and the defendant relied on the privity rule, arguing that the rule of *Thomas v. Winchester* did not apply. The court rejected the defendant's argument, holding in effect that the manufacturer of anything that could foreseeably harm a third party if negligently made was subject to liability under *Thomas*. This holding of course totally eviscerated the limitations contained in the *Thomas* rule and functionally overruled the contract privity requirement. Many other states followed *MacPherson* in the years that followed.

Clearly the decision in *MacPherson* was very significant. But it is important to see what *MacPherson* did and did not do for plaintiffs in product liability actions,. By eliminating the privity requirement the

[2] 6 N.Y. 397 (1852).

[3] 217 N.Y. 382, 111 N.E. 1050 (1916).

case obviously made it possible for plaintiffs to sue manufacturers with whom they had no direct contractual relationship. This was important not only because immediate sellers sometimes had few assets. In addition, with the rise of pre-packaged, mass-produced goods, often the retail seller was a mere conduit for the transfer of the product. As such, the retailer had not been negligent in any way. In such cases *MacPherson* did not create the right to sue an *additional* defendant; in the typical case *MacPherson* created the right to sue the only party who could possibly be found liable for negligence.

Although this was a necessary step for plaintiffs, it was far from sufficient to make recovery automatic, because the plaintiff still had to prove negligence. As a result of *MacPherson* manufacturers could be held liable to remote purchasers or users of their products, but only for negligence. Proving negligence was often far from a simple task. Consider the broken wheel in *MacPherson*, which the defendant had purchased from a maker of component parts. The plaintiff might be able to show that the wheel was defective, if it was not destroyed in the accident that injured him. But unless the standard to which manufacturers are held is perfection rather than due care, merely showing that there was something wrong with the wheel does not prove that the manufacturer was negligent in placing it on the vehicle. One way to prove negligence would be to attempt to show that the defendant was under a duty to inspect component parts such as wheels, and that the defendant's inspection in this case was negligent. That approach could require evidence regarding the defendant's methods of training inspectors, inspection standards, the rate at which defects went undetected given these inspection standards, and so forth. All this might have been available in discovery, but only at a cost. And even then the plaintiff had to hope that what he discovered would help to prove negligence rather than show how careful the defendant had been.

Without such evidence, the defendant could contend, whether the defendant was negligent in failing to discover the defect in the wheel of the plaintiff's automobile be speculative, and it would be improper to submit the case to the jury. In some cases *res ipsa loquitur* could solve this problem for the plaintiff. As products and manufacturing techniques become increasingly complex, however, typically it becomes less appropriate to invoke *res ipsa* because of uncertainty as to whether the type of accident in question does or does not ordinarily happen in the absence of negligence. In short, because products are not perfect, sometimes they caused injuries even the absence of the manufacturer's negligence. And even when the manufacturer was negligent, plaintiffs could not always prove it. Thus, *MacPherson* ushered in a new era in products liability, but created new problems for plaintiffs at the same time that it solved old ones.

III. The Era of Transition and the Rise of Warranty Rules

At about the same time that the cause of action against manufacturers for negligence emerged, several other bases of recovery under certain limited circumstances began developing. Each arises out of the notion of "warranty." A warranty is a promise or guarantee. When a warranty about the safety or quality of a product is breached, that breach may give rise to a cause of action, not only for losses flowing immediately from the breach (e.g., lost value), but also for such consequential losses as personal injury or property damage. During a period that overlapped with the era of negligence, several causes of action based on breach of warranty were slowly recognized.

A. *Express Warranty*

Warranties may be either express or implied. An express warranty is simply that—a promise or guarantee, for the breach of which liability may ensue. Sometimes the warranty is contractual, sometimes less formal and part of an advertising campaign. By the 1930's some courts began to hold immediate sellers and sometimes even manufacturers liable for breach of express warranties.[4] This development was not unimportant, especially when liability was extended to manufacturers. But proving that claims of product quality amounted to an express warranty was difficult, and this form of liability was never an important basis for the imposition for liability for product injuries. Over a period of decades the real action took place in the field of implied warranties, three forms of which are discussed in the following Sections.

B. *Liability of the Immediate Seller*

The first form of implied-warranty liability arose out of a provision of the Uniform Sales Act enacted in many states after the turn of the twentieth century. The Act provided that a warranty of "merchantability" was implied in every contract for the sale of goods. To be merchantable the goods had to be of fair average quality. If they were not,

---

[4] See, e.g., *Baxter v. Ford Motor Co.*, 168 Wash. 456, 12 P.2d 409 (1932).

the seller had liability for personal injuries resulting from breach of the warranty regardless of negligence or its absence. But the liability ran only from the immediate seller, and typically only to the purchaser and not to other users or bystanders. And, being a creature of the Sales Acts, the implied warranty of merchantability was implied but not mandatory. That is, it was what contract-law theorists today call a "default" rule: an implied warranty could be disclaimed by contract. Nonetheless, limited though it was, this was the first instance of strict liability for injuries caused by product defects.

If one stops and thinks about it, there is nothing at all extraordinary or even counterfactual about the implied warranty of merchantability, especially if it is disclaimable. In the case of mass produced, homogeneous goods, to a very great extent the warranty of merchantability was implied not only by law but also in fact. The Sales Acts simply reversed the old common law rule of *caveat emptor*—"let the buyer beware"—under circumstances in which the reasonable assumption of a buyer would be that what he was purchasing met minimal standards of quality and safety. The legal implication simply followed the factual assumptions of the parties. And because the warranty was implied wherever there was privity, in the absence of a disclaimer the seller held liable for personal injuries itself had a claim for indemnification from its wholesaler (with whom it was in privity), which in turn had a claim against the manufacturer. In this way liability ultimately would be shouldered by the manufacturer, with a consequent incentive created for the manufacturer to provide an optimal mix of quality, safety, and price in its products. But the manufacturer was still insulated from the ultimate user by several layers of litigation.

C. Impure Food: Liability of the Manufacturer

Shortly after the Uniform Sales Act was promulgated and began to make its way through the state legislatures, a few courts went one step further. They held that the manufacturer of food could be held directly liable to the consumer for personal injuries resulting from the consumption of impure food, on a theory of breach of implied warranty.

This was perhaps the greatest conceptual leap ever made during the period of transition from negligence to strict liability. As I have just argued, the idea that a contractual sale of a product by an immediate seller to a purchaser contains an implied warranty of merchantability is factually and legally unremarkable, though this approach does reverse the ingrained rule of *caveat emptor*. The theory behind the immediate seller's liability is still largely contractual, both because it is reasonable to suppose that the warranty is implied in fact as well as in law, and because this implied warranty remains disclaimable—i.e., subject to express contractual modification.

In contrast, ordinarily there is no contract of sale between a manufacturer (of food or anything else) and a purchaser. To hold that there is nonetheless an implied warranty running from the manufacturer to the purchaser which, if breached, gives rise to liability, is to create something out of nothing. It is not necessarily wrong to do this; but what is created has little to do with any contract. The cause of action for breach of the manufacturer's implied warranty therefore much more closely resembles tort than contract. And because the cause of action requires no showing of negligence, the tort it resembles is strict liability. The focus is on the product's quality (its "merchantability"), not on the manufacturer's conduct. Admittedly, certain aspects of the cause of action contained residue of the contractual soil out of which warranty law grew: often a contract statute of limitations and the notice requirements of contract law applied, for example. And this form of implied warranty also remained disclaimable, though the only place to disclaim it was in the contract between the retailer and the purchaser. But the fact remains that the core of the cause of action was largely indistinguishable from strict liability in tort for injuries caused by an unmerchantable product.

D. The Fall of the Citadel: Liability of Manufacturers Generally

The rise of the food manufacturer's liability for breach of implied warranty was important conceptually, but for practical purposes the first half of the twentieth century remained mainly an era of negligence liability. The key player—the manufacturer of durable consumer and commercial goods—was liable only for negligence, and only when the plaintiff could prove negligence. In the 1950's there was a slight erosion of this liability limitation, as some courts began to apply the implied warranty theory to manufacturers of products that were not food but were intended for intimate bodily consumption—such as perfume and hair dye.

But the first real fall of the "citadel," as Dean Prosser once called it, occurred when a manufacturer of an ordinary product was held liable for breach of an implied warranty of merchantability. That occurred in 1960 in *Henningsen v. Bloomfield Motors, Inc.*.[5] The plaintiff there was the injured wife of the purchaser of a new Plymouth, which mysteriously left the road after the steering failed. The decision was double-barreled. The court first held that an implied warranty of merchantability ran not only from the immediate seller, but also from the manufacturer.

The problem for the plaintiff, however, was that the contract of sale contained some fine-print labelled "warranty" that was actually a disclaimer of liability for personal injury. The court's second move was to invalidate this disclaimer, on grounds that did not make it entirely clear whether some disclaimers—if clearly labelled and pointed out to the purchaser—would be binding. But the opinion soon came to be understood to hold that the manufacturers' implied warranty of merchantability could not be disclaimed in connection with personal injury. Once this step was taken, there could no longer be any doubt as to what the cause of action really was. A cause of action for breach of an implied warranty that cannot be disclaimed, running from a manufacturer to a party who suffers injury but is not in privity with the manufacturer, is simply strict liability in tort masquerading under another name. The transition from negligence to strict liability was now virtually complete; it only remained for the courts of other states to follow *Henningsen* and to acknowledge what they were really doing.

IV. The Modern Era: "Strict" Liability for Defective Products

Those acknowledgments followed quickly. The first case to make what had happened absolutely clear was the Supreme Court of California's decision in *Greenman v. Yuba Power Products, Inc.*[6] But the courts were moving very quickly—so quickly, in fact, that by 1965 the Restatement (Second) of Torts § 402A, only slightly ahead of its time, indicated that any seller of a product in a "defective condition unreasonably dangerous to the user" was strictly liable in tort for personal injury or property damage resulting from that defective condition. Soon that was in fact the law in most states. And it remains the law today, although a few states still cling to warranty terminology in holding manufacturers and other sellers strictly liable.

[5] 32 N.J. 358, 161 A.2d 69 (1960).

[6] 59 Cal.2d 57, 377 P.2d 897, 27 Cal. Rptr. 697 (1963).

The language of the Restatement was a bit confusing. Could a product be defective without being unreasonably dangerous, or unreasonably dangerous without being defective? Probably not, and the drafters of the Third Restatement have read the subsequent case law and chosen to drop the phrase "unreasonably dangerous" from their formulation, employing only the adjective "defective." In fact, the draft of the Third Restatement in circulation at the time this book goes to print does not even use the phrase "strict liability" to describe products liability generally. Rather, the forms of liability for injuries caused by defective products are set out separately, using categories that the case law has come to employ in the more than three decades following the adoption of § 402A. These categories—manufacturing defects, design defects, and warning defects—shape virtually all current thinking about products liability.

A. Manufacturing Defects

A product contains a manufacturing defect when, as produced, it does not conform to the manufacturer's own design. Sometimes called a "construction" defect, a product with a manufacturing defect is different from most of the others coming off the assembly line. Presumably the wheels on most of the Buicks made by the defendant in *MacPherson* and the steering mechanisms on the most of the Plymouths made by the defendant in *Henningsen* did not contain the defects that made the plaintiffs' particular cars dangerous. A manufacturing defect thus results when something goes wrong in the manufacturing process and a product departs from its intended design.

Strict liability for injuries caused by manufacturing defects circumvents the difficulties of proof posed for plaintiffs after *MacPherson* made it possible to sue the manufacturer for negligence. There is no need for the plaintiff to show that the manufacturer used inadequate materials, failed to conduct a proper inspection, or otherwise took a risk whose potential costs were greater than its potential benefits. On the contrary, once the plaintiff shows that the product departed from its intended design and that this departure caused the plaintiff's injury, the plaintiff has proven a manufacturing defect. The manufacturer is then liable even if has exercised reasonable care in every aspect of the manufacturing process.

The arguments in favor of this form of strict liability are the arguments in favor of strict liability generally. First, many manufacturing defects probably are the result of some hard-to-pinpoint negligence.

Strict liability may therefore produce more accurate results, from the standpoint of optimal deterrence, than negligence. Second, as between the manufacturer and the victim, the manufacturer is in the superior position to conduct research or otherwise discover cost-effective methods of reducing the risk of harm resulting from manufacturing defects, ordinarily by reducing the incidence of those defects. And in general the manufacturer probably is in a better position to spread the cost of the defects that it is not cost-effective to eliminate.

B. Design Defects

In contrast to a manufacturing defect, which occurs in only a (usually small) portion of any particular mass-produced product, a design defect is one that occurs in an entire product line. For example, a car model with a gas tank in a place that makes it vulnerable to explosions in rear-end collisions is designed to have the gas tank in that position. If the placement of the tank in that position makes the car defective, that is a design defect that afflicts every vehicle coming off the assembly line in the condition it was intended to be.

In the case of alleged manufacturing defects there is a readily available standard against which to measure whether there was a defect in the product that injured the plaintiff—departure of the product from the manufacturer's own design. But in the case of design defects that standard obviously is not appropriate, because it is never breached. Of course, a product design can never be risk-free. Perfectly safe products are impossible and in any event would result in products too expensive for most people to purchase. Consequently, it was never expected that "strict" products liability would mean that every injury caused by a product would be compensable. Knives are made to cut; if I cut myself with a perfectly good knife the manufacturer is not liable, because the knife was not defective. The courts have therefore had to develop standards for use in determining whether a product design is defective. Two such standards occupy the field.

The first test measures the safety of the design against *consumer expectations*. Under this test, if the design is not as safe as consumers expect it to be, it is defective. Unfortunately, in most cases this test is either unworkable or circular. If the consumer expectations test were empirical, then it would require statistical evidence of consumer expectations to prove design defect. This is not required and would hardly be practical if it were. On the other hand, if the consumer expectations test is not rigorously empirical but is instead to be applied through some form of reasoning by the jury, what is it? The ordinary juror would probably think that what the typical consumer expects from a design is a reasonable amount of safety—i.e., all the safety that it is cost-effective to provide. A motor vehicle is expected to be "crashworthy," i.e., to be reasonable safe in a collision. But no consumer expects that if he does not emerge completely uninjured from a crash, the design of his car is automatically "defective." Only "reasonable" crashworthiness is expected.[7] Yet that looks curiously like a negligence test—the very standard that strict liability is supposed to replace.

An alternative to the consumer expectations test acknowledges that, in fact, deciding whether a design is defective is very much like deciding whether the design is negligent. This *risk-benefit* or *risk-utility* test asks whether the risks posed by the design outweigh its benefits. This is nothing more than a negligence test without a foreseeability requirement. Over time the courts and commentators have tended to adopt this hindsight risk-benefit test, increasingly recognizing that design defect liability is not really strict liability, or at least is a lot less "strict" than manufacturing defect liability. A product design is not defective unless its risks outweigh its benefits, whereas that balance does not matter in manufacturing defect cases. Admittedly, the absence of a foreseeability requirement removes much of the blameworthiness that inheres in a true negligence standard. But except in the case of truly unpredictable harms such as rare long-latency diseases, few products whose risks in retrospect outweigh their benefits do so in unforeseeable ways. So in most design defect cases the plaintiff could prove the foreseeability of these risks if that were required. The crux of the issue in design defect cases is how to compare a product's risks compare to its benefits.

Much of the controversy surrounding design defect liability involves the difficulty of making this risk-benefit comparison in practice. Two problems are especially acute. First, in cases involving technical design choices for complex products such as motor vehicles, the design defect test in effect asks jurors to engage in a task for which they do not have the relevant expertise. As in medical malpractice cases, expert testimony is virtually always necessary to provide the jury with the basis for making a decision. Yet unlike medical malpractice cases, in design defect litigation there is no "respectable minority" rule to guide the jury's task. It is not enough that a respectable minority of designers would conclude that the defendant's design was not defective. On the

---

[7] See *Volkswagen of America, Inc. v. Young*, 272 Md. 201, 321 A.2d 737 (1974).

contrary, if the risks of the design outweigh its benefits, the design is defective. In effect, the jury is asked to choose the best design or, as some have put it, the jury is asked to redesign the product.

Second, any complex product is a combination of many design choices regarding safety, cost, attractiveness, and functionality. An entire product design, however, does not cause injury. One feature of the design does that. If I am injured in a collision because of the angle and hardness of my steering wheel, the design of my Ford has not injured me; rather, the design of the steering wheel is responsible. The focus of the product liability action I bring will therefore be whether the design of the steering wheel was defective. The jury's tendency will be to evaluate the risks and benefits of that design in isolation from the other elements of the overall design. Of course the steering wheel could have been made more safely, for a price. So could many other features of the design. But at some point what that requires is a Mercedes, not a Ford. Since I purchased a Ford and not a Mercedes, the real question ought to be how safely a Ford must be designed as a whole. But that is the very kind of question that jurors are not terribly well-suited to answer, even with the help of experts. Many courts have attempted to deal with this problem by requiring that the plaintiff prove not only that the risks of a particular design outweigh its benefits, but also that there was a reasonable alternative design that would have reduced the risks in question. Yet that requirement asks the jury to make a second design decision for which it is ill-suited—whether the alternative design proposed by the plaintiff is reasonable and feasible.

All this is far from ideal. The dilemma posed by these weaknesses in design defect liability, however, is that there is no particularly suitable alternative to the current approach. Stronger safety regulation by government is one such alternative, but that does not seem either likely or likely to be effective. Another alternative is to allow the market to decide how much safety it wants, on the model of the *Winterbottom* approach. Just as there is a market for attractiveness and functionality, there is a market for safety. Some people want more safety than others and are willing to pay for it. But the complexity of designs and the latency of design dangers make it very difficult for the ordinary consumer to assess safety in anything but a very general way. If I want the most safety money can buy, I choose a Mercedes. If I want considerable safety but not the most money can buy, I may choose a Ford. Because I can never be fully informed about design safety, however, my choice of a Ford will not necessarily result in Fords having an overall level of design safety that is optimal for Ford purchasers. There is therefore a considerable role to be played by the threat of liability for design defects, especially those defects that are latent rather than obvious.

As a consequence, we face a choice between the imperfections of the regime of tort liability for design defects, the imperfections of governmental safety regulation, and the imperfections of the model of consumer sovereignty that *MacPherson* long ago rejected in overruling *Winterbottom*. Tort law's design defect approach now dominates, but not without considerable dissatisfaction on the part of many observers of this field.

C. Warning Defects

If it were possible to provide product purchasers with complete information about product risks and benefits, there would be little need for manufacturing defect or design defect liability. Complete information could be transmitted and consumers could make their own choices about the desirable mix of safety, price, attractiveness, and functionality in the products they purchase. Because that is an impossible ideal, consumer sovereignty cannot totally displace product liability. But consumer sovereignty can play a major role in the domain addressed by liability for warning defects.

Warning law occupies the area in which it is feasible to transfer risk-benefit information to the purchaser and thereby to put the purchaser in a position to decide for himself whether the risks posed by a product design are worth its benefits. When providing a warning or instructions in proper use is feasible, then the product seller generally is relieved of liability for harm caused by the risk about which an adequate warning or instructions were provided. The theory underlying liability for the failure to warn is that, once an adequate warning has been given, the purchaser rather than the product seller is the superior bearer of strict liability. That is, with adequate information, the consumer can make the activity-level and other choices necessary to optimize the combination of risk and benefit derived from the product.

The duty to warn users of pharmaceuticals about side effects illustrates the point. Suppose that I buy a bottle of aspirin warning me about the risk that a small percentage of the users of aspirin will develop ulcers as result of prolonged use. Since there are aspirin substitutes, I can use the aspirin once or twice and then compare its effectiveness with that of a substitute. I can then make an informed decision whether to risk the side effects of aspirin. On the other hand, if the drug in question has no adequate substitutes, then the provision of a warning at least puts me in a position to decide whether to risk the drug's side effects or, instead, to tolerate the medical condition that causes me to seek treatment. Once I have the necessary information— or if the drug requires a prescription, once a learned intermediary such as my physician has the information and consults with me about it— then I am in at least as good a position as the manufacturer of the drug to decide whether its risks are worth its benefits. Restatement (Second) of Torts § 402A (Comment k) and much of the case law refer to this kind of product as "unavoidably unsafe" and decline to impose liability for the injuries that result after an adequate warning of the risk of these injuries is given.

Two areas of controversy dominate warning law: the adequacy-of-warning issue and the connection between warnings and design defect liability.

1. Adequacy of Warning

If complete risk-benefit information could be transmitted in warnings or instructions, it would be easy to determine whether the warning or instructions given were sufficient to insulate the manufacturer or seller from liability. But of course providing complete information is never possible. What is required is an "adequate" warning or instruction, typically of foreseeable risks. Warning liability is therefore not truly "strict" liability, since adequacy determinations inevitably take into account the feasibility and cost of providing a warning, as well as the kind of information that purchasers want and need.

The great problem here is that there are diminishing returns from providing additional information. The more risks a warning discloses and the more detailed the instructions in safe use that are given, the less likely the user actually is to digest and heed the warning or to follow the instructions. The term "label clutter" is often used to describe the problem. Since the adequacy issue ordinarily is for the jury, however, there is likely to be a tendency for liability to be imposed in cases in which fairly low probability risks were not disclosed, or the particular phraseology used in the warning is alleged not to have conveyed the nature of the risk in question with an adequate degree of specificity. In *MacDonald v. Ortho Pharmaceutical Corp.*,[8] for example, the warning on birth control pills manufactured by the defendant referred to the risk of blood clots that could lodge in the brain and

---

[8] 394 Mass. 131, 475 N.E. 2d 65 (1985).

could be fatal, but did not use the word "stroke." The plaintiff suffered a stroke, and in the plaintiff's suit the court held that her contention that the warning was inadequate raised a jury question. Given the number of different risks that might be disclosed about any given product, the issue is somewhat analogous to asking a jury in a design defect case to decide whether the risks posed by a particular design feature were worth that feature's benefits, without looking at the entire product design. A jury is very likely to conclude that the particular risk that was not disclosed to the plaintiff is the one additional risk about which there should have been a warning. That is an unfortunate effect of the current approach. But like design defect liability, there does not seem to be any more suitable alternative approach to the adequacy-of-warning issue. If there is to be a requirement that an adequate warning be given, at some point we must rely on juries—as well as on courts granting directed verdicts—to decide when a warning was or was not adequate.

2. The Warning/Design Defect Connection

The risks posed by some products outweigh their benefits when there is no warning or instructions, but are outweighed by their benefits when the product does carry an adequate warning or instructions. There is no dispute that in such cases there is a duty to warn, and that if that duty is satisfied there is no liability for a risk that is the subject of an adequate warning or instruction. But what about a product that has no reasonable alternative design and whose risks still might outweigh its benefits after an otherwise adequate warning or instruction is given? Can such a product be found to have a design defect, or does the provision of the warning or instruction insulate the seller from liability?

Outside the field of prescription drugs, which are subject to the rule governing "unavoidably unsafe" products permitting a warning alone, the answer is not entirely clear. The "patent danger" rule that once prevailed in many states implied that a warning was always sufficient, since this rule provided that when the dangers posed by a product were obvious ("patent" rather than "latent") the manufacturer could not be held liable for injuries that resulted. Because many risks are even more obvious when a product carries an express warning about them than when the risks are merely visible, it would seem that under the patent danger rule there should be no design defect liability once an adequate warning has been given. But the patent danger rule has been overruled in many jurisdictions.[9] And a few prominent decisions have implied that a jury may find that certain products are too dangerous to be on the market at all, even when their risks are known and understood. For example, in *O'Brien v. Muskin Corp.*,[10] the court held that it was for a jury to decide whether an above-ground swimming pool that was 3 and 1/2 feet deep was defectively designed because of the risk of injury from diving into it, even when the risk was obvious. Yet above-ground swimming pools inherently pose a risk to those who dive into them.

It is therefore difficult to see *O'Brien* as anything other than a rejection of consumer sovereignty even in the face of adequate information, although the case was quickly overruled by statute. If consumers are permitted to choose Fords lacking rear-seat airbags without Ford's incurring liability for injuries to passengers that would have been prevented by such devices, then why must the makers of above-ground swimming pools pay for injuries that result because their pools have obviously shallow depths and hard bottoms? Nor is the problem solved by saying that the issue is one for the jury and that the obviousness of the risk can be taken into account, since the issue is whether there should ever be liability under these circumstances. Rather, in this area involving the intersection between design defect and warnings law, the tension between consumer sovereignty and the protective goals of tort law that has been present at least since *Winterbottom v. Wright* will not go away. As long as we simultaneously trust and distrust the consumer, trust and distrust the market for safety, trust and distrust design defect liability, the law governing liability for injuries caused by obviously dangerous products will be unsettled.

V. Products Liability Defenses

Most of the defenses to products liability actions are the same defenses available in other negligence and strict liability cases. Contributory or comparative negligence tends to be a defense when the essence of the action is negligence. And assumption of risk is typically available as a defense whether the action is regarded as sounding in negligence or in strict liability.

---

[9] See *Micallef v. Miehle Co.*, 39 N.Y.2d 376, 348 N.E.2d 571, 384 N.Y.S.2d 115 (1976).

[10] 94 N.J. 169, 463 A.2d 298 (1983).

One defense that is distinctive to products liability, however, is product misuse. Suppose that I use a garden rake to boost myself up to a high window sill outside my house, the rake breaks while I am in midair, and I am injured in the fall. In my suit against the rake manufacturer for designing a rake too weak to bear my weight, the manufacturer has a misuse defense, even assuming that I can prove that the rake was defectively manufactured or designed. This misuse defense has become complicated, however, by the development of an exception for injuries caused by a "foreseeable" misuse. The manufacturer remains liable for these misuses. For instance, if I try to use a kitchen knife as a screwdriver and this use causes the knife to splinter into shards that put out my eye, it is probably a jury question whether this is a foreseeable misuse. This exception to the misuse defense can be trumped, however, by the plaintiff's assumption of risk. That is, if the plaintiff knowingly and negligently takes the risk entailed by a foreseeable misuse, the manufacturer is not liable.

Whether all this is described as a matter of available versus unavailable defenses or as proximate versus remote cause does not much matter, as long as what is really at stake remains clear. The question is which party under the circumstances at issue is the best bearer of the cost of the injuries at issue, the plaintiff or the defendant. Liability for foreseeable misuses is best shouldered by the manufacturer or seller; liability for unforeseeeable misuses, and for knowing and negligently encountered foreseeable misuses, is best shouldered by the plaintiff.

VI. Disclaimers, Bystanders, and Consumer Sovereignty

In exploring modern products liability law I have tried to suggest that although it is not be appropriate for consumer sovereignty to be the dominant principle in the field, consumer sovereignty might play a greater role than it does. For example, it is virtually never possible to disclaim liability for injury caused by a defective product—i.e., to contract out of that liability in advance. That possibility died after *Henningsen*, as warranty was displaced by strict liability in tort as the principal basis of liability. The law in this field, however, need not be a slave to conceptualism. Why not permit disclaimers of products liability under circumstances in which the market for safety appears to be functioning properly?

One of the reasons, I think, is distrust of the market's ability to regulate safely effectively. But of course this would not necessarily preclude permitting disclaimers when the market was working effectively. Some products pose one major, salient, danger. Chain saws, for instance, pose such a risk. Some potential purchasers are adept and experienced in the use of chain saws and are therefore willing to risk cutting off their fingers for a lower-priced saw. Others are not. It is certainly possible to imagine a regime in which all the major risks posed by chain saws were disclosed, and purchasers then chose between tort and no-tort options, or between full-compensation and partial-compensation options, for different prices.

The reason such regimes have not developed, however, is that the courts probably do not consider themselves to be in a very good position to decide under what circumstances the market for safety could and could not function with sufficient effectiveness to warrant validating disclaimers of or limitations on tort liability. On this view the near-blanket prohibition on disclaimers in products liability can be seen as a rule fashioned at a very high level of generality. Although the rule is not perfectly accurate in that there are some situations in which disclaimers ought to be permitted, the blanket rule generates considerable savings on transactions costs and yields acceptable accuracy in the majority of cases. The critical question would then be whether there may eventually be enough situations in which permitting disclaimers would be desirable, so that relaxing the blanket prohibition and fashioning an effective method of identifying these situations would make sense.

As we saw from the outset in imagining what a modern regime premised on the *Winterbottom* rule might look like, however, missing from this equation is a factor that makes the whole problem somewhat more complex: the role of bystanders. The argument that consumer sovereignty should play a greater role in determining the scope of products liability is premised on the notion that individual consumers know best for themselves what is the optimal combination of product safety, price, attractiveness and functionality. But by definition a bystander is a party who is not in the chain of product distribution, and therefore has no means of contractually waiving or otherwise limiting her tort rights by agreement with potential defendants in return for a better priced or more attractive product. Even if consumer sovereignty were made dominant and full disclaimers were permitted, it can hardly be imagined that bystanders injured by defective products would be left without a cause of action. Rather, two parallel legal regimes would develop—one for those purchasers whose liabilities were governed by a contractual disclaimer or limitation of liability, and another for others, including bystanders. For this reason, manufacturers of products who effectively disclaimed liability to their purchasers would still face liability to bystanders. It may be that this would in fact be the best arrangement—choice for purchasers, automatic tort protection for bystanders. But perhaps the prospect that moving toward greater consumer sovereignty could never entirely substitute contract for tort, but instead would result in the development of two separate products liability regimes, has also served to preclude more serious consideration of this alternative.

Some confirmation of the accuracy of these explanations is afforded by the state of the law governing liability for "commercial" losses resulting from product defects. Such losses occur when a product defect causes no personal injury or property damage but does cause such economic loss as a decline in the value of the product itself, or lost profits. The courts in such cases generally hold that the plaintiff's claim is governed by contract law, including the law of sales.[11] Thus, although the very sale of the product in question may carry an implied warranty of merchantability, under the law of sales the disclaimer of such a warranty is virtually always valid if the disclaimer does not pertain to liability for personal injury or property damage.

Why are such disclaimers permitted? When only commercial losses are at stake, the factors that influence the courts to stay within the tort-law orbit of mandatory liability are much less likely to be present: distrust of the market is much less pronounced, people's safety is not at stake, and there is hardly any threat to bystanders. Moreover, as in the tort arena, the rule governing the issue also is set at a very high level of generality, although the rule is precisely the opposite of the tort law rule. The courts rarely inquire into the circumstances surrounding the disclaimer of liability. Rather, disclaimers of liability for pure commercial losses are virtually always valid. Given this structure, it is no surprise that the one area where the courts have had trouble developing an entirely consistent set of rules is the case in which a physically-dangerous defect has (luckily) resulted in only commercial loss.

Because this kind of case falls right on the borderline contract and tort, the principles of contract and tort law each exercise sufficient gravitational pull to make the problem difficult for the courts to resolve, and the rule governing the issue has remained uncertain.

---

[11] See, e.g., *East River Steamship Corp. v. Transamerica Delaval, Inc.*, 476 U.S. 858, 106 S.Ct. 295, 90 L.Ed.2d 865 (1986).

10

Damages

When lawyers litigate tort cases, their concern is at least as much with the magnitude of the damages that may be awarded as with the imposition of liability itself. Awarding damages in tort cases performs two functions: achieving corrective justice by compensating the plaintiff for losses resulting from the defendant's tortious act, *and* promoting deterrence by threatening defendants with liability for the costs resulting from their tortious acts. Consequently, the law governing damages in tort cases is unavoidably linked with the purposes underlying the imposition of tort liability themselves. With that linkage in mind, this Chapter examines the basic rules regarding compensatory damage awards; the "collateral source" rule, which affords the plaintiff the right to recover damages even for benefits that have been paid to the plaintiff from her own sources of insurance; damages in cases involving "wrongful death;" and punitive damages.

I. Compensatory Damages

The general rule is that the successful plaintiff is entitled to recover damages to compensate her for the losses proximately resulting from the defendant's tortious act or omission. In a case involving injury to property, those damages are measured by the loss in value of the property or the cost to repair (or replace), whichever is less. In addition, the plaintiff may recover damages for consequential loss, such as diminished profits.

The successful plaintiff in a personal injury case is entitled to recover 1) the "special," or out-of-pocket, losses proximately resulting from the defendant's tortious action and 2) "general" damages for pain and suffering. Out-of-pocket, or tangible, losses in personal injury cases typically consist of health-care expenses and lost wages. In contrast, pain and suffering damages for intangible losses are awarded to compensate the plaintiff for physical and emotional suffering, embarrassment, inconvenience, loss of life's enjoyments, and other similar intangible losses. The ordinary rules governing the burden of proving the elements of the plaintiff's claim apply to proof of damages. The plaintiff must prove by a preponderance of the evidence that she has suffered, or will in the future suffer, the losses for which she claims damages.

Two significant features of this setup are worth exploring in more detail: 1) the principle of a single recovery, and 2) the function of awards for pain and suffering.

A. The Principle of a Single Recovery: Compensation for Both Past and Future Loss

Perhaps the most salient feature of the law governing damages in tort cases is that in the ordinary case the plaintiff gets only a single recovery, providing compensation not only for past but also for future losses, if any. Naturally, this principle of a single recovery has both advantages and disadvantages.

1. Advantages

The great advantage of the principle is that the case does not go on forever. Once there has been a trial and appeals have concluded, there is legal closure. For the plaintiff, the benefit of closure is that she can get on with her life, both psychologically and physically. The more injured and hurting the plaintiff appears to be at trial, the more damages the jury is likely to award. Under the principle of a single recovery, once that recovery is obtained, the legal incentive for the plaintiff to stay sick or injured disappears. The defendant derives enormous benefits from closure as well. The defendant gets repose that is very similar to the effect of the running of a statute of limitations. Once a case has concluded the defendant's financial exposure and vulnerability to the plaintiff have ended. Economic planning can proceed without uncertainty about whether there will be further liability to the plaintiff in the future. Finally, for the legal system, the advantage of a single recovery is the avoidance of multiple judicial proceedings and their consequent administrative cost.

2. Disadvantages

There can be no doubt, however, that there are disadvantages to the principle of a single recovery. One is that there is almost certainly less accuracy in estimating future damages than there would be if determinations were made periodically as losses were incurred. Predicting how injured (if at all) the plaintiff will be in the future, and then calculating the amount of medical expenses, lost wages, and pain and suffering that will result from the plaintiff's injuries is bound to be an exercise in informed estimation at best. If awards were made periodically as losses were incurred, surely greater accuracy could be achieved. A second disadvantage is that the plaintiff must be a good investor or she will not have the award when she needs it in the future. This need for investment of awards for future losses is underscored by the practice of discounting awards to present value.

3. Discounting Awards to Present Value

The principle of a single recovery requires the jury to "discount to present value" awards made for future losses by awarding less than the absolute dollar amount of those losses. The reason for this requirement is the "time" value of money that is invested today for future needs. For example, if the plaintiff is injured today and will continue for the next ten years to incur medical expenses and suffer physical pain from that injury, making an accurate award for her future losses requires two steps. First, the jury must determine what medical expenses the plaintiff will incur and how much physical pain she will suffer in each future year, and place a dollar value on those losses. One way to do this is to assume that there will be no inflation in the future. Another approach, which requires even more speculation about what the future will bring, is to estimate what effect future inflation will have on such items of loss as medical expenses and wages, and then to take this inflation into account in predicting the dollar value of the plaintiff's future losses.

Either way, a second step is required. Because the function of an award of damages is to compensate the plaintiff for her losses *and no more*, then an award today of the full amount that the plaintiff will lose in the future will constitute overcompensation. If invested today that sum will earn interest or otherwise appreciate in value. By the time the losses for which the damages intended to compensate the plaintiff are actually incurred, the plaintiff will have a sum greater than the amount of those losses. The amount of a future loss must therefore be discounted to present value—i.e., reduced to a sum which, if invested, will equal the amount of the future loss at the time it occurs.

This is a mathematical exercise which can easily be accomplished using "present value" tables. But to use a present-value table one must determine what "discount" rate to use. The discount rate is simply the reverse of an assumption about what rate of interest the plaintiff's damages award will earn while it is invested by the plaintiff. If the amount of the award was arrived at on the supposition that there will be no inflation in the future, then a "pure" rate of interest (one which ignores the possibility of inflation) will be used to determine the appropriate discount rate. But if the award assumed that there would be inflation, then an inflation-adjusted interest rate will have to be used to determine the discount rate.[1]

These seeming technicalities have two important implications. First, unless a jurisdiction has adopted uniform rules regarding the appropriate discount rate to be employed in determining the present value of an award, then any case involving potentially substantial future losses is likely to involve testimony by experts about future inflation and the appropriate discount rate. This has always seemed to me to be an unnecessary as well as an unfortunate exercise, since the result is that different juries will make different findings about how much inflation there will be in the future or, what is equally speculative, what the market rate of interest would be in the future if there were no inflation. It would make a lot more sense to have a uniform discount rate, promulgated annually by rule of court or otherwise arrived at.

Second, as I noted in discussing the disadvantages of the principle of a single recovery, for the theory underlying the principle of a single recovery to work in practice, the plaintiff must be at least an average investor. The discounting of damage awards to present value assumes that the portion of a single recovery awarded for future losses will appreciate over time through investment. If that appreciation does not occur as assumed by the discount rate used, then the plaintiff will ultimately find herself without sufficient funds to compensate her for losses when they are incurred, and a major purpose of the law of tort damages will not be served.

B. Pain and Suffering Awards

1. The Functions of the Award

Awards for pain and suffering perform a number of functions. First, in the case of serious injuries, few people would think that providing compensation for out-of-pocket loss alone could ever make the plaintiff "whole." Money paid for pain and suffering may not remove

---

[1] See *O'Shea v. Riverway Towing Co.*, 677 F.2d 1194 (7th Cir. 1982).

that loss, but it does acknowledge rather than ignore the plaintiff's intangible losses.[2] Second, even if the plaintiff's pain and suffering cannot ever be fully compensated for with money, the plaintiff may be able to use an award to provide activities or enjoyments that substitute for those lost as a result of the injury in question. For instance, if the plaintiff no longer can play soccer because of paralysis, he might use the money from an award of general damages to purchase a satellite dish that will bring televised soccer from around the world into his home, or the plaintiff might use the award to take up an entirely new hobby.

Third, regardless of whether money can compensate in any way at all for pain and suffering, there can be little question that pain and suffering is one of the consequences with respect to which the law aims to achieve optimal deterrence when it threatens potential defendants with tort liability. That is, even if there were no benefit obtained from paying pain and suffering awards to victims, it would make sense to hold injurers liable for these damages. From the standpoint of optimal deterrence it really does not matter whether the defendant pays these damages to the plaintiff, or to a charitable foundation instead, or the amount of pain and suffering damages the defendant is required to pay is put in a bucket and burned in the courtroom. What matters is that the defendant have to pay the money. The requirement of payment assures that other potential injurers are threatened with liability not only for out-of-pocket, but also for pain and suffering damages. And this threat promotes optimal deterrence by encouraging potential defendants to take into account the cost of the pain and suffering that their activities may cause in deciding what safety precautions are worth taking.

Admittedly, in certain contexts this deterrence argument is less persuasive than in others. For example, whenever potential plaintiffs are in a direct or indirect contractual relationship with potential injurers—in fields such as medical malpractice or products liability—the right to bring a tort action can be understood as insurance for which potential plaintiffs pay in advance through increased medical expenses or product costs. Strong arguments have been made and contested in the literature about whether rational purchasers of medical services and products would want to pay for insurance against pain and suffering. If they would not, some commentators argue, then pain and suffering

---

[2] See Margaret Jane Radin, *Compensation and Commensurability*, 43 Duke L.J. 56 (1993).

awards should not be made at all.[3] Other commentators have suggested that it is rational to want to purchase pain and suffering insurance.[4] This issue remains contested. But as long as we have a general law of damages rather than damages rules applying separately to malpractice and products liability—and as long as tort law is conceived as more than a mere "insurance" system—the deterrence arguments for awarding pain and suffering damages seem highly likely to prevail.

The last argument in favor of awarding pain and suffering damages is practical in the extreme. Attorneys representing plaintiffs in personal injury cases virtually always work on a contingent-fee basis: if the plaintiff loses, she owes the attorney nothing except expenses, and sometimes not even that; but if the plaintiff succeeds, the attorney receives a percentage of the plaintiff's award, sometimes as much as 40 percent. Given the prevalence of this type of contingent-fee arrangement, even a plaintiff fully compensated by a jury for her out-of-pocket expenses would receive less than full compensation after she paid a percentage of this award to her attorney. Among other things, therefore, the award of damages for pain and suffering provides the plaintiff a sum out of which to compensate her attorney. It might be a lot more sensible to treat the plaintiff's counsel fees as another item of compensable out-of-pocket expenses rather than using pain and suffering awards as an under-the-table method of paying counsel fees. But as things now stand, juries almost universally understand how counsel fees really are paid and take this into account in making pain and suffering awards.

2. Limitations on Awards

Notwithstanding these justifications for awarding pain and suffering damages, it does not necessarily follow that awards of such damages should always be unlimited. The major criticism of awarding pain and suffering damages is that, because assessment of the value of pain and suffering is so subjective, valuations vary enormously from jury to jury. Predicting the amount of an award is therefore difficult. Critics argue that this unpredictability creates uncertainty on the part of poten-

---

[3] See, e.g., Alan Schwartz, *Proposals for Products Liability Reform: A Theoretical Synthesis*, 97 Yale L.J. 353 (1988).

[4] See, e.g., Steven P. Croley and Jon D. Hanson, *The Nonpecuniary Costs of Accidents: Pain-and-Suffering Damages in Tort Law*, 108 Harv. L. Rev. 1785 (1995).

tial defendants that results in overdeterrence and in the consequent reluctance of certain enterprises, such as pharmaceutical companies, to develop legally risky product lines at all.

In theory, most of the functions of pain and suffering awards can be well-served even when subject to certain kinds of limits on what can be awarded for pain and suffering. The traditional approach to the problem of variability in award levels has been to permit courts to restrict awards through the practice of *remittitur*. Under this practice, when a jury award is in excess of what a reasonable jury could award in light of all the evidence, the trial court affords the plaintiff a choice between a new trial and acceptance of a specified reduction in the award. A similar practice known as *additur* is available when the award is unduly low. But this is an *ad hoc* approach that many courts are in any event reluctant to apply except in the most egregious cases of jury error.

The problem posed for those who would favor a more systematic effort to make pain and suffering awards predictable, however, is to develop standards of limitation that are both fair *and* workable. It is easy enough to satisfy one of these criteria at a time, but very hard to fashion an approach that can satisfy both simultaneously. For example, a number of states have placed absolute dollar ceilings on the amount that may be awarded for pain and suffering—typically in the neighborhood of $250,000. Ceilings make the average size of awards much more predictable, since no award can exceed the ceiling. But ceilings accomplish this aim at the cost of possible unfairness to the most seriously injured victims—those whose pain and suffering a jury would value at more than the ceiling if this were permissible. Disproportionately these are young, seriously injured victims, since these victims have life expectancies and injuries that are most likely to involve long-term, severe pain and suffering. Ceilings therefore exact much of the sacrifice necessary to achieve predictability from those who are young and seriously injured. Conversely, anyone whose pain and suffering the jury values at less than the ceiling makes no sacrifice at all and receives compensation for 100 percent of his or her pain and suffering.

The alternative would be to exact some sacrifice from all categories of victim, regardless of how modest their pain and suffering, through a "schedule" of pain and suffering awards.[5] This approach

---

[5] See Randall R Bovbjerg et al., *Valuing Life and Limb in Tort: Scheduling "Pain and Suffering,"* 83 Nw. U. L.Rev. 909 (1989).

would be more fair than dollar ceilings, but less workable. To make this approach work, it would be necessary to construct a schedule of permissible pain and suffering damages calibrated to the age and severity of injury suffered by each victim: a certain amount for death at a given age, a certain amount for paralysis at a given age, a certain amount for loss of an arm at a given age, and so forth. Then the jury in every case would be required to determine in what category in the schedule the plaintiff's injuries fell. The damages awardable by category might be mandatory, or they could serve merely as guidance for the jury. This approach would be cumbersome, though it could eventually work effectively. Workers compensation awards for specified permanent disabilities work in roughly this way. But certainly the creation of a pain and suffering damages schedule of this sort cannot be accomplished through judicial action. Legislative action would be required. This approach, however, has seemed much less attractive to legislatures than the enactment of absolute ceilings on pain and suffering recoveries that ignore the problem of equity among victims. Consequently, many states still operate with only *remittitur* and *additur* to control damage awards, while others have absolute ceilings on the sums that can be awarded for pain and suffering.

II. Collateral Sources and Benefits

The traditional collateral source rule provides that evidence of payments made or to be made to the plaintiff by "collateral" sources such as insurance is not admissible in the plaintiff's tort action against the defendant. The result is that the plaintiff is entitled to recover damages from the defendant that have already been paid by the plaintiff's own insurer. The modern economy is chocked full of insurance, both private and public. Plaintiffs are often insured for all or part of their losses, by health, disability, fire, and other forms of insurance. Whether the payment of collateral benefits to the plaintiff is taken into account in setting damage awards can make a substantial difference in the amount of an award. The treatment of the benefits paid to plaintiffs by these and similar sources of compensation that are collateral to any tort recovery is therefore of considerable importance in any tort case.

A. *The "Prudence" Issue*

The traditional argument for the collateral source rule is that the plaintiff who has invested in insurance coverage should not be penalized for his prudence in doing so. There is something to this argument, but less than there seems to be at first glance. The plaintiff who has purchased insurance would not be "penalized" if insurance benefits were taken into account in setting damages, any more than a plaintiff who invested in a sprinkler system is "penalized" when his recovery for a negligently-started fire is lower than it would be if the sprinkler system had not prevented some of the damage to his property. Rather, the plaintiff's own action has mitigated the amount of the loss he actually has suffered. After all, the defendant must suffer the disadvantage of injuring an unusually vulnerable plaintiff and must "take his victim as he finds him" when the victim has a thin skull. Why not also permit the defendant the advantage of injuring an economically "strong" victim—i.e., one who has insurance? If there were a need to avoid "penalizing" the plaintiff for his prudence in purchasing insurance, the way to do that would be to reimburse the plaintiff for the insurance premium he had spent unnecessarily, rather than permitting him a recovery for a monetary loss he did not suffer.

Moreover, health, disability, and fire insurance cover losses however caused, and therefore insure against far more than losses caused by a third-party's tortious act. What the plaintiff in a tort action paid his insurance premiums for he did substantially receive—broad insurance protection against medical expenses, lost wages, or fire losses. Offsetting a damage award by the amount of benefits paid to the plaintiff by any of these sources of insurance would "deprive" him of only a small portion of the insurance he had purchased. Finally, vast amounts of insurance covering potential victims is not purchased voluntarily through an individual's prudence, but is provided automatically as a fringe benefit of employment or by government entitlement programs such as veteran's benefits or Medicare. It is much harder to see how the "reward for prudence" argument has any bearing on whether the plaintiff should get the benefit of payments made by this very large category of collateral sources.

B. The "Double Recovery" Issue

One of the most common arguments made against the collateral source rule is that it permits the plaintiff to recover twice—once from his insurer and then a second time from the plaintiff. Such duplication of payment, the argument goes, violates the principle underlying all of damages law—that compensation should as nearly as possible make the plaintiff whole, but that the plaintiff should not obtain a net financial gain as a result of a tort recovery. Like the "reward for prudence" argument in favor of the collateral source rule, this argument also is

215

less strong than it first appears to be. First, as I noted at the very outset of this Chapter, there are dual purposes underlying the law of damages: corrective justice through compensation *and* optimal deterrence. Even when corrective justice does not support the collateral source rule, the desirability of promoting deterrence may do so. The expenses incurred as a result of the plaintiff's injury are real costs even if they are incurred, for example, by his health insurer rather than by the plaintiff himself. If the collateral source rule did not permit recovery of these expenses, then defendants would no longer be threatened with liability for them, and deterrence would be sub-optimal. So there is a tension between the desirability of avoiding overcompensation and the desirability of optimally deterring potential injurers. The collateral source rule resolves that tension in favor of optimal deterrence, even if this means occasional overcompensation.

A second reason that the double recovery argument is less strong than it may appear to be involves the contingent-fee system. Since the plaintiff must pay his attorney out of his award, even if the collateral source rule did permit "gross" overcompensation, probably it does not often result in "net" overcompensation after payment of a percentage of the total award to the plaintiff's attorney. This may not be the most sensible way to help to assure the plaintiff a means of paying counsel fees, but because the collateral source rule is already in place, the contingent-fee system that has grown up around it should influence the decision whether to retain the rule.

C. The Subrogation Issue

Both the prudence and double recovery arguments regarding the collateral source rule presuppose that the plaintiff keeps whatever "excess" payment results from the rule. Proponents of the rule therefore attempt to justify double recovery and opponents attack double recovery. But in fact the double-recovery issue is largely, though not entirely, a red-herring. There is a third alternative that much more accurately describes what actually happens in practice: The plaintiff gets a judgment that includes a double recovery of that portion of his losses that are already insured, but then reimburses his insurance company out of the judgment for the amount of the benefits paid by the company. Under this alternative, both of the purposes of the law of damages are achieved. The plaintiff is fully but not overcompensated, yet the defendant is held liable for the full amount of the costs resulting from his tortious act.

This all takes place through the legal device known as "subrogation." Subrogation occurs under the terms of the insurance contract between the plaintiff and his insurer. The insurer with a right of subrogation steps into the shoes of the plaintiff (is "subrogated to" the plaintiff's rights) to the extent of payment made by the insurer to the plaintiff. Thus, whatever rights the plaintiff has against the defendant, to the extent of its payment, the plaintiff's insurer has those rights also. The plaintiff's insurer therefore has the right to sue the defendant for negligence and to recover the amount of payments the insurer has made to the plaintiff. But this suit is usually unnecessary, since the plaintiff is already suing the defendant. So the insurer's rights of subrogation are translated into a right to be reimbursed (in insurance language, "indemnified") for the amount of payment out of the plaintiff's tort recovery. And by virtue of the collateral source rule, that tort recovery will be for all the losses incurred as result of the defendant's act, including those paid by the insurer. After reimbursing the insurer, the plaintiff keeps what he lost, the insurer receives what it had paid, and the defendant ends up paying the full amount of the losses he caused.

The fact that subrogation is available in this way certainly adds strength to the case for retaining the collateral source rule. Unfortunately, however, subrogation reimbursements paid to plaintiffs' insurance companies are not systematic. One reason is that it may take considerable effort to secure such reimbursement. Insurance benefits typically are paid long before any tort recovery is obtained. For example, a health insurer normally pays hospitals and physicians treating injuries within months of billing. But the patient may not obtain a tort recovery or settlement until years later. To secure reimbursement out of that subsequent tort recovery, the insurer must first have identified the portion of its many claim payments that are potentially reimbursable—i.e., those in which the patient's injury may have been caused by tortious action. The insurer must then determine whether the plaintiff later brought suit to recover these losses from a third party. Then the insurer must monitor the course of this legal action. Finally, the insurer must make known to the parties to the suit its putative right to reimbursement and then seek to vindicate that right before a judgment or settlement is paid, or at least before the plaintiff disburses or sequesters the award. Making this effort is likely to be worthwhile for insurers only in cases involving payment of very substantial health or disability insurance benefits.

A second reason that subrogation reimbursements are less than systematic results from the fact that most tort payments are the product of settlements, not judgments. Almost by definition, settlements are for less than the full amount of the plaintiff's damages. As a consequence, the portion of any settlement that should be paid to an insurer in reimbursement of already-paid benefits is contested. Paying the insurer the full amount of these prior payments off the top of any settlement would deprive the plaintiff of compensation; yet computing what fraction of prior payments should be reimbursed requires some formula that would specify the portion of the plaintiffs' total losses that the amount paid in settlement constituted. For example, if we knew that the plaintiff's total losses were $100,000 and he settled for $60,000, then the settlement would be for 60 percent of his losses. It would therefore make sense to reimburse the plaintiff's health insurer for 60 percent of its prior benefit payments. But this $100,000 valuation of the plaintiff's total losses is not available when there has been a settlement: litigating the total amount of the plaintiff's losses is precisely what the settlement was designed to avoid. So there is a dilemma about how to divide the settlement. In some states fairly firm rules have emerged to guide the division of settlements in order resolve this dilemma. But in many states the rules are underdeveloped and the entire process is more a matter of lore than law. The result is unsystematic reimbursement of collateral sources. Thus, whereas subrogation reimbursement can prevent double recovery by the plaintiff even while the defendant pays the full amount of the losses it caused, sometimes such reimbursement of past payments occurs and sometimes it does not.

As to future payments of insurance benefits the issue is even more cloudy. Suppose that the plaintiff secures a large judgment under a general verdict for both past and future losses, and then reimburses his health insurer in full for prior payments. But then the plaintiff continues to incur medical expenses resulting from his earlier, tortiously caused injuries. Presumably part of the judgment has compensated him for these losses. In theory his insurer health insurer should not have to pay these medical expenses. But in practice the insurance does pay, because ordinarily the plaintiff has secured a general verdict that does not indicate what sum has been paid for future medical expenses. At least with respect to that portion of any judgment compensating the plaintiff for future losses that turn out also to be covered by collateral sources, then, there often is double recovery. In short, as to both past and future benefits paid by collateral sources, the collateral source rule achieves only mixed success at simultaneously securing the proper level of compensation for plaintiffs while optimally deterring potential defendants.

As a result of pressure from defendant's interest groups, over the past few decades a number of state legislatures have reexamined the collateral source rule. Finding the rule unsatisfactory, over a dozen have enacted statutes that either partially or completely eliminate the rule. The operation of these statutes varies. Some direct that there be a reduction in the plaintiff's award equal to collateral benefits paid in the past or payable to the plaintiff in the future; others merely make evidence of such payments admissible. Some make exceptions in cases in which the insurer paying prior benefits to the plaintiff has a right of subrogation—thus acknowledging that in some sense the purpose of the statutes is to prevent double recovery only when that is a real threat. But other statutes draw no such distinction and apply more generally.

The great problem that is faced in implementing these statutes arises in cases involving substantial future losses. To be faithful to the purpose behind the statutes, the plaintiff's recovery of damages for future losses should be reduced by the amount of the collateral benefits that more probably than not will be paid to the plaintiff in the future. But determining the amount of such future benefit payments to the plaintiff requires predicting what sources of insurance, public and private, the plaintiff will have in the future, sometimes the distant future. The more serious and long-term the plaintiff's injuries are, the more speculative the entire exercise is likely to be, and the less likely it is that there will be any substantial offset of future losses by the amount of estimated future collateral benefits.

III. Damages in Wrongful Death and Survival Actions

At common law a plaintiff's cause of action died with him. But in the nineteenth century, statutes enacted in both England and the United States altered this rule. The law governing recovery in death cases is in the first instance still a creature of statute. There are two general classes of statutes, with variations within each. By far the most important are *wrongful death* statutes, which create a new cause of action on the part of those who survive the decedent. In contrast, *survival* statutes preserve the deceased's cause of action.

A. *Wrongful Death Actions*

Typically a wrongful death statute provides that upon the death of an individual caused by the wrongful act of another, the person or entity "that would have been liable had death not ensued" continues to be liable. Although this phrasing implies that the decedent's cause of action survives, in fact it does not. Statutory treatment of three issues makes this clear.

1. Beneficiaries

Wrongful death statutes provide that recovery is for the benefit of designated individuals. Typically these are the "heirs at law" of the decedent—those who would by statute inherit his estate if he died "intestate," that is, without a Will. Such statutes of "descent and distribution" direct, for example, that the estate of an intestate go to a surviving spouse, or half to the spouse and half to surviving children, or if there is no surviving spouse in equal shares to surviving children, and so forth. The exact terms of the statutes vary from state to state. Under wrongful death statutes these statutorily designated "heirs at law" are the beneficiaries of the wrongful death cause of action even if the decedent did have a Will leaving his estate to others.

2. The Measure of Damages

A beneficiary's recovery is measured by the losses she suffers as a result of the decedent's death. In the past these were limited to out-of-pocket, economic losses that would have been paid in support of the beneficiary, and there were statutory ceilings on the dollar amount that could be recovered in a wrongful death action. Both these limitations are a thing of the past in most states. Damages for emotional loss are recoverable, usually in unlimited amounts. Thus, if the beneficiaries are the parents of a deceased ten year old their recovery is likely to be substantial, whereas when the beneficiary is an estranged, adult child who is the only living relative of a deceased parent his recovery will be small. Regardless, the principle that what is recovered is measured by the *beneficiary's losses* makes clear that, for all practical purposes, the cause of action is the beneficiary's and not the decedent's.

3. Defenses

Because a cause of action exists only if the deceased would have had one had death not ensued, the defendant can invoke any defense it would have had against the decedent. But most courts also hold that defenses that would be available against the beneficiary in an ordinary action also are available in wrongful death action. Thus, if the decedent was negligent then the recovery is reduced in accord with the applicable comparative negligence statute. But even if the deceased was not negligent, if the beneficiary was negligent, then the contributory or comparative negligence of the beneficiary is available as a defense in the beneficiary's action. Once again, this setup makes it clear that for most practical purposes, even if not for all, the cause of action is the beneficiary's.

B. Survival Actions

All states have enacted statutes that preserve a cause of action for losses suffered by a decedent before he died. Thus, if before he died the decedent incurred medical expenses or experienced pain and suffering as a result of the defendant's tort, by statute damages for these losses are recoverable in an action by his estate, and pass through his estate to those entitled to inherit it. These are one form of "survival" statute.

A number of states have gone further, however, and have provided by statute for a cause of action to recover economic losses that are incurred as a result of the decedent's death. Typically the measure of these losses is the amount that would have been in the decedent's estate had he or she lived a full life expectancy. To make this computation a jury must predict the decedent's gross future earnings, and then subtract all payments and expenditures that he would have made in his lifetime, including support that he would have provided to his family, but also any money he would have spent on himself. This cause of action also is for the benefit of the decedent's estate and any recovery passes through the estate, to whomever is entitled to inherit. Entirely depending on the decedent's Will if he has one, this may be a surviving spouse, children, or anyone else. In the absence of a Will, this recovery will pass with the rest of his estate to his heirs at law under the applicable statute of descent and distribution.

C. The Underdeterrence Problem

Any state that has enacted only a wrongful death or only a survival statute has a potential underdeterrence problem. A wrongful death statute imposes liability only for losses suffered by those who survive a decedent; there is no liability imposed for sums that would have been in the decedent's estate when he died a natural death. Conversely, a survival statute imposes liability only for sums that would have been in the decedent's estate when he died a natural death; there is no liability for losses suffered by those who survive a decedent. Some states, partly for this reason and partly out of solicitude for survivors, have enacted both types of statutes.

Notice, however, that even states that have enacted both types of statutes still face a potential deterrence gap, though a smaller one. Even both statutes together impose liability on the defendant only for the losses of the decedent's heirs at law and for everything that would have remained in the decedent's estate had he lived a full life expectancy. Neither statute imposes liability for the losses of any other person for whom the defendant would have provided support, or for the sums the decedent would have earned and spent on himself during his lifetime. Partly for this reason, the grotesque adage that a defendant is better off killing than badly maiming a victim tends to remain true, even in states that have enacted both types of statutes. Since dangerous behavior is just as likely to result in serious injury as in death, however, this apparent gap in the amount of deterrence created by the law governing recovery of damages in death cases may be more theoretical than real. Nonetheless, it is worth noting that despite all the apparent concern of modern tort law with deterrence in personal injury cases, the law governing the damages that are recoverable in the most serious of all such cases—those involving death—is at least theoretically flawed as a means of deterring wrongful conduct.

IV. Punitive Damages

In exceptional cases the plaintiff is entitled not only to recover compensatory damages, but also to an award of damages designed to punish the defendant. These are known as "punitive" or "exemplary" damages. The states vary in their descriptions of the behavior that warrants an award of punitive damages, but almost always behavior more blameworthy even than gross negligence is necessary. In addition to punishment, punitive damages often are said to be designed to deter extremely blameworthy behavior. Presumably the defendant who has acted with something approaching knowledge that his behavior was highly likely to cause harm has been insufficiently deterred by the threat of liability for compensatory damages. This might be because the defendant knows that potential plaintiffs face difficulty in proving causation and therefore does not expect them to sue, because the defendant wishes to harm the plaintiff and is willing to pay compensatory damages to be able to do so, or simply because the defendant has been paying insufficient attention to the threat of liability for compensatory damages. The threat of liability for punitive damages in such cases puts a thumb on the scale, so to speak, in an effort to alter the defendant's risk-benefit calculations and get his attention.

The controversy over the unpredictability of pain and suffering awards has been paralleled in recent years by criticism of punitive damage awards on the same ground. In an effort to respond to this criticism, a number of the state statutes that have placed ceilings on awards of pain and suffering damages apply to punitive damages as well. In addition, in recent years the United States Supreme Court has reviewed punitive damages awards in a variety of cases in response to defendants' claims that excessive awards violate the Constitutional requirement of due process of law. Unfortunately, clear standards have not emerged from the Court's decisions in these cases. Factors to be considered appear, among other things, to include the proportion between the amount of harm the defendant caused or might have caused and the amount of the punitive damages award, as well as the relation between the blameworthiness of the defendant's behavior and the amount of the award.[6] But based on the decisions rendered thus far, the Constitutional restrictions on awards of punitive damages are very loose. Few plaintiffs will be affected by these restrictions, and few defendants will be protected by them.

---

[6] See, e.g., *BMW of North America v. Gore*, ___ U.S. ___, 116 S.Ct. 1589, 134 L.Ed.2d 809 (1996).

11

Limited Duty

"**D**uty" is a largely question-begging concept that can be safely used if one is not misled by it. To support a cause of action in tort, of course, there must be proof of duty, breach of duty, damages and causation. In the ordinary negligence case the defendant is alleged to have had and to have breached the duty to exercise reasonable care. Asking whether the defendant had a duty to the plaintiff and whether that duty was breached is therefore just another way of asking whether the defendant was negligent, and whether that negligence was a proximate cause of the plaintiff's harm. Analyzing the problem in terms of duty adds nothing, and could lead to the mistaken conclusion that even after the negligence and proximate cause questions have been answered, there is still no liability unless the defendant owed the plaintiff a duty independent of the obligation to exercise reasonable care. In the ordinary case this conclusion is mistaken, because the defendant's negligence is precisely the breach of duty that is alleged.

There is a class of cases, however, in which the defendant is not liable for negligence. This class of cases can accurately be described as involving "limited duty," in the sense that because the defendant is not liable for harm caused by his negligence, he owes no duty to exercise reasonable care to avoid injuring the plaintiff. This Chapter analyzes four classes of cases that traditionally involve limited duty, as well as their exceptions: rescue situations; the obligations of owners and occupiers of land to those who enter on the land; "pure" emotional loss; and "pure" economic loss.

I. Rescue

The traditional rule, still almost universally in force, is that in the absence of special circumstances or a special relationship, one person has no duty to rescue another person from a position of danger. This rule holds even if the risk to the defendant is small or non-existent, and the danger to the plaintiff is great. I have no duty to rescue a drowning person, even if I need not enter the water to do so, but could throw him a life preserver or extend a nearby pole to help him.

It is easy enough to explain this rule, though often it is very hard to stomach the rule. As a matter of principle, the common law cares enough about individual liberty that typically it does not ask people to do more than mind their own business. And as a practical matter, it would not be easy to develop rules about *who* would be liable when more than one individual could have accomplished a rescue but no one did. These considerations have led the law of torts to bite the bullet, so to speak, and to continue to decline to impose a duty to rescue even in the pure one-stranger to one-stranger rescue situation in which there would be no question as to which party might have accomplished a rescue. Most courts see tort law's maintenance of this no-duty stance in one-stranger to one-stranger cases as a defense against stepping onto a slippery slope of permitting liability for the failure to rescue to be imposed under a reasonable-behavior-under-all-the-circumstances standard, although permitting recovery in this kind of case alone would be very appealing.

Over time, however, recovery has been permitted in a whole series of cases that involve special circumstances or a special relationship between the party in danger and the party who might have rescued him. These are precisely the cases in which the parties' relationship is not stranger-to-stranger. First, a defendant who has negligently placed the plaintiff in a position of danger may be held liable for negligently failing to rescue him from that danger. Here the distinction is drawn between mere failure to rescue the plaintiff—so-called "nonfeasance"—for which liability ordinarily is not imposed, and negligently placing the plaintiff in danger to begin with—"misfeasance"—which may give rise to liability for negligent failure to rescue.

Second, landlords, universities, shopping centers and other such proprietors of property have on occasion been held liable in negligence for harm foreseeably suffered by tenants, students, or customers because of the misconduct of third parties. The classic case on this issue is *Kline v. 1500 Massachusetts Avenue Apartment Corp.*,[1] in which the defendant landlord was held liable in negligence for injuries suffered by a tenant who was assaulted in the hallway of the defendant's apartment house. In these cases two factors are necessary prerequisites to

---

[1] 439 F.2d 477 (D.C. Cir. 1970).

recovery: a pre-existing relationship between the plaintiff and defendant, and circumstances that put the defendant on notice of the risk of harm to the plaintiff from third parties. Then the question is whether the risk is sufficiently probable, the potential harm sufficiently great, and the cost of reducing that risk sufficiently small, to render the defendant negligent for having failed to "rescue" the plaintiff by taking precautions that would have avoided the harm: installing better locks, providing emergency telephones, using better lighting, etc.

Finally, in rare cases, professionals such as psychiatrists have been held liable in negligence to persons injured by their patients after the patient has communicated to the psychiatrist an intention to cause such harm to the third person. The seminal case on the issue is *Tarasoff v. Regents of University of California.*[2] *Tarasoff* has come in for much criticism, not only for the obvious reason that the psychiatrist there (and in most similar cases) had no relationship whatsoever with the victim, but also because the threat of liability in such cases forces the therapist to choose between his professional obligation to keep his patients' confidences and the legally-created duty to the third party. But the rule in *Tarasoff* is rarely invoked, and in any event appears to be limited to cases involving a specifically identified third party.

II. Owners and Occupiers of Land

The law in this field always begins with the tripartite classification of entrants onto the land of others: invitees, licensees, and trespassers. Owners and occupiers of land (simply called "owners" hereafter) owe a duty to exercise reasonable care to those whom they invite onto their property. Such invitees include anyone on the property for business purposes, i.e., for the benefit of the owner. Somewhat surprisingly, not everyone who is "invited" qualifies as an invitee to whom a duty of reasonable care is owed. Rather, in most states people who are social guests, though of course they have been invited onto the property, are classified as "licensees." Owners and occupiers owe such licensees a lesser duty of care. The courts say that for a licensee the owner must make the premises as safe as he makes them for himself. What this boils down to is that the owner must warn the licensee of hidden dangerous conditions, but need not eliminate these conditions. Finally, to trespassers—those who enter property without express or implied

---

[2] 17 Cal.3d 425, 551 P.2d 334, 131 Cal.Rptr. 14 (1976).

permission—the owner owes only a duty to refrain from wantonly and wilfully injuring them, e.g., by setting hidden traps that will injure trespassers.

Over time some exceptions to these rules developed. For instance, in many states owners owe "discovered trespassers" reasonable care. And the doctrine of "attractive nuisance" has created a qualified but well-recognized exception for actually foreseen (as opposed to merely foreseeable) child trespassers who trespass because of some particularly "attractive" dangerous condition maintained by the owner, such as a railroad turntable or ferris wheel, especially when the danger the condition poses can be eliminated at a comparatively low cost. To these children the owner owes reasonable care. But these are limited exceptions to what are otherwise fairly rigid, categorical rules.

Notice the effects of this rigidness. The rules governing the duties of owners and the correlative rights of entrants are established at a high level of generality. Whenever it is clear what category an entry falls into—and often that will not be in dispute—the scope of the duty owed to that entrant is also clear. This makes for comparatively high predictability of outcome and comparatively low adjudication costs. This efficiency is tolerable, indeed desirable, as long as the tripartite set of duties to the different entrants onto land reflects widespread agreement about the proper rights of these entrants and the proper obligations of owners. Under such circumstances commonly-held norms and the rigid categories coincide. But as that agreement breaks down, then rules about these rights and duties set at a high level of generality are seen often to produce inaccurate or undesirable outcomes.

Until about thirty years ago, the tripartite categorization of entrants onto land, and the distinctions among duties owed to them, remained largely intact. But then some courts began to find this categorization unacceptable. The first and still one of the most far-reaching decisions was the Supreme Court of California's wholesale rejection of the categories in *Rowland v. Christian*.[3] In place of the categories, the court determined that a series of factors should be taken into account in determining the scope of the defendant's duty, including the foreseeability of harm, the closeness of the connection between the defendant's conduct and the plaintiff's harm, and the moral blame attached to the plaintiff's conduct. The court reasoned that because there is not necessarily a connection between these and other relevant factors and

---

[3] 69 Cal.2d 108, 443 P.2d 561, 70 Cal.Rptr. 97 (1968).

the classifications of trespasser, licensee, and invitee, the classifications should be rejected in favor of a reasonable-conduct-under-all-the-circumstances test. The entrant's status could still be taken into account in applying this test, but that status could no longer be determinative. In the decade or so that followed over a dozen other courts followed this approach, either completely abolishing the categories, or abolishing the distinction between invitees and licenses even while preserving the separate, lower duty of care to trespassers.

But wholesale change has not occurred. Most courts have chosen to retain the traditional tripartite categorization and the rules that go with it. The main reason, I think, is not that the courts in the remaining, majority of states still consider the old categories to be entirely satisfactory. On the contrary, I believe that most courts understand the inaccuracy and unfairness that can result in occasional cases from rigid reliance on the categories. These flaws can be mitigated to some extent, though certainly not entirely eliminated, by flexible application of the exceptions to the categories that already exist, such as the higher duty of care to discovered trespassers and the attractive nuisance doctrine. But the majority of courts also seem to have recognized that a wholesale shift to a duty of reasonable care under all the circumstances would make results in owner-and-occupier liability cases much less certain. The amount of care expected would vary radically from jury to jury, and prediction of outcomes would be much more difficult. These courts have chosen not to incur these costs.

The ideal solution would be rules set at an "intermediate" level of generality that were less rigid than the tripartite categorization, but still drew sufficiently bright lines to render duties clear and outcomes reasonably predictable. For a few courts the trespasser/non-trespasser distinction has served this function, but only for a few. Apparently for most courts, no such intermediate rule has seemed suitable. As a consequence, the courts have had to choose between retaining the tripartite categorization largely in tact, and rejecting the classification almost entirely. Since neither approach is wholly satisfactory, it is no surprise that the states differ as to the proper choice, and that the law is now divided in this field into the majority of states that still accept the traditional approach and the minority that do not.

III. "Pure" Emotional Loss

The appeal of rules set at an intermediate level of generality as a substitute for highly categorical rules is nowhere more evident than in the development of the cause of action for negligently-caused emotional loss. To understand what is and is not at stake here, remember that there is a separate cause of action for *intentional* infliction of emotional distress (see Chapter Two), and that the right to recover for emotional loss that results from negligently-caused physical injury—pain and suffering—is of course well-recognized (see Chapter Ten). In contrast, the issue here is whether there is a cause of action in negligence for "pure" emotional loss—i.e., emotional loss that is not the result of negligently-caused physical injury.

Interestingly, many of the cases involve women who suffer emotional loss because of fear for the personal safety of their husbands or children. Some commentators have therefore viewed this body of law as being anti-feminist, since the rules long placed significant limits on the right to recover for pure emotional loss.[4] On the other hand, it might be argued that over time this body of law relaxed the limits on liability precisely to benefit the women who were so typically the plaintiffs in emotional loss cases. Certainly the law today is very different from what it was a century ago, and that change has been for the benefit of the many female plaintiffs in these cases.

The original rule was that there is no cause of action for pure emotional loss. This is of course a rule set at a very high level of generality. The two rather circumscribed exceptions were for loss suffered when the defendant negligently mishandled the corpse of a loved one, and for loss suffered when the defendant negligently sent a telegram incorrectly announcing the death of a loved one. The rationale underlying the general rule (and by implication, the exceptions) was that there was too great an opportunity for fraud in the typical case in which a plaintiff claimed that he or she was frightened or upset by the defendant, and that in any event the "floodgates" of litigation would be opened if a cause of action for negligently-caused pure emotional loss were recognized. These legitimate concerns, as we will see, have moti-

---

[4] See, e.g., Martha Chamallas with Linda A. Kerber, *Women, Mothers, and the Law of Fright: A History*, 88 Mich. L. Rev. 814 (1990).

vated the courts to fashion rules that take the concerns into account even as the courts have recognized, and then expanded, the cause of action for negligently-caused emotional loss.

A. *The Impact Rule*

The first major qualification of the general rule was the *impact* rule, which permitted recovery in negligence for pure emotional loss only if the defendant's conduct resulted in some physical impact on the plaintiff's body. Some especially cautious courts required that the emotional loss resulting from the impact also manifest itself in physical symptoms (e.g., nausea, inability to sleep, stomach trouble, etc.). But there was no requirement that the plaintiff be physically injured by this impact. This intermediate rule is a pretty crude way of distinguishing the claims that are likely to be valid from those that are not, as well as limiting the number of cases that may be brought. But that is what the rule was designed to do. The impact rule was anything but a "reasonable-under-all-the-circumstances" test. Either there was an impact and a cause of action was permitted, or there was no impact and no cause of action.

The impact rule can generate very arbitrary results. If you lose control of a car going at a speed of ninety miles per hour and almost collide with my two year-old son on the sidewalk, I have no cause of action no matter how much fright and emotional suffering I experience, and no matter how long that suffering persists. But if you carelessly back out of your driveway and brush me at two miles per hour, then there has been impact and I can sue for my emotional suffering. How much I will recover depends on how much suffering I can prove, and I may not be able to prove that I suffered much, but the law recognizes the possibility in the latter case only. One of the funniest opinions in the history of tort law, Justice Mussmano's concurrence in *Bosley v. Andrews*,[5] pokes fun at this all-or-nothing feature of the impact rule.

B. *The Zone of Danger Rule*

Over time the courts became increasingly dissatisfied with the arbitrariness of the impact rule and replaced it with a zone of danger rule. But just as the complete bar to recovery was replaced with the impact

[5] 393 Pa. 161, 142 A.2d 263 (1958).

rule permitting some recoveries even while rigidly excluding other claims, so the impact rule was replaced with a rule that was also couched at an intermediate level of generality, albeit one that permitted more recovery. Under the zone of danger rule the plaintiff could recover for negligently caused emotional loss even if there was no impact, if the plaintiff was in the "zone" in which physical injury was threatened, and feared for her own safety. A number of courts adopting the impact rule also required that the resulting emotional loss manifest itself in physical symptoms as well. On the other hand, in time some courts relaxed the zone of danger rule a bit, permitting recovery by those in the zone of danger even when their emotional loss resulted partly from fear that another person in the zone (such as one's small child) would be physically injured.

Like the impact rule, the zone of danger rule attempts to reduce the risk of both fraudulent claims and an excessive number of claims, by identifying a limited class of cases in which it is plausible that there will be emotional loss even in the absence of direct physical injury. Having to adjudicate any claim by a plaintiff within the zone of danger was something the courts were willing to do under the new rule, in order to circumvent the arbitrariness of the impact rule. By the same token, undoubtedly the courts adopting the zone of danger rule recognized that there would be cases in which a plaintiff who was outside the zone of danger nonetheless suffered emotional loss. But denying recovery in those admittedly "legitimate" cases was the price these courts were willing to pay in order to avoid the prospect of being forced to adjudicate an unlimited number of potentially plausible claims.

C. The Dillon Rule

Then the same sort of thing happened again. Like so many of the cases that had preceded it, *Dillon v. Legg*[6] involved a claim by a mother would had witnessed her daughters' injury. In *Dillon* the Supreme Court of California, which in the years between about 1960 and 1985 was something of a leader in the expansion of tort liability generally, discarded the zone of danger rule. The court held that the plaintiff in a pure emotional loss case need not have been in the zone of danger and therefore need not have feared for her own safety in order to recover for her emotional loss. But like the rule it replaced, the new rule did not employ an "under all the circumstances" test. Rather, the

---

[6] 68 Cal.2d 728, 441 P.2d 912, 69 Cal.Rptr. 72 (1968).

court indicated that three factors would have to be taken into account in deciding whether the claim was one that warranted recovery—presumably not only in jury deliberations, but also in the judicial determination whether a claim could even go to the jury.

The three factors were proximity, visibility, and relationship. The court indicated that the closer the plaintiff was to the accident, the more visible the accident was to the plaintiff, and the closer the relationship between the plaintiff and the party within the zone of danger, the greater the foreseeability of emotional harm to the plaintiff and the stronger the argument was for recovery of the plaintiff's emotional loss. It would have been possible for these factors to degenerate into mere guidelines surrounding what would amount to an "under all the circumstances" test. But that is not what has happened. The courts that have adopted a *Dillon* test—and many have not, preferring to retain the zone of danger approach—have been adamant about drawing bright lines between the kinds of cases that do and do not warrant recovery. Thus, hearing but not seeing an accident typically is insufficient; and a close friend or lover is apparently not in a close-enough relationship with the plaintiff to warrant recovery even when the plaintiff witnesses the injury.

In summary, over a period of almost a century there has been a progressive relaxation of the rule that there can be no recovery in negligence for pure emotional loss. But at each stage of that relaxation, one bright-line rule after another was substituted for its predecessor. This evolution contrasts with what happened, for example, in the field of owner's and occupier's liability. There the courts never were able to identify satisfactory bright-line alternatives to the traditional approach based on the status of entrants onto land. But in the field of pure emotional loss, the courts fashioned a series of such "intermediate" rules that permitted more recovery than in the past and were serviceable for decades at a time, but were couched at a level of generality that prevented their degenerating into an "under all the circumstances" approach to liability.

IV. "Pure" Economic Loss

The last example of a limited duty involves cases of negligently-caused economic harm, occurring in the absence of personal injury or property damage suffered by the plaintiff. Again it is important to understand what is and is not at stake here. There is a cause of action in tort for *intentional* infliction of economic loss, known as interference with contract rights or prospective advantage (see Chapter 14). In addition, there is of course a right to recover for economic loss that is the consequence of, or as is sometimes said, is "parasitic" on one's own personal injury or property damage. The out-of-pocket medical expenses and lost wages that injured plaintiffs recover in ordinary *negligence* cases are economic losses, as are lost profits resulting from property damage. But that is not what is at issue in cases involving negligently-caused "pure" economic loss.

Rather, in the cases with which we are concerned here, physical injury to the person or property of one party also results in purely economic harm to another party. That is, this latter party's losses are not parasitic on any personal injury or property damage that he suffered. For example, suppose that the defendant's negligent driving causes a collision on a bridge that necessitates the closing of the bridge for half a day. A party whose business is located on the far side of the bridge is deprived of an essential source of supply because the bridge is closed, and suffers economic loss as a result; or a general contractor is prevented from hand-delivering a construction bid to an office on the other side of the bridge by the 12:00 noon deadline, and would have submitted the low bid. Can either of these parties recover from the defendant for the economic losses that they have suffered as a result of the defendant's negligence?

The traditional answer has been to deny such recovery outright.[7] Like the traditional prohibition of recovery in negligence for pure emotional loss, this is a rule at the highest level of generality. Unlike the law governing recovery for pure emotional loss, however, in this field there has been virtually no evolution away from the bright-line rule denying recovery. Although a few exceptions have been created, the rule as it now stands is very similar to the rule as it stood a century ago.

The reason is that the considerations that supported the rule a century ago still largely support it. First, notwithstanding that pure economic loss is often a highly foreseeable result of negligent conduct, the amount of liability that could result if there were a cause of action for pure economic loss could be enormous, but its scope would be very difficult to predict. This unpredictability would render the sale of insurance against such liability a very risky undertaking. Such liability might therefore be uninsured. The threat of wholly uninsured liability

---

[7] *Robins Dry Dock & Repair Co. v. Flint*, 275 U.S. 303, 48 S.Ct. 134, 72 L.Ed. 290 (1927).

would probably discourage many potential defendants from engaging in valuable activities that, nonetheless, entail a risk of enormous consequential economic loss if the activities are conducted negligently. For example, think of the size of the economic losses that would be suffered by third parties as a result of the negligent repair of an electric line on a busy urban street, or negligently colliding with a utility pole. Second, although in theory a deterrence shortfall results from the denial of recovery for pure economic loss, the defendant in all such cases is already threatened with substantial liability for the personal injury or property damage that may result from its negligence. So the defendant ordinarily is not immunized from all liability as a result of the rule. Third, and conversely, often the third-party economic losses that result from negligently-caused personal injury or property damage, even when sizable, are distributed among large numbers of people. Given such already-existing broad loss distribution, the loss-distribution rationale for imposing liability on the injurer is weak, especially since many of these losses can be insured by victims through business-interruption insurance.

Finally, the economic losses resulting from an act of negligence could be traced far and wide. A pure economic loss suffered by one party may then result in a pure economic loss suffered by someone with whom he deals, and so on *ad infinitum*. If there were to be some recovery for pure economic loss, a workable and fair distinction between the cases in which recovery would and would not be permitted would have to be developed. But no logical "intermediate" rule seems available. If no such bright-line can be developed, then permitting recovery would require a general foreseeability or under-all-the-circumstances test that in every case would threaten unlimited liability, even if that were not always the result. For practical purposes, therefore, the law has chosen to draw the line at no liability rather than to venture into an arena where there would be few if any guidelines for adjudication.

The courts have, however, occasionally created exceptions to the rule. Perhaps the most noteworthy involve cases in which there has been natural-resource damage for which no party seems to have a cause of action. In such cases, liability for economic loss serves as a kind of surrogate for a cause of action for physical damage to natural resources. For example, in *Union Oil Co. v. Oppen*,[8] the defendant's negligence caused oil pollution in the Santa Barbara Channel off Cali-

---

[8] 501 F.2d 558 (9th Cir. 1974).

fornia. Among other things, this pollution killed fish and resulted in economic loss to the plaintiffs, who were commercial fishermen. Conceivably the State of California could have sued for the overall environmental damage that resulted from the defendant's negligence, but the State made no such effort. The court allowed the plaintiffs to recover, adopting a test which it said was based mainly on foreseeability. But the absence of a proper plaintiff to sue for the physical damage in question, together with the fact that the defendant was a sufficiently large enterprise (a major oil company) to be capable of bearing that liability, probably influenced the result. In a few similar cases recovery has also been permitted by commercial fishermen, but denied to seafood sellers.[9] For the most part, however, recovery has been denied even in cases closely analogous to *Union Oil*. Most of the courts faced with the question have subscribed to the traditional rule and have declined to venture onto the potentially slippery slope of permitting some recoveries.

---

[9] See, e.g., *Pruitt v. Allied Chemical Corp.*, 523 F.Supp. 975 (E.D.Va. 1981).

12

Tort Reform, Workers Compensation, and No-Fault Systems

M ost tort law is common law, made by the courts over a period of centuries. In the past several decades, however, the state legislatures have entered the tort law arena, modifying a number of traditional rules of tort law. Prior to the enactment of this legislation, there were only two examples of major legislative intervention in the tort system: workers compensation and auto no-fault. This Chapter surveys each of these three developments, as well as the possibility of extending the no-fault model to other areas such as medical and product-related injuries. Our purpose here is not to examine every detail of these approaches, but to gain the perspective that an understanding of their structure and function can shed on the nature of tort law itself.

I. Statutory Tort Reform

First in the mid–1970's and then again in the mid–1980's, there were tort liability "crises" across the country, involving escalating rates of suit and increasing liability insurance costs. In response to these crises, nearly every state legislature modified its state's tort law in one way or another. It is not possible to capture all the nuances of this legislation with a single sweeping generalization. More than anything else, however, the legislation modified various aspects of the law governing damages in tort cases. A reasonably accurate sense of this common theme can be gleaned simply by noting the three reforms that were most frequently enacted: absolute dollar ceilings on the amount of awards for pain and suffering and punitive damages; limitations on or complete elimination of joint and several liability; and abolition of the collateral source rule.[1] Each of the reforms has been discussed in earlier Chapters.

---

[1] See Joseph Sanders & Craig Joyce, *"Off to the Races": The 1980s Tort Crisis and the Law Reform Process*, 27 Hous. L. Rev. 207, 217–23 (1990).

Interestingly, none of these legislative reforms touches the core of tort liability for personal injury. None affects the standard of care, or rules governing proof of causation, for example. And none precludes any plaintiff who could have obtained a judgment against a defendant prior to its enactment from obtaining a judgment thereafter. Those defendants who were liable before the enactment of tort reform continued to be liable after enactment, but often for less. The reform legislation accepted the incidence of tort liability as it stood, but restricted the measure of damages a successful plaintiff is entitled to recover.

This legislation can be viewed in either of two ways. One view is that as the frequency of tort suits and the size of average awards increased, the need of potential defendants to be able to predict the scope of their tort liability exposure increased as well. When liability insurance and tort liability were only a tiny percentage of the costs of conducting a business or profession, predictability was less necessary. But as liability insurance and tort costs increased, predicting their magnitude came to be more important, because the effect of an unexpected increase in costs would be more substantial. State legislatures responded to this need by enacting legislation that would make awards more predictable, without changing the core rules of tort liability in any way. A more cynical view, however, is that as insurance and tort costs increased, potential defendants wanted relief from these costs. And what defendants care about most is the amount of their liability, not whether they are held liable. Consequently, defendants sought and received the relief they wanted in the form of legislation that would decrease—or at least slow the increase in—their insurance and tort costs. Moreover, this reasoning goes, if the amount of damages that can be recovered in a tort suit is limited, then potential plaintiffs' incentives to sue will be reduced, and the incidence of tort liability will decline even without any formal change in liability standards.

Whether one takes the former or the latter view, there can be no disputing the fact that the tort reform legislation of the past several decades has been limited and incremental. This legislation has left the basic structure of tort liability untouched, even while tinkering around the edges by modifying the measure of damages in a variety of ways. To gain an understanding of the possibilities for more fundamental reform, we must look to other developments.

II. Workers Compensation

The nineteenth century was a period of enormous industrialization and urbanization in the United States. It is only a slight exaggeration to say that we went from being a nation of rural farmers to being a nation of city-dwelling factory workers. With all this industrialization came a whole series of problems, one of which was industrial injuries. At the dawn of the twentieth century there was growing recognition that workplace injuries were not merely a legal, but also a social problem. The tort system itself was not providing compensation for such injuries in an adequate way. Legal doctrines restricted workers' rights of recovery on grounds of assumption of risk, contributory negligence, and the "fellow-servant" rule that precluded recovery from an employer for injuries caused by another employee's negligence. In addition, many workplace injuries were not the result of anyone's negligence and therefore were not subject to tort liability, because employers were liable only for negligence. After some years of controversy and, at first, the enactment of partial or optional systems, a new system of "workers compensation" replaced tort liability for workplace injuries.

Any injury compensation system, including tort law and workers compensation, has three major components: the compensable event, the measure of compensation, and the payment mechanism. In tort law, for example, the prevailing compensable event is an injury caused by negligence; the measure of compensation is full payment of both tangible and intangible losses; and the payment mechanism is the injurer's liability insurance or (so to speak) self-insurance.

Workers compensation modified the first two of these components of the tort system, but left the third component in place. The compensable event in tort was an injury caused by an employer's negligence. In contrast, in workers compensation the compensable event is non-negligently-caused injury. Workers compensation abolishes the tort liability of the employer and provides compensation to employees through an administrative system for injuries "arising out of or in the course of employment." And the only defense available is that the employee intended to cause his own injury or acted with wanton disregard for his own safety. This is strict liability of a very broad sort. "Fault" has been replaced by "cause" as the basis of liability.

Workers compensation also modifies the measure of compensation. Because of the expansion of the compensable event and the elimination of defenses, vastly greater numbers of workers are entitled to receive compensation. Vastly increased costs could therefore be expected if the measure of compensation were not reduced. Some administrative cost savings could be expected because of the greatly reduced cost of determining eligibility for compensation. In tort it typically would have taken litigation to determine whether an employer was negligent. But most employees who enter the job uninjured and at the end of the day are injured have incontestably suffered a compensable event. Indeed, what dispute resolution there is takes place out of court, before an administrative board. Despite these administrative cost savings, if the measure of compensation had not been changed the new workers compensation system would have cost many times what the tort system did.

Consequently, the amount that an employee could recover was limited. At first, recovery was limited to medical expenses and a portion of several weeks' wages. There was no recovery for pain and suffering at all. Over time the number of weeks' wages that were recoverable has increased to the point where there is no limit in some states and the limit is several years in others. Both wage losses and medical expenses are paid periodically as they are incurred. And there has also developed a rough but restricted substitute for pain and suffering—lump-sum awards for partial and total permanent disability have been enacted. For example, the statutes specify particular sums to be awarded for loss of a hand, loss of an eye, paralysis of both legs, and so forth. Typically these sums are considerably more limited than the pain and suffering awards that could be obtained in a tort suit for the same loss—usually the lump-sums are less then $10,000.

The changes that workers compensation made in the compensable event and the measure of compensation are important, but what was not changed also matters. The payment mechanism did not change— that is, the employer remained liable, though on a new basis. The employer might purchase liability insurance—workers compensation insurance, as it is called—to cover its liability for benefits, or might self-insure. But regardless, because it remained liable, the employers' incentive to compare the cost of workplace accidents (its responsibility for workers compensation benefits) with the cost of reducing workplace accidents, was retained. Indeed, in a sense that incentive was strengthened, because the employer was now liable for many more claims than in tort, though for a much lower average amount per claim. To put it another way, from the deterrence standpoint workers compensation constituted a shift from negligence to strict liability, and therefore had the potential to capture many of the advantages of strict liability described in Chapter Eight.

And what the theory of strict liability suggests, the facts confirm. Studies show that despite eliminating the threat of tort liability, workers compensation has generated substantial safety incentive effects. Indeed, no definitive study has shown that workplaces are less safe than they would have been had tort liability been preserved, and many show otherwise. That is not to say that workers compensation is without its critics. Benefit levels are criticized as too low, periodic payment encourages some malingering, and with the rise of diseases that may be caused by long-term exposure to hazardous substances, determining whether a workers' disease is or is not work-related has become more complicated and more expensive. But over many decades, workers compensation has remained an effective approach that has achieved its goals by providing swift compensation to injured workers on a no-fault basis.

III. Auto No-Fault

In the period after World War II the automobile became an essential feature of American life. As more vehicles and miles were driven, however, there inevitably came more auto accidents. Just as there was a point at which workplace injuries went from being perceived merely as a legal problem to being a social problem, so by the 1960's uncompensated auto-related injuries had become sufficiently frequent and serious to be recognized as a social problem.

One approach to this "compensation gap" was the enactment of legislation in many states requiring all drivers to be covered by liability insurance. Such a requirement was meant to assure that no one who was the victim of negligent driving would be left without a solvent source of recovery. In addition, the insurance industry developed a number of other devices that addressed the problem outside of tort law. "Uninsured motorist insurance" covers the victim in the event that a negligent defendant is uninsured; and "medical payments coverage" affords small amounts of insurance for the medical costs resulting from auto accidents, whether there was negligence involved or not. But these devices still leave gaps in the fabric of compensation for auto-related injuries: not all drivers comply with the requirement that they purchase liablity insurance; uninsured motorists insurance only covers losses caused by the negligence of another driver; and medical payments insurance usually has very low limits of coverage. In short, these devices supplement rather than replace tort law as the principal avenue of recovery for those who suffer auto-related injuries.

Naturally the workers compensation model came under consideration as a possible substitute for tort law's approach to the provision of compensation for auto injuries. But it had been recognized for some time that the auto accident problem did not fit neatly into this model. In the employment situation there are two differently-situated parties, the employer and the employee. It was reasonable to conceive of the employer as the injurer and the employee as the victim, because the employer is generally in the superior position to manage the risk of workplace injuries. Placing liability on the employer on a strict liability, or "no-fault," basis therefore made sense in the workplace context. In the typical auto-accident situation, however, the two parties are similarly situated in a number of respects. Both parties tend to be ordinary individuals who cannot be identified in advance as injurer and victim; both parties may be injured; and sometimes there is only a single victim without any other party involved as an "injurer" at all. Moreover, even when there are two parties involved in an auto accident and only one suffers injury, it does not follow at all that the uninjured party is an injurer. If am carefully stopped at a red light when another driver runs into my car from behind and injures himself, no one would say that I injured him. In the absence of an inquiry into the negligence of the parties, it is not terribly meaningful to ask whether the party who did not suffer an injury was an "injurer" or merely was involved in an accident that happened to injure someone else.

For these reasons, the workers compensation model of injurer-based strict liability did not (and still does not) transfer comfortably to the auto-accident situation. It took two law professors, Robert Keeton and Jeffrey O'Connell, to think their way through to a solution of this problem. Where workers compensation had left essentially untouched the third element of any compensation system—the payment mechanism—Keeton and O'Connell proposed a wholesale change.

Keeton and O'Connell's idea was to replace tort liability for auto injuries not with automatic injurer liability on the model of workers compensation, but with automatic victim liability. Instead of imposing liability in tort on those who negligently caused auto-related injuries, victims would bear their own injury costs by purchasing insurance against their losses.[2] Thus, auto no-fault consists of two prongs: the abolition of tort liability and the mandatory purchase of insurance directly protecting victims. While this may seem at first to reject the strict liability approach of workers compensation, in fact this approach does not reject strict liability. Rather, auto no-fault adopts strict liability on the part of the victim, not the injurer, even when there is an injurer. To put it another way, once the element of negligence is removed from the equation, it is just as accurate to think of the victim as causing his own injuries as it is to think of the other party involved in the accident (who may also be a victim) as the cause.

Soon after this idea emerged, it began to be debated in the state legislatures. In the 1970's a somewhat modified version of the idea was enacted in more than a dozen states, and a number of other states have borrowed selected features of the no-fault idea and enacted them into law. For purposes of exposition, I will call Keeton and O'Connell's idea *pure* no-fault, the modified version that was actually enacted in about a dozen states in the 1970's *real* no-fault, and the third, very selective version *add-on* no-fault.

A. "Pure" No-Fault

Pure no-fault—though not enacted in any state—would modify all three elements of the tort system. First, tort liability for auto-related injuries is abolished. Instead, no-fault compensation is provided to the those who suffer auto-related injuries. The compensable event under this system is an injury "arising out of or in the course of" the operation, maintenance, or use of a motor vehicle.

Second, as under workers compensation, the measure of compensation is reduced. Compensation for pain and suffering damages is eliminated. Compensation for a percentage of wage loss and medical expenses is afforded, however, at least up to a comparatively high (e.g., $50,000) automatic minimum, but drivers are entitled at their option to purchase coverage in excess of this minimum.

Third, the payment mechanism is insurance purchased by potential victims rather than by potential injurers. In the language of insurance, compensation is paid by "first-party" rather than by "third-party" (i.e.,

---

[2] See Robert E. Keeton & Jeffrey O'Connell, Basic Protection for the Traffic Victim: A Blueprint for Reforming Automobile Insurance (1965).

liability) insurance. To make this insurance automatically available to victims, no motor vehicle can be registered or legally driven in a state adopting this regime unless the owner has purchased insurance covering any driver of or passenger in the vehicle, or pedestrian in an accident involving the vehicle.

One of the principal reasons this system has not been enacted in any state is deep disagreement about whether it is sensible and fair to eliminate recovery of damages for pain and suffering. As in workers compensation, a system that afforded compensation for pain and suffering on a no-fault basis would be enormously expensive, and therefore impossible to enact as a practical matter. Consequently, whether to preclude no-fault compensation for pain and suffering is not merely a question about one feature of the system, but goes to the heart of the auto no-fault idea. Critics of no-fault argue that eliminating tort liability, especially for pain and suffering damages, will cause an increase in the accident rate because drivers will no longer face the threat of tort liability for negligent driving. In addition, the critics argue, in cases involving serious injury resulting from negligent driving, corrective justice requires that the injurer be made to compensate the victim. No-fault would relieve injurers of this obligation.

Proponents of no-fault respond to these criticisms as follows. First, as to the possible loss of deterrence resulting from the abolition of tort liability for negligent driving, any driver who is not already sufficiently concerned for his own safety to drive carefully will not drive any less carefully once the threat of tort liability is eliminated. As for the corrective justice argument, most acts of negligent driving are momentary lapses of attention. Typical drivers commonly commit acts of negligence, and whether their negligence causes serious injury or none at all depends more on luck than on the degree of blame that can be ascribed to them. Moreover, liability insurance protecting drivers from the financial consequences of their own negligence is very prevalent, and in many states is required. Victims and injurers both pay into the same liability insurance pool, and premiums are only very roughly calibrated to the individual driver's accident record. Corrective justice between injurer and victim in this situation is therefore attenuated at best. Finally, because of the administrative cost savings it would achieve and the reduced need for attorneys, no-fault would put more money into the pockets of accident victims and less into the pockets of attorneys and insurance companies.

Whether an impartial observer would assess these arguments to weigh more heavily in favor of or against no-fault, the proponents of pure no-fault have never succeeded in convincing a single state legislature to enact this approach. The reasons vary to a degree from state to state, but certainly one major factor has been the opposition of attorneys who regularly represent plaintiffs in auto cases, who have lobbied strenuously against no-fault. A second major factor has been the principled concern of many legislators who have proved reluctant to support the complete abolition of tort liability for auto-related injuries. But this did not end the issue. A hybrid version emerged as an alternative to pure no-fault. This alternative, which I shall call "real" no-fault, garnered enough support to be enacted in some states and to remain in force today.

B. "Real" No-Fault

The legislative impasse over pure no-fault was broken in about a dozen states by fashioning a system that includes only a partial abolition of tort liability. Like pure no-fault, real no-fault also has both tort-abolition and victim-insurance prongs, but under real no-fault tort liability is abolished only for less serious injuries. Thus, the obstacle that stood in the way of the enactment of pure no-fault on both political and principled grounds—concern over abolition of tort liability for injuries involving substantial pain and suffering— is removed.

In real no-fault the distinction between injuries that are compensable only on a no-fault basis and injuries for which a cause of action in tort is preserved is drawn through the use of a "threshold." Claimants whose injuries surpass the threshold may bring tort actions; claimants whose injuries do not surpass the threshold have no cause of action in tort. There are two types of thresholds. A *monetary threshold* specifies the dollar amount of medical expenses that a claimant must incur to preserve her cause of action in tort. A *verbal threshold* lists the various "serious" injuries that qualify for recovery in tort regardless of the medical expenses incurred to treat them. Other than soft tissue injuries and simple fractures, most injuries of any seriousness typically qualify. But since the vast majority of auto-related injuries are not "serious" in this sense, the size of the monetary threshold is critically important. There is considerable variation. These thresholds are as low as a few hundred dollars in some states and as high as several thousand dollars in others.

The result is that in low-threshold states only the most modest tort claims are precluded, while in other states only the most serious are permitted. The effect of this difference, however, depends in part on how the second, mandatory-insurance prong of no-fault is handled. If the minimal level of insurance is high (e.g., $50,000) then most victims are automatically entitled to recover most of their out-of-pocket losses from their own insurance company and typically do so. Since no-fault statutes normally offset tort recoveries by the amount of prior insurance payments (i.e, reverse the collateral source rule with respect to no-fault benefits), for these victims the major effect of preserving their cause of action is that they may recover damages for pain and suffering. In contrast, in states with low minimum levels of mandatory no-fault insurance (e.g., $2000), many victims do not have enough of their own insurance to cover all of their out-of-pocket losses. The preservation of a cause of action permits full recovery of out-of-pocket losses by these victims.

Beyond these general differences lie more subtle, though significant, choices embodied by the distinctions between approaches. The states adopting low thresholds have removed "nuisance" claims from the tort system and assured all victims quick, automatic compensation for their losses. But since the bulk of tort actions are preserved in these states, this form of no-fault looks a lot more like mandatory first-party insurance than like tort reform. By contrast, high thresholds that are difficult to surpass have the potential to shrink the tort system in a significant way. In these states the two prongs of no-fault—mandatory insurance and partial abolition of tort liability—bear an important relation to each other. The higher the insurance-benefit levels that a particular state's no-fault statute mandates, the higher the threshold can comfortably be, for a high threshold will tend to assure full or near-full payment of victims' out-of-pocket losses without the need for tort recoveries.

The shape of the system adopted also affects one of the key questions about no-fault: how much it costs. Critics often charge that no-fault is not cheaper than the tort system, and point to changes in insurance costs after the adoption of no-fault to prove their point. But the comparison of before-and-after costs can be simplistic and misleading. When there is tort liability alone, then drivers must purchase liability insurance only. After no-fault with only partial abolition of tort liability is enacted, however, drivers must purchase both liability insurance protecting them against the liability for "serious" injuries that has been preserved, and first-party insurance covering themselves and their passengers for all out-of-pocket injury costs up to the mandated benefit level. If that benefit level is high, then of course the total cost of real no-fault (tort plus no-fault) will exceed the former cost of tort liability alone. Under the new system the most expensive part of the old system (liability for serious injuries) has been preserved, while another system (mandatory first-party insurance) has been added onto it. The only appropriate cost comparison would be between tort liability and pure no-fault. But that is a comparison that cannot be made in practice, because pure no-fault has never been enacted.

C. "Add-on" No-Fault

The third and last version of no-fault is the most prevalent but least significant. This version has one prong only. Under this version no-fault insurance is an "add-on" to the tort system. Tort liability remains untouched, but there is mandatory purchase of insurance for victims.

Formally, this add-on form of no-fault is merely auto-insurance reform without any tort reform whatsoever. But informally, even add-on no-fault may have some impact on the incidence of tort liability. By providing an automatic source of recovery for at least a portion of every victim's out-of-pocket losses, add-on no-fault eliminates the need to sue for these losses. Some victims still will wish to bring suit, especially in cases of severe pain and suffering. But for victims with comparatively small claims and modest injuries, suit is not necessary, and some may decline to sue because their out-of-pocket losses have been paid. In this way even a reform that has no direct effect on the incidence of tort suits may have an indirect effect. It may be that over time, as the scope of add-on benefits increases, the attractiveness of retaining the right to sue in tort will decline. But at present in most states the legislatures show no particular inclination to move beyond the add-on approach by abolishing any portion of tort liability for auto injuries. Instead, tort liability and add-on no-fault peacefully co-exist.

IV. The Future of No-Fault: Beyond "Comp" and Auto?

The no-fault revolution is at a standstill. No state has enacted real auto no-fault in two decades, although California voters came within a percentage point of doing so in 1996. Nonetheless, long after workers compensation had been put in place it inspired auto no-fault. Is it possible that these two no-fault systems could now serve as models for reform of other aspects of the tort system?

247

The prospects are not rosey, but it is highly instructive to understand why. The central problem is how to define the compensable event in a suitable way. In the employment and auto settings, defining the compensable event is straightforward and simple: an injury "arising out of or in the course of" employment or motoring. Such a definition works because people virtually always go to work or get into a car uninjured. If they emerge from work or driving injured, it is highly likely that they have suffered a work-related or auto-related injury. Using so straightforward a compensable event, however, is not feasible in such other settings as medical or product-related injuries.

A. Medical No-Fault

By analogy to workers compensation and auto no-fault, could no-fault benefits easily be made available to anyone suffering an injury "arising out of or in the course of medical treatment?" Unfortunately, determining whether the claimant had suffered a compensable event would require complex fact-finding in a large percentage of such claims. Many people seek medical treatment because they are already ill or injured. In such cases there would have to be a fact-finder who could distinguish injuries or illnesses that were caused by medical treatment from conditions associated with the patient's underlying injury or illness. Whether the physician had committed malpractice would no longer be at issue. But the causation question under medical no-fault—"did the patient suffer an injury arising out of medical treatment?"—would still be at issue in many cases. The swift and certain compensation of victims that is so characteristic of and so much an important part of workers compensation and auto no-fault would therefore often be unavailable. Nonetheless, some research has been undertaken in an effort to assess the feasibility of making medical no-fault determinations, and the results are mildly encouraging.[3] Although these efforts have as yet not gone beyond the research stage, limited experiments in medical no-fault compensation are likely to be undertaken in the coming years.

B. Product No-Fault

A somewhat different problem, also involving the compensable event, would plague efforts to develop product no-fault. No one would want a system of insurance against all product-related injuries. If you

---

[3] See Paul C. Weiler et al., A MEASURE OF MALPRACTICE: MEDICAL INJURY, MALPRACTICE LITIGATION, AND PATIENT COMPENSATION (1993).

fall off a perfectly suitable ladder or cut yourself with a high quality steak knife, I do not want to pay into an insurance pool that will cover you against the losses you suffer as a result of these products doing exactly what they are supposed to do. I would rather take care of myself and not pay for your careless climbing or cutting. Consequently, the product no-fault compensable event would have to be limited to something like injuries "arising in the use of defective products." But of course the difficulty of determining whether a product is "defective" is precisely what so troubles current product liability law, and precisely what makes finding some alternative outside of tort attractive. There would be little point in adopting a no-fault system that replicated the problems it was designed to avoid.

One approach that might avoid some of these problems would be to authorize elective, contractual no-fault for medical and/or product injuries. If legal theorists cannot collectively define a compensable event that is suitable for general use in product no-fault, it may still be possible for individual companies or industry groups to develop more focused alternatives that will work in more limited settings. For example, chain saw manufacturers might want to fashion their own no-fault system for their purchasers. Standing in the way of this alternative, however, is the courts' extreme reluctance to permit contractual disclaimers of tort liability. Potential defendants are therefore reluctant to invest in the development no-fault alternatives when they know that their investment may be lost when the courts invalidate the approach they have tried to use. Without advance validation there is not much incentive to develop a no-fault alternative to tort liability.

Thus, ideally, legislation would authorize the adoption of such alternatives in advance. Ironically, however, authorizing legislation is unlikely to be enacted until a particular scheme has been developed. The result is a chicken-and-egg problem in which a particular scheme is unlikely to be developed in the absence of authorizing legislation, and authorizing legislation is unlikely to be enacted before a particular scheme is developed. Partly for this reason elective no-fault has not yet gotten off the ground, although at least in theory it is an attractive approach.

13

Reputational and Dignitary Harms: Defamation and Invasion of Privacy

Virtually everything in the first twelve chapters of this book has been concerned with liability for personal injury and property damage, or for the consequences of such harm. In this Chapter and the next one we take up very different forms of liability involving intangible rather than physical harms. This Chapter concerns causes of action that protect reputation and, for want of a better term, "dignity": defamation and invasion of privacy.

I. Defamation

The development of most of the tort law of the twentieth century is the story of the progressive expansion of liability. This is not true, however, of liability for defamation, which is the only major field of tort law that has undergone a reduction in its scope during the modern era. Until 1964 the law of defamation had remained largely unchanged for a very long time. Beginning in that year, however, the U.S. Supreme Court entered the field and began a still-continuing effort to define and elaborate the limitations on the scope of the law of defamation required by the First Amendment to the U.S. Constitution. Since those limitations are only partial, however, the challenge in this field is both to understand the common law of defamation and to identify the features of this body of law that have been modified by constitutional dictate.

A. *The Core Principles of the Common Law of Defamation*

Defamation is the making of a statement to a third party that injures a person's reputation. Reputation itself is not one thing, but a cluster of values. Sometimes reputation is much like property—one's creditworthiness, for example, has monetary value. On the other hand, sometimes reputation is a form of honor, built up over time through accomplishment or behavior. Finally, sometimes reputation is more closely akin to dignity, which can be lost through ridicule or satire. The law of defamation is designed to protect each of these forms of reputation.

A defamatory statement may be oral, in which case it is *slander*, or it may be made in written or otherwise more "permanent" form such as on television, in which case it is *libel*. Because libelous statements are permanent and therefore often are capable of doing more damage than slander, the common law of defamation made them more easily actionable, in the ways noted below.

The common law of defamation law reflected a particular set of values, placing much more emphasis on the protection of reputation than on freedom of speech. There was strict liability for making a defamatory statement—or for republishing someone else's statement. There was no requirement that the defendant intend to harm the plaintiff, or that the defendant know that the statement was false. Indeed, technically speaking, falsity was not even an element of the tort. To be defamatory the statement merely had to injure the plaintiff's reputation. The truth of the statement could in fact be relevant, because truth was a defense. But it was just that—a defense that the defendant had to plead and prove in order to avoid liability.

1. The *Prima Facie* Case

In general a libel was actionable without proof of special damages—i.e., out-of-pocket loss resulting from damage to the plaintiff's reputation. Some states applied this rule only to libel "per se," defined as a statement that was defamatory on its face and therefore required no extrinsic evidence to explain its defamatory character. The great advantage to the plaintiff in a libel per se action was that he could recover compensation for "presumed" damage to his reputation and for consequent emotional loss without proving that damage. In contrast, slander was not actionable per se—i.e., there could be no presumption of damage—unless it was defamatory in one of four ways: by accusing the plaintiff of committing a major crime, having a sexually transmitted or other "loathsome" disease, conducting himself in a way that made him unsuited for his business or profession, or engaging in infidelity or other serious sexual misconduct.

Thus, simply by showing that the defendant had made a statement to a third party that was damaging to the plaintiff's reputation, a plaintiff could prove a *prima facie* case of defamation. In a broad variety of libel and slander per se cases, this showing would trigger a presumption that the defamation had caused compensable damages. Among other things this meant that the plaintiff could survive the defendant's motion for a directed verdict by making this simple showing, and that unless the defendant could make out a defense as a matter of law, the plaintiff's case would go to the jury. The message sent by this structure was clear. Any person who considered making a statement damaging to someone else's reputation was putting himself at risk of liability. As between the interest in one's reputation and the right to speak freely, the common law seemed clearly to favor the former at the expense of the latter.

2. Defenses

When the available defenses are added to this mix, the picture becomes somewhat cloudier, but the overall emphasis remains the same. As I noted above, truth was an absolute defense. There was also a series of privileges, some absolute and some conditional. Aside from consent, there was an *absolute privilege* to make defamatory statements in legal proceedings of one sort or another—legislative, judicial, or administrative. And high officials of government had an absolute privilege for any statement made as part of their conduct of office, whether or not the statement was made in a formal proceeding. A *conditional privilege* was one that protected the maker of a defamatory statement from liability only if the statement was made with knowledge that the statement was false or with reckless disregard for the truth or falsity of the statement. This standard was sometimes referred to as "actual malice," a term that the Supreme Court was later to employ.

The conditional privileges to make defamatory statements applied in a variety of contexts. What linked them together was that these were the kind of statements that had to be made in order for ordinary business and important family matters to be conducted. For example, there were conditional privileges for making defamatory statements in letters of recommendation, in reports to proper authorities about the commission of crimes, and in communications to family members about the character of people with whom they were dealing or had personal relationships—such as prospective spouses. And lower governmental officials enjoyed a conditional privilege to make defamatory statements as part of the conduct of their office. Finally, there was a conditional privilege to engage in "fair comment" on artistic, literary, and other public matters, including public officials. But in the majority of states the fair comment privilege applied only to the expression of opinions, not to assertions of fact.

The effect of the privileges was to give those who held them some room for making false statements without facing liability for defamation. If only the defense of truth were available, then any false statement could result in liability. Armed with a conditional privilege, however, the maker of a statement who had an honest belief that it was true would be protected against liability. And if the maker happened to enjoy an absolute privilege, even an honest belief in the truth of a defamatory statement was not necessary. So the privileges created some "breathing space" for speech under circumstances where the fear of liability for making a false statement might otherwise have discouraged the making of valuable true statements.

Since it was the defendant's burden to prove defenses and privileges, however, the law of defamation encouraged even a defendant who believed he was privileged to make a defamatory statement to think twice before he made it. Nonetheless, at least on paper, potential defendants had protection against liability for a wide variety of negative statements about other people that they might make in the ordinary course of business or personal life. For making volunteered, gratuitous, wholly optional statements, however, there was less likely to be a conditional privilege and much more likely to be liability. Two such non-privileged categories of statements stand out especially. Ordinary gossip was unprotected at common law and is unprotected now. The private individual, newspaper, or television station that makes or repeats a defamatory statement about an ordinary individual who is uninvolved in public issues faces strict liability and has only the defense of truth as protection. Similarly unprotected at common law was political speech, broadly conceived, with the exception of the assertion of opinions subject to the fair comment privilege. Those who made factual statements about government officials, candidates for office, or people involved in public issues enjoyed no privileges and only had the defense of truth to protect them. In contrast to ordinary gossip, however, political speech was about to receive powerful constitutional protection.

254

B. *Defamation Law and the Constitution*

Beginning in 1964, the U.S. Supreme Court entered the field. There can be no doubt that the Supreme Court's rulings regarding the constitutional limits on the scope of liability for defamation have had great significance. Once utterly untouched by constitutional limitations, defamation law cannot be understand at all without appreciating these limitations. On the other hand, important as the so-called "constitutionalization" of defamation law is, what has actually happened should not be exaggerated. After over three decades of constitutional elaboration, it is only a modest oversimplification to say that the major development has merely been the establishment of a new constitutional conditional privilege, for "political speech."

1. *New York Times v. Sullivan*

The most important of the Supreme Court's decisions in this field was its first, *New York Times Co. v. Sullivan.*[1] The plaintiff in that case, Sullivan, was one of three elected City Commissioners of Montgomery, Alabama in 1960. The individual defendants signed a political advertisement published in the New York Times containing a series of accusations regarding the City of Montgomery's conduct toward civil rights demonstrators, some of which were false. The plaintiff was not mentioned by name, but he sued the Times and those whose names were published in the ad for libel. Under Alabama law, if the jury found the statement to be "of and concerning" the plaintiff, the statements were actionable without proof of special damages because the statements were libelous per se and not privileged. Punitive damages also could be awarded if malice were proved, because a retraction the defendant had demanded was not published.

The jury awarded Sullivan $500,000 in compensatory and punitive damages. But the U.S. Supreme Court overturned the verdict, holding that the First Amendment guarantee of freedom of speech (applied to the states through the Fourteenth Amendment) requires that the makers of statements about public officials be afforded a conditional privilege to make those statements. To defeat the privilege, the Court held, a public official suing for defamation had to prove with "convincing clarity" that the statement was made with "actual malice"—i.e., with knowledge that the statement was false or with reckless disregard for

---

[1] 376 U.S. 254, 84 S.Ct. 710, 11 L.Ed.2d 686 (1964).

its truth or falsity. In addition, to be actionable there had to be sufficient proof that the statements were "of and concerning" the plaintiff to assure the required constitutional freedom to criticize the government.

In one sense the decision in *New York Times v. Sullivan* is unremarkable. If the existing common-law privileges were designed to afford "breathing space" for speech necessary to the ordinary functioning of business and family affairs, then surely the functioning of a democracy requires that there be at least a similar amount of breathing space for political speech. For example, all that *Sullivan* did substantively was to create a conditional privilege to make defamatory statements about public officials equivalent to the privilege that employers and teachers have when writing letters of recommendation. That can hardly be controversial.

On the other hand, for nearly two hundred years the state courts had operated without any federally-set limits on the scope of defamation law. Now, suddenly, there was a potential federal "presence" in every defamation suit brought by a public official. The context in which *Sullivan* was decided helps to explain how the Supreme Court could have made a decision with the potential to so intrude on the traditional province of the state courts. A civil rights dispute gave rise to Sullivan's lawsuit. The defamatory statements made in a northern newspaper—the New York Times—were technically false in certain respects but were not misleading overall. The plaintiff's suit was then tried in the still-segregated south. And the Alabama jury awarded Sullivan one-half a million dollars without proof that the statements had caused Sullivan any monetary loss at all.

Moreover, the record before the Supreme Court showed that the trial judge in the case had insisted on segregated seating in the courtroom, and had introduced the case with the statement that the Fourteenth Amendment (which guarantees due process of law) is a "pariah and an outcast," indicating also his belief that "the white man's justice * * * will give the parties * * * equal justice under law."[2] Add to this inflammatory setting the fact that the civil rights movement, which by 1964 was at a fever pitch, drew much of its political support from the North, through the mechanism of media coverage. It was therefore understandable for the Supreme Court to be concerned that the threat of large judgments imposing strict liability for defamatory statements made in the course of public controversy over civil rights would be

---

[2] See Rodnew A. Smolla, SUING THE PRESS 32–33 (1986).

used as a segregationist weapon against those who favored civil rights. Viewed in this light, the Supreme Court's willingness to begin creating a whole new constitutional jurisprudence of defamation is somewhat more understandable, especially since 1960's were a period of venturesome lawmaking by the Supreme Court in other areas as well.

2. Beyond *Sullivan*

Once established, however, the new regime automatically had a life of its own beyond civil rights disputes. In short order the rule in *Sullivan* was applied to not only to public officials, but also to what the Court called public "figures"—individuals who were not elected or appointed officials, but whose prominence in politics, entertainment, sports, or other pursuits made them a subject of public interest. Eventually it also became clear that the Constitution required the plaintiff to prove falsity, rather than putting the burden of proving truth on the defendant. And in *Gertz v. Robert Welch, Inc.*,[3] the Court was confronted with the inevitable question of how the law of defamation could be squared with constitutional requirements when the plaintiff was neither a public official nor figure, but the defamatory statement about the plaintiff concerned a matter of public interest.

The Court responded with two rules. First, *Gertz* held that the Constitution does not permit the imposition of strict liability for defamation in cases involving matters of public interest, but that the states were free to adopt any other standard as long as the plaintiff was required to show at least negligence on the part of the defendant. In effect, in cases involving matters of public interest where the plaintiff was not a public official or public figure, the states could adopt a conditional privilege that would be defeated either by a showing of negligence, or, in some states, only by showing actual malice. Second, the Court ruled that in any of these cases now subject to constitutional limits, "presumed" damages were not permissible in the absence of a showing of actual malice. Thus, when the plaintiff had shown only that the defendant was negligent but still was permitted to recover, there could be no recovery without a showing of actual loss, though this did not have to be out-of-pocket loss.

For a time it was unclear whether *Gertz* had constitutionalized all or only a part of the law of defamation, since some of its language was very broad. But in *Dun & Bradstreet, Inc. v. Greenmoss Builders,*

---

[3] 418 U.S. 323, 94 S.Ct. 2997, 41 L.Ed.2d 789 (1974).

Inc.,[4] the Court ruled that the states were permitted to continue impos-ing strict liability in cases that do not involve matters of public interest, and apparently free to continue the practice of awarding "presumed" damages in such cases as well. Clearly this rule applies in cases involv-ing private plaintiffs suing non-media defendants. To what extent the rule can coherently apply when a private plaintiff sues a media defen-dant is unclear, however, since defamatory statements published by the media are likely almost by definition to have somewhat more public "interest" than utterly private statements. Over a period of three dec-ades a series of other rules governing important but "subsidiary" issues also has evolved.

The upshot of all this is that there is no a whole set of constitu-tional limits on the scope of defamation liability. There are now two separate constitutionally-required standards (actual malice and negli-gence) in cases involving public officials/figures and matters of public interest, respectively. But the states are still free to apply the old strict liability standard in other cases. There is a set of cases in which dam-ages cannot be presumed (when proof of at least negligence is required but actual malice has not been proved). There is a new burden of proof regarding falsity. There is a heightened scope of review in cases where the "of and concerning" the plaintiff issue is raised. And there is resid-ual uncertainty about whether different standards apply in some of the cases involving media as distinguished from non-media defendants.

This legal framework is not only complicated, but has produced unanticipated side effects. For example, the actual malice requirement in public official and public figure cases has obviously made it harder for plaintiffs to recover; but because so much blame on the part of the defendant is required for a recovery in such cases, defendants have a tendency to fight defamation suits more strongly than they did in the past, when a finding of liability did not necessarily imply fault or professional misconduct on the part of a newspaper, magazine, or T.V. program. Moreover, what had once been a simple strict liability issue is often transformed into a complicated and costly inquiry into the nature of the defendant's publication and fact-verification process, be-cause constitutional fault or malice must be proved. And if the plaintiff does succeed in proving actual malice, the judgment awarded is likely to be much larger than in the past, because the defendant has been proved to have been highly blameworthy. For this reason also, defen-

---

[4] 472 U.S. 749, 105 S.Ct. 2939, 86 L.Ed.2d 593 (1985).

dants have an increased incentive to invest whatever it takes to defeat a defamation suit. Finally, studies have shown that for many plaintiffs, merely bringing suit and proving falsity constitutes vindication, even if they lose because they cannot show actual malice. The result is more litigation, that is more complicated, than in the past. Many plaintiffs win by suing, even if they do not win by winning.

3. Assessment

At this point the Supreme Court cannot turn back the clock, and might not wish to do so even if it could. But in retrospect some of the concers with which the Court begann—the threat of liability for large sums in cases involving minor factual inaccuracies—might have been addressed in another way. Conceivably the Court might have focused on the threat of "presumed" damages to the constitutional guarantee of free speech, and limited its intervention in state defamation law to the regulation of such damages. Strict liability might then have been permitted to continue in cases in which the plaintiff—typically a public official or figure—wished to vindicate his or her reputation but was not seeking to bankrupt or intimidate the plaintiff.[5] A few states now have enacted statutes permitting such name-clearing actions through proof of falsity alone, but the statutes might not have been necessary had the Court chosen to pursue the damages route in order to assure that the necessary constitutional protections were available.

Nor is the increased protection that media enterprises have come to enjoy entirely consonant with the other legal and economic developments of the past thirty years. At the same time that the rest of tort law was moving closer to enterprise-based forms of liability such as strict products liability and relaxed rules governing proof of causation in toxic harm cases, defamation law moved in the other direction. One of the principal changes in the world of print and electronic media during this period has been the recognition that "news" is a "product." Yet whereas other product defects now result more liability, the media's main product results in less liability than in the past, not more.

Finally, although at some level *New York Times v. Sullivan* was intended to take at least some of defamation law out of politics, many of the most noteworthy defamation trials of the post-*Sullivan* period have carried into the courtroom the very political struggles that were the subject of the defendant's reporting. The suit against the television

---

[5] See Pierre Leval, *The No-Money, No-Fault Libel Suit: Keeping* Sullivan *in its Proper Place*, 101 Harv. L. Rev. 1287 (1988).

program "Sixty Minutes" by the commander of the United States forces during much of the Vietnam War, General William Westmoreland, is only the most celebrated example of many.[6] Ironically, then, not only does the constitutionalization of defamation law run against the grain of the rest of modern tort law; in addition, much of what that constitutionalization has brought probably has not been anything like what the Supreme Court may have expected. Unanticipated side effects that make litigation more complicated and costly rather than simply creating additional breathing space for political speech now figure in virtually every major defamation suit.

II. Invasion of Privacy

The first principle of the tort of invasion of privacy has been repeated so often that it is almost a cliche. Invasion of privacy is not one tort, but four: 1) appropriation of the plaintiff's name or likeness; 2) unreasonable public disclosure of private facts; 3) intrusion on the plaintiff's solitude or privacy; and 4) portrayal of the plaintiff in a false light. Although these categories are now well-established, all four causes of action emerged clearly only in the twentieth century.

Each privacy tort is concerned with a different form of invasion and, to some extent, a different form of loss. What links the four torts together is not simply the umbrella term privacy, but their general concern for the protection of personal dignity. In keeping with this concern, none of the four torts requires proof of special damages to be actionable. Rather, although (unlike common law libel and slander per se) damages are not "presumed" in invasion of privacy actions, the plaintiff is entitled to recover for the rather abstract non-monetary harm to dignity suffered from the invasion, as well as for resulting mental distress suffered. Given the requirements of the privacy torts described below, the conduct that gives rise to the invasion very often also warrants imposition of liability on the defendant for punitive damages.

As the four privacy causes of action emerged, the courts had not only to decide whether an invasion ever was actionable, but (when it was actionable) under what conditions. Because the privacy torts are of comparatively recent vintage and are not the frequent subject of litigation, their contours still are not clear in every detail. The need for continued clarification of the interests they protect, the basis upon

---

[6] See *Westmoreland v. CBS, Inc.*, 596 F.Supp. 1170 (S.D.N.Y. 1984).

which liability for each form of intrusion may be imposed, and the countervailing concerns that limit the scope of liability, make the privacy torts open-ended and subject to evolutionary modification.

A. Appropriation

A person's name and the way he or she looks are a central part of her identity. For this reason it is tortious for the defendant to appropriate the plaintiff's name or likeness for commercial purposes, and in many states for non-commercial purposes. When the benefit the defendant obtains from appropriation is commercial, the main interest the tort of appropriation protects is the economic value of one's name or likeness. In this sense the interest is much like property, and the defendant's wrong is much like taking property without consent. But even if the plaintiff's name or likeness is not used for commercial purposes the appropriation is a wrong. For example, using the plaintiff's name without permission to publicize a charity ball would also be actionable in many states.

The limits on the tort of appropriation derive from what in a very rough sense can be understood as assumption of risk by the plaintiff. Anyone who attends a public gathering or even goes out onto the street must ought to recognize that her photograph may be taken and used as an exemplar by the news media or even by a private person. Thus a fan at a sporting event has no claim against the magazine that publishes his picture, and a person passing by a gruesome accident is not protected against publication of his picture in the background of a newspaper photograph of the scene. The First Amendment probably also exercises some gravitational pull in this field, though there are few decisions actually applying it. Because for the news and entertainment media commercial profit and free speech are inextricably linked, it is not always possible to distinguish a purely commercial appropriation of the plaintiff's likeness from legitimate reporting of matters of public interest. Thus the tort of appropriation may provide less protection for plaintiffs who are public figures and especially entertainers, who must tolerate use of their names and likenesses when publicity is given to their exploits. On the other hand, since these are the very people whose names and likeness will help to sell products, the damages they recover when they are successful in an appropriation suit may be substantial.

B. Disclosure

In general people have a right to be left alone. It is an intrusion on my privacy—on my right to be left alone—if you disclose private facts about me to a third person or persons and under the circumstances your disclosure is "offensive." But because some people have voluntarily placed themselves in the public eye, they have a right to expect less protection against the disclosure of private facts about them than do private individuals. And occasionally the rights of someone who has involuntarily become a subject of publicity must be balanced against the public's legitimate, though not necessarily admirable, interest in them.

The leading case on this score is *Sidis v. F–R Publishing Corp.*,[7] in which the New Yorker magazine profiled a reclusive genius who had received publicity as a child prodigy many years before. The plaintiff had become an "insignificant clerk," was living in a rooming house, and had gone to some lengths to avoid public attention. Nonetheless, the court held that he had no cause of action, on the ground that the facts about the plaintiff, though embarrassing to him, were in an attenuated sense "newsworthy." Apparently the newsworthiness of the facts about the plaintiff influenced the determination that the disclosure was not offensive. Other courts have let the issue whether the plaintiff's fame (or infamy[8] has faded sufficiently to render the disclosure offensive go to the jury. And the U.S. Supreme Court has ruled that the First Amendment precludes recovery for the disclosure of the name of a rape victim obtained from public records,[9] though subsequent decisions have left unclear exactly how "public" a record must be to afford the defendant this protection.

The lesson of these decisions is that, regardless of the precise point at which the line is drawn, the right to be free from offensive public disclosures of private facts must at some point yield to the public's right to know about matters of public interest. Whether a disclosure is actionable will tend to be a highly context-dependent decision, taking into account the extent to which the plaintiff has or has not voluntarily subjected himself to publicity in the past, the character of the informa-

---

[7] 113 F.2d 806 (2d Cir. 1940).

[8] See *Briscoe v. Reader's Digest Ass'n*, 4 Cal.3d 529, 483 P.2d 34, 93 Cal.Rptr. 866 (1971).

[9] *Cox Broadcasting Corp. v. Cohn*, 420 U.S. 469, 95 S.Ct. 1029, 43 L.Ed.2d 328 (1975).

tion disclosed, the manner in which the defendant came into possession of the information, and the legitimacy of the public interest in the information disclosed.

C. Intrusion

Nothing comes closer to invading the core of what we think of as "privacy" than physical or electronic invasion of a place or space from which the plaintiff has a right to exclude others. The bedroom is the classic venue, but a physician's examination room, and even one's mail also qualify. The intrusion need not literally be physical—visual or auditory surveillance from afar may also be actionable. The only requirements are that the invasion be highly offensive to a reasonable person and that it be into a place or space in which the plaintiff has a reasonable expectation of privacy.

In contrast to the other privacy torts, there is usually no counter-vailing interest that the defendant can point to justify instrusive conduct. The only real limit on the tort, it seems, is practical. The invasion must be sufficiently objectionable that it is worth the court's time to impose liability for it. Most allegedly actionable invasions can be resolved with an "I know it when I see it" test that takes the entire context into account. After all, although one can articulate why an intrusion does or does not seem "offensive," ultimately offensiveness is more a matter of indignation than logic.

One difficult problem involves "stalking" and other persistent intrusions that take place in public spaces rather than on private property. Even on the street, in a park, or at a museum, one's personal space may be offensively invaded by the repeated, harassing presence of the defendant. The plaintiff may not be entitled to maintain that space against intrusion by multiple, nameless individuals; but a single individual day after day may be said to invade the "moving circle" of privacy that follows everyone around, even in public spaces. Celebrities as well as private individuals have a right to protection against this kind of invasion, once it becomes harassment. Unfortunately, however, although the threat of civil liability and even punitive damages may deter business enterprises from becoming involved in such harassment,[10] the disturbed individual is less easily deterred by conventional means.

---

[10] See, e.g., *Nader v. General Motors Corp.*, 25 N.Y.2d 560, 255 N.E.2d 765, 307 N.Y.S.2d 647 (1970).

Here tort law reaches the limits of its capacities, and injunctions or statutorily prescribed criminal penalties become necessary to curtail the ongoing invasion of the plaintiff's privacy.[11]

D. False Light

Finally, it is an invasion of the plaintiff's privacy to portray him in a false light if that is done with actual malice (in the constitutional sense)[12] and the portrayal is highly offensive. Often a portrayal in a false light will also constitute defamation, but conceivably a portrayal can be in a false light without injuring the plaintiff's reputation or otherwise defaming him. The interests protected by false light and defamation are extremely close if not identical, however, and indeed in some cases only a narrow definition of the interest in "reputation" protected by the tort of defamation seems to qualify as a portrayal false light without its also being defamatory.

---

[11] See, e.g., *Galella v. Onassis*, 487 F.2d 986 (2d Cir. 1973).

[12] See *Time Inc. v. Hill*, 385 U.S. 374, 87 S.Ct. 534, 17 L.Ed.2d 456 (1967).

14

Economic Harms: Misrepresentation and Interference with Actual or Prospective Contractual Advantage

This last Chapter concerns torts that typically arise out of contractual or commercial relations and result mainly in economic losses rather than physical harm. These torts reflect business customs and ethics, and therefore have evolved over time in response both to economic change and new business practices.

I. Misrepresentation

The classic form of misrepresentation is intentional: fraud. But under limited circumstances liability may also be imposed for economic losses caused by negligent misrepresentation, and sometimes even for innocent misrepresentation. Although there is liability for fraud outside of business and commercial settings, most of the litigation involving this cause of action arises out of economic dealings rather than personal relations. For this reason, and before we address the elements of a cause of action for misrepresentation, it is useful to begin by considering what the tort is all about.

A misrepresentation is a false statement of fact. The tort of misrepresentation is therefore intended to redress harm caused by the communication of false information, mainly in the course of business and commercial relations. Not all false statements are actionable, however, because the degree of care that is expected of the party making a statement of fact varies. In virtually every setting—though even here there are a few exceptions—it is expected that one party will not lie to another. On the other hand, there probably is no firm expectation among business people that they will exercise reasonable care that the statements they make to each other in the course of transacting business are true. Only in settings where information is transferred as part of a service purchased—such as legal or accounting advice—is such an expectation commonly held. And still less is there an expectation that the accuracy of statements made in commercial relations is guaranteed to be true, in the absence of an express guarantee of accuracy.

The law governing liability for misrepresentation pretty well coincides with these expectations. There is liability for fraud almost without regard to the business setting in which a lie causes economic harm to its recipient. But liability for merely negligent misrepresentation is not imposed in ordinary commercial settings, being reserved mainly for professional and fiduciary relationships where reasonable care is supposed to be exercised. And although the scope of liability for innocent misrepresentation varies somewhat between jurisdictions, in general tort liability for innocent misrepresentation (as distinguished from an obligation to rescind a contract based on it) is imposed only when the defendant has warranted the truth of his statement.

A. Fraud

There are five elements to a cause of action for fraud. 1) The defendant must have made a false statement of fact; 2) with knowledge of the falsity or with reckless disregard of the truth or falsity of the statement; 3) intending the plaintiff to rely on the statement; 4) the plaintiff must have justifiably relied; and 5) the plaintiff must have suffered damage as a result. In addition, something like a proximate cause requirement limits the scope of liability for fraud.

1. False Statement of Fact: Misrepresentation and Nondisclosure

There can be no false statements of fact about the future, and there are no false opinions. Typically, therefore, fraud consists of a false statement about a present (or occasionally a past) state of affairs. On the other hand, a person's present state of mind is as much a fact as anything else. It is therefore possible to make a statement about one's intention's regarding the future or about one's opinion that is false, if the statement misrepresents the defendant's present state of mind. For example, if I promise to pay your way through college if you give up smoking, never intending to do so, my promise is a false representation of my state of mind. Similarly, if I say that I believe that John Doe is to be trusted when I have no such belief, I have misrepresented my opinion.

The failure to disclose a material fact may also constitute fraud. But the law's longstanding reluctance to impose tort liability for the failure to act, and the norm of *caveat emptor* that animated much of the common law of contract, together meant that traditionally there was little such liability. The general attitude of the law is that it is incumbent on the injured party to ask about material information. A false answer by a party would result in liability for fraud, and that party's an unwillingness to give any answer at all would tell the inquirer everything he needed to know. There are some exceptions in which the law imposes an affirmative duty to disclose information not asked for, but most involve unusual situations rather than straightforward withholding of information: for example, for incomplete statements that are half-truths; and for statements that are not knowingly false when made but which the defendant later learns were false. In recent years, however, there has been something of a move toward imposing liability for fraud when the defendant has failed to disclose facts that are "basic" to the transaction. Partly such liability reflects changing norms regarding proper business behavior. But some decisions are an effort to lead rather than follow business ethics.

One of the problems associated with liability for nondisclosure is that neither the case law nor ordinary norms are clear about the situations in which disclosure is and is not expected. A failure by the seller of a home to disclose that it is infested with termites is often actionable;[1] but a buyer's failure to disclose his belief to the seller of land that it contains deposits of oil is not. Some of this difference in treatment reflects the differences between buyers and sellers, since buyers are often uninformed consumers, whereas sellers are at least sometimes sophisticated and informed repeat players in the market. But that is not always the case, and in any event much of the case law cannot be explained on this basis.

One interesting effort to explain the scope of liability for nondisclosure argues that there is no duty to disclose when the information in question is the product of a costly search, whether by the buyer or seller.[2] On the other hand, when the information was not the result of a costly investment or search and is basic to the transaction, liability for fraudulent failure disclose is more likely to be imposed. Thus, the seller of a house infested with termites has come into possession of that

[1] See Restatement (Second) of Torts §551.

[2] See Anthony T. Kronman, *Mistake, Disclosure, Information, and the Law of Contracts*, 7 J. Legal Stud. 1, 9 (1978).

information without making a costly effort to do so, whereas the buyer of land under which there may be oil often has invested in geological research. Imposing liability for the former's failure to disclose will create little if any disincentive to acquire useful information, whereas liability for the latter's failure to disclose would do exactly that.

2. Scienter

The defendant must make the false statement of fact with actual knowledge of its falsity or with reckless disregard of its truth or falsity. This state-of-mind requirement is termed "scienter." The ordinary expectation is that statements of fact are made with an honest belief that they are true. A statement that is knowingly false or made with disregard of its truth or falsity contains a false implication that the maker believes it to be true, when in fact he does not, or has no belief one way or the other. The requirement that disregard be "reckless" adds an element of blame that would be absent from merely casual or inadvertent disregard for the truth or falsity of what one is said.

3. Intent that the Plaintiff Rely

The plaintiff has not committed fraud unless he intends that the plaintiff rely on his false statement. This requirement is sometimes called an "intent to deceive," but this latter way of describing the requirement can be misleading. A defendant who knowingly makes a false statement and intends the plaintiff to rely on it automatically intends to deceive. On the other hand, a defendant who acts only with reckless disregard may intend the plaintiff to rely, but does not necessarily intend to deceive the plaintiff. It could be argued that if such a defendant intends the plaintiff to rely on the statement, he must also intend to give the plaintiff the mistaken impression that he (the defendant) has an honest belief that the statement is true. But it seems just as possible that a defendant who disregards whether what he says is true or false is at the same time simply disregarding whether the plaintiff will suppose that the defendant believes the statement to be true. Admittedly, however, the two are very close, and any defendant who has an actual intent that the plaintiff rely normally also has an actual intent to deceive the plaintiff about his (the defendant's) state of mind.

4. Justifiable Reliance

This element adds a causation requirement to a claim for fraud. If the plaintiff did not rely on the defendant's false statement, then the statement did not cause the plaintiff's loss and there can be no recovery. That reliance also must be justifiable, however, which means both that i) the statement must be material—i.e., would be of substantial importance to a person involved in the transaction in question—and ii) is not so preposterous or otherwise lacking in credibility that the plaintiff should not have relied on it.

The materiality and credibility criteria thus require weighing the importance and character of the statement in context. A false statement that a house being sold is not infested with termites will virtually always be material, whereas a statement that the house has a dry basement when in fact small puddles appear twice per year probably is not material in the absence of special circumstances. As to credibility, the plaintiff is not justified in relying on the defendant's statement that his fifty-year old house is in "perfect condition" and "is strong enough to stand up in a tornado." An exaggerated statement of high quality is the kind of "puffing" that so often takes place in the course of negotiation that people must learn to discount it. It may be justifiable, however, to rely on more precise assertions made under circumstances in which exaggeration is not to be expected. For instance, it is *not* mere puffing for a defendant who has applied for credit to exaggerate the amount of money he has in a bank account.

5. Damages

This element raises more complicated issues than might be supposed in the first instance. Ordinarily the measure of damages in tort is designed to make the plaintiff "whole"—that is, to put him in the same position she would have been had his loss not occurred. In fraud, compensation for the plaintiff's *out-of-pocket* losses would accomplish this goal. For example, suppose that defendant represents his house to have copper plumbing and new wiring when in fact it has neither. If these statements were true, the house would be worth $100,000, but in fact it is worth only $85,000 in its actual condition. The plaintiff buys the house for $90,000. His out-of-pocket loss is $5000—the difference between what he paid and what the house is actually worth. Note that if the plaintiff had paid only $85,000 for the house then he would have no out-of-pocket damages and would recover nothing.

However, the defendant's statement caused another form of harm that the out-of-pocket measure does not capture: it deprived the plaintiff of the *benefit-of-the-bargain* he had made. Had the property been in the condition represented by the defendant, the plaintiff would have purchased a $100,000 house for $90,000. His loss in this respect was $10,000. In fact, therefore, the plaintiff has lost a $10,000 bargain and has suffered a $5000 "out-of-pocket" loss. Courts and commentators occasionally also describe this total ($15,000) loss as the benefit-of-the-bargain, on the theory that what the plaintiff should recover is the difference between the value of what he bargained for ($100,000) and what the value of what he received ($85,000). This measure of damages puts the plaintiff in a better position than he would have been in had the misrepresentation never occurred—something tort law does not typically do. But that is precisely what contract law does when it awards expectation damages for breach of contract, measured by the difference between the value of what was promised and what was delivered. The benefit-of-the-bargain measure simply recognizes that even in an action that is brought in tort (perhaps because the plaintiff is also seeking punitive damages), fraudulent misrepresentations made in the course of contractual negotiations may have a promissory character that warrants an award of damages for loss of the promisee's benefit of the bargain.

Many courts permit the plaintiff to choose his preferred measure of damages, because there are times when the benefit-of-the-bargain measure does not maximize the plaintiff's recovery.[3] Of course, where there was no contract between the plaintiff and the defendant, the plaintiff's out-of-pocket or consequential loss is the only measure of damages available. But suppose that the values stated in the earlier hypothetical case were that the same except that the plaintiff paid $110,000 for the house. The plaintiff's out-of-pocket loss would be $25,000. Of course, one might question whether the plaintiff should receive such an award, since in effect it disregards the fact that he would have lost money had the defendant's statement been true. But the courts permitting such a recovery have subscribed to the principle that the defendant who commits fraud should not be heard to complain that part of the plaintiff's loss results from his poor bargain. In effect this is simply a rejection of contributory negligence as a defense to fraud.

6. The Scope of Liability

Something like a proximate cause requirement obtains in fraud, and serves to limit the right of recovery to those persons whom the defendant actually knows will rely on his false statement or whose reliance is highly foreseeable. When the fraud occurs in the course of contractual dealings, of course, the other party is known. But some-

---

[3] See, e.g., *Selman v. Shirley*, 161 Or. 582, 91 P.2d 312 (1939).

times third parties can be expected to rely either on representations made to a contracting party or otherwise. For example, potential investors can be expected to rely on statements made by auditors, future creditors can be expected to rely bank references, etc. There is naturally a concern that the threat of liability to a large number of unidentified parties will deter desirable involvement in these activities. The law has therefore tended to draw the line short of liability to all foreseeable foreseeable plaintiffs, though there is liability to plaintiffs who are actually foreseen and to those who are "highly" foreseeable.

B. Negligent Misrepresentation

There may of course be liability for negligent misrepresentation that foreseeably causes personal injury or property damage. If you ask me whether it is safe to stand on a ladder that I have carelessly inspected and I answer that ladder is safe, I am liable for any injuries that you suffer when the ladder collapses. This is ordinary negligence. In Chapter Eleven, however, we saw that in general there is no liability in negligence for pure economic loss. That rule applies to negligent misrepresentation as well, for in general business and personal relationships there is no firmly established expectation that people will exercise reasonable care that their statements are true before they speak. Rather, people are expected only to be honest—i.e., not to make knowingly false statements. In certain settings, however, reasonable care is expected, and in these settings there is liability for economic loss caused by negligent misrepresentation.

Aside from *scienter*, proof of the other elements of a cause of action for fraud (falsity, intent that the plaintiff rely, justifiable reliance, and damages) is also required for negligent misrepresentation. Two other important issues do arise in connection with negligent misrepresentation: 1) the incidence of liability—when there can be any such liability at all; and 2) the scope of liability—when there can be such liability, to whom the defendant may be held liable.

1. The Incidence of Liability

The principle example of liability for negligent misrepresentation involves what amounts to malpractice by professionals and other providers of expert services. Accountants, attorneys, weighers, surveyors, real estate agents, and other similarly situated experts are liable for negligence because they are expected to exercise reasonable care in accordance with the standards of their callings. And most often that negligence is memorialized in the form of some advice, information, opinion or conclusion that is negligently inaccurate. Holding these parties liable to their clients or customers for negligent misrepresentation is unremarkable. Such liability is sometimes imposed on those who stand in a special relationship to those whom a negligent misrepresentation injures, such as the directors of a corporation to investors, or a bailee to a bailor.

Liability for pure economic loss resulting from negligent misrepresentation is virtually unheard of in situations that do not fall into one of these two categories. The theory behind this limitation of liability is not that other parties are never expected to behave carefully. Rather, the rule that there is no liability for negligent misrepresentations except in the professional and special relationship cases reflects the ordinary expectations of the parties to other kinds of transactions. If the expectation is otherwise in an ordinary commercial situation—i.e., if the parties do expect more than honesty—then they are always free to provide by contract that one or both parties promise that they have exercised or will exercise reasonable care that their statements are accurate and that they will be liable for the harm that results if they were negligent. In the absence of such agreement, however, the law assumes that they expect to be held liable only for fraud.

In fact, in practice, contractual provisions requiring the exercise of reasonable care are rare, for two reasons. First, when parties in a commercial transaction want more than honesty, they tend to want guaranteed accuracy, not just reasonable care. As a consequence, the typical contract provision representing a fact to be true is a warranty whose breach results in liability automatically—i.e., on a strict liability basis. Second, outside the professional services context, what constitutes a "reasonable" degree of care to assure the accuracy of representations is difficult to inform by reference independent norms. Professionals and other "experts" tend to follow common practices and to comply with common standards. They impliedly hold themselves out as following these practices and complying with these standards. The failure to do so is at least some evidence of their negligence. In contrast, non-professional and non-expert pursuits tend not to be governed or even "ordered" by common practices or standards regarding the transmission of accurate information. For example, it is unclear how meaningful it would be even to talk about whether a clerk in a movie-supply business had exercised "reasonable" care to assure that the descriptions of the movies in its catalogue were accurately matched-up with the movie titles. For this reason, neither the law of misrepresentation nor the parties acting for themselves by contract tend to find a negligence standard appealing in such settings.

2. The Scope of Liability

Supposing that the defendant has made an actionable negligent misrepresentation, to whom may he be held liable? Here, what amounts to proximate cause becomes central. The courts have long been concerned about the scope of various forms of liability for negligence that does not cause personal injury or property damage, because of the unpredictable and potentially unlimited extent of pure economic losses. As a consequence, although the defendant may be held liable in appropriate cases to his client or customer for negligent misrepresentation, the liability has reached only a very little beyond those with whom the defendant is in privity of contract.

In the paradigm case in this field, *Ultramares Corporation v. Touche*, then Chief Judge Cardozo expressed in often-repeated terms this concern about the dangers of "liability in an indeterminate amount for an indeterminate time to an indeterminate class."[4] Although the law may have all three of these concerns, in practice the focus has been on the last. *Ultramares* and other similar cases involve the common situation in which independent auditors are paid to inspect and then to certify the financial condition of a business. The owner or manager of the business misleads the auditors by overstating assets or understating liabilities in some way that the auditors do not detect. The auditors know that third parties will see and rely on their certification—that is its purpose. Of course, the primary wrong is committed by the party who engaged in the fraud. But typically he has disappeared or is judgment-proof. The auditors are likely to be certified public accountants covered by malpractice liability insurance and with assets of their own.

The plaintiffs seeking a deep-pocketed defendant are third parties such as investors or creditors who have lost money by relying on the certification provided by the auditors. So they sue the auditors for negligent misrepresentation. Fairly early it was settled that if a defendant such as the auditor had actual knowledge of the specific identity of a party who would rely on its statement, then that party could recover even in the absence of privity of contract. Since then the scope of liability has expanded, but not very much. In most jurisdictions there can be liability to more than one person who is not in privity with

---

[4] 255 N.Y. 170, 179, 174 N.E. 441, 444 (1931).

the defendant, but only if that person is a member of a "limited group" of actually foreseen individuals, though their specific identities ordinarily need not be known by the defendant. In some jurisdictions that group may in theory be larger, if only one individual in the group (such a a future owner in the chain of title to real property) is ultimately likely to rely on and be injured by the misrepresentation. This state of affairs is to be contrasted with claims for actual fraud, in which liability extends to anyone whose reliance was highly foreseeable.

There is no deep explanation for this limitation on liability for negligent misrepresentation, any more than there is a deep explanation for the limitations on liability for negligently-caused emotional distress discussed in Chapter Eleven. The explanation is largely practical. The courts' objective is to permit the imposition of liability to those beyond the boundary of privity, but to contain the scope of that liability within manageable proportions under a rule with sufficient texture to make results predictable. The rule extending liability to a "limited number of actually foreseen" individuals does this. But if history is any guide, over time the limits of this rule will erode and it will have to be replaced with another more expansive rule that also has sufficient texture to make results predictable.

C. Innocent Misrepresentation

Typically there is no liability for innocent misrepresentation outside the contracting context. However, when one contracting party has expressly or impliedly warranted to the other the truth of a fact material to the transaction, then liability for breach of warranty amounts to strict liability for innocent misrepresentation. Benefit-of-the-bargain damages may be awarded in such cases. In contrast, when an innocent misrepresentation does not amount to a warranty, the law is far less clear. Suppose that in negotiations for the sale of my house I innocently misrepresent it to be free of termites. In some jurisdictions the statement is not actionable at all. In others the statement is actionable, but only the equitable remedy of rescission or its legal equivalent, liability for out-of-pocket loss, is available. Indeed, under some circumstances the plaintiff in such a transaction may not obtain rescission but may only recover the cost of repair.

These rules are unsettled largely because the expectations on which they must be based if they are to work effectively also are unsettled. We simply do not have uniform and firm standards about responsibilities for innocent misrepresentations. What is perceived as a "warranty" or a guarantee will vary from individual to individual, as will moral intuitions about what an innocent misrepresenter ought to be required to do, if anything, to make things right. As long as these intuitions vary so much from setting to setting, the tort law rules governing liability for innocent misrepresentation will remain unsettled, and will have to be specified by contract or litigated on a case by case basis.

II. Intentional Interference with Contract

It is a tort to interfere *intentionally* with a contract between two other parties or to induce breach of such a contract. On the other hand, *negligent* interference with contract rights ordinarily is not actionable, as we saw in the Chapter Eleven's discussion of negligent infliction of pure economic loss. Of course, other torts—such as fraud, or false imprisonment, or others—may be committed with the intent of causing a breach of contract. But the cause of action for intentional interference exists even if the means of interference is not itself an independent tort.

The modern tort of intentional interference derives from the English case of *Lumley v. Gye*,[5] in which the defendant induced an opera singer to breach her contract to sing at the Queens Theater. The complaint in *Lumley* alleged that the interference was with malice, and for some time it was unclear whether maliciousness was an element of the tort. It is now well-established that maliciousness is not required. On the other hand, not every interference is tortious. To be tortious, the interference must be for an "improper" purpose. However, most interferences—including those intended merely for the defendant's economic benefit—are held to be improper. Indeed, it would be more accurate to say that there is liability unless the defendant had an especially "proper" purpose, except that this way of putting the matter inaccurately suggests that defendant always bears the burden of proof on this issue. Some of the purposes that are "proper" and that therefore exempt an interfering defendant from liability have included preventing immoral behavior, and influencing a child not to marry the "wrong" person. On the other hand, a boycott in service of the desire to pressure a contracting party to take some collateral action—such as settling a labor dispute—ordinarily is not a "proper" purpose.

---

[5] 2 El. & Bl. 216 118 Eng. Rep. 749 (Q.B. 1853).

In recent years the commentators have disagreed about whether the tort of intentional interference should exist at all. On the one hand, the theory of "efficient breach of contract" suggests that sometimes it is value-enhancing for a contract to be breached and for the breaching party to pay damages. On this view the tort should not exist, since it inhibits efficient breach, for which the plaintiff will be compensated by the breaching party anyway.[6] On the other hand, the kinds of on-going "relational" contracts (employment, commercial requirements or supply arrangements, etc.) that are involved in the typical intentional interference action may be best served by promoting cooperation rather than efficient breach.[7] Neither view has clearly prevailed or exercised much influence on the courts.

III. Intentional Interference with Prospective Advantage

It is not only a tort to interfere interfere with contract, but also to interfere intentionally with prospective economic advantage. Typically, though not always, such economic advantage is a possible contract. In fact, prospective commercial economic advantage (as distinguished, for example, from inheritances or gifts) is the typical interest protected by this tort.

The major difference between this tort and intentional interference with contract is that it is emphatically not a tort to engage in "fair" economic competition that is designed to deprive a competitor of a *prospective* contract and garner that advantage for oneself. Thus, as in intentional interference with contract, whether the interference is done for a "proper" purpose is key, but ordinary competition is proper in the absence of a contract that will be interfered with. Beyond that, the forms of improper interference have crystallized into categories of "unfair competition" that have developed to the point that they are separate "sub-torts" whose contours are beyond the scope of this book: trademark infringement, false advertising, misappropriation of intellectual creations, industrial espionage, and boycott, as well as a catch-all category that is called *prima facie* tort in the State of New York. The entire area is further complicated by the existence of causes of action based on federal statutory protections for trademarks, copyrights, and patents. As various forms of intellectual property such as computer software become an increasingly important part of our economy, the

---

[6] Harvey S. Perlman, *Interference with Contract and Other Economic Expectancies: A Clash of Tort and Contract Doctrine*, 49 U.Chi. L.Rev. 61 (1982).

[7] Lillian R. BeVier, *Reconsidering Inducement*, 76 Va. L.Rev. 877 (1990).

scope of protection afforded to their creators will be increasingly litigated, but almost certainly any common law protection will be provided in the shadow of the federal statutory schemes that expressly address the problem.

TABLE OF CASES

References are to Pages

———

INDEX

References are to Pages